ACBL Bridge Series

More Commonly Used Conventions

in the
21st Century

ISBN 978-0-939460-95-3

Updated ACBL Bridge Series

More Commonly Used Conventions in the 21st Century is the fifth in a series of texts developed by the American Contract Bridge League.

These materials were written in 1986 by Audrey Grant. In 2006, the ACBL enlisted Betty Starzec, a Senior TAP Teacher-Trainer, to update the series to more accurately convey the latest duplicate bridge ideas and philosophy. The update complements the *Learn to Play Bridge* computer programs written for the ACBL by world champion Fred Gitelman.

There are five textbooks and teacher manuals with coordinating E-Z Deal decks of cards:

Volume One —
  Bidding in the 21st Century – *The Club Series*
Volume Two —
  Play of the Hand in the 21st Century – *The Diamond Series*
Volume Three —
  Defense in the 21st Century – *The Heart Series*
Volume Four —
  Commonly Used Conventions in the 21st Century
    – *The Spade Series*
Volume Five —
  More Commonly Used Conventions in the 21st Century
    – *The Notrump Series*

Trained teachers across North America offer bridge courses using these materials. Information on teachers in your area is available on the ACBL website **www.acbl.org** through the Find a Teacher link.

Coordinated decks of E-Z Deal Cards, which allow the reader to deal out the exercise hands at the end of each chapter, are available for each bridge text.

These materials can be purchased through Baron Barclay Bridge Supply 1-800-274-2221.

The American Contract Bridge League

The American Contract Bridge League (ACBL) is dedicated to the playing, teaching and promotion of contract bridge.

The membership of more than 165,000 includes a wide range of players — from the thousands who are just learning the joy of bridge to the most proficient players in North America.

ACBL offers a variety of services, including:

- **Tournament play.** Thousands of tournaments: North American Bridge Championships (three a year), as well as tournaments at the regional, sectional, local and club levels — are sanctioned annually.

- **A magazine.** The Bridge Bulletin, a monthly publication, offers articles for all levels of players on tournaments, card play, the Laws, personalities, special activities and much more.

- **A ranking plan.** Each time a member does well in any ACBL event, whether at the club level or at a North American Bridge Championship, that member receives a masterpoint award. Players achieve rankings and prestige as a result of their cumulative masterpoint holdings.

- **A teaching program.** ACBL has trained more than 5,000 people through the Teacher Accreditation Program (TAP) to teach beginning bridge lessons. You can find a teacher in your area at ACBL's website — **www.acbl.org**, Find a Teacher.

- **A newcomer program.** ACBL offers special games and programs for players new to bridge and new to duplicate. The Intermediate-Newcomer (IN) Programs at the three North American Bridge Championships are very popular and are offered as examples of what ACBL hopes regionals and sectionals will offer to their local newcomers.

- **Access to 3,200 bridge clubs.** ACBL offers sanctioned bridge play at clubs across the United States, Canada, Mexico, Bermuda, on cruise ships and even at a few foreign-based bridge clubs. You can locate a club in your area at ACBL's website — **www.acbl.org**, Find a Club.

- **A charity program.** Since 1964, the ACBL Charity Foundation has made substantial contributions to a wide range of charitable organizations, now with $100,000 in annual allocations.

- **A cooperative advertising program.** ACBL assists teachers, clubs, units and districts by subsidizing costs incurred for advertising programs designed to recruit students and promote bridge lessons and games.

- **A Junior program for players age 25 and under.** ACBL offers a funded teaching program, a funded school bridge lesson series program, student membership, a youth website — youth4bridge.org — and special events.

- **Membership benefits.** The Bridge Bulletin, a toll free line for member services, recognition for levels of achievement, online games, 10% discount at Baron Barclay Bridge Supply, 35% FedEx Office discount on printing, OfficeMax discount card and discounted Hertz car rental are offered.

ACBL has been the center of North American bridge activity since it was founded in 1937. You can enjoy the fun, friendship and competition of bridge with an ACBL membership available online at www.acbl.org.

Be an ACBL member
Join the
www.acbl.org

TABLE OF CONTENTS

CHAPTER 8 — Two-Over-One

APPENDIX

INTRODUCTION

The American Contract Bridge League's (ACBL) *More Commonly Used Conventions in the 21st Century* student text is the fifth in a series of bridge books for beginning and advancing players. It is preceded by four additional texts: *Bidding in the 21st Century, Play of the Hand in the 21st Century, Defense in the 21st Century* and *Commonly Used Conventions in the 21st Century.* The books focus on introducing students to all aspects of the game of bridge.

The ACBL, the sanctioning body for bridge in North America, developed these books to address the needs of students and teachers. They are a comprehensive set of materials that reflect current bridge bidding and playing standards. This series of books, written originally for the ACBL by Audrey Grant, a professional educator, has been used successfully by bridge teachers and students for more than 20 years.

In the late 1900s, the ACBL produced a computer program, *Learn to Play Bridge I* and subsequently *Learn to Play Bridge II,* written by bridge champion, Fred Gitelman. The response to these programs has been tremendous with more than 150,000 copies now in circulation. (LTPB can be downloaded for free by visiting the ACBL's web site, **www.acbl.org**, or Fred Gitelman's website at **www.bridgebase.com**).

In this current publication of the *More Commonly Used Conventions in the 21st Century* text, the ACBL has updated the material not only to convey more accurately the latest bridge ideas and philosophy but also to be used as a tool in conjunction with the *Learn to Play Bridge* programs.

The *ACBL Bridge Series* updated material encompasses these changes:

- 25 total points are required for games of 3NT, 4♠ and 4♥.
- Opening bids still require 13 total points or more. Therefore, the opener's bidding ranges as well as responder's ranges were adjusted slightly in order to conform to the 25 total points required for game. For example, responder's ranges are 6-9 total points for the minimum range, 10-11 total points for the medium range and 12+ total points for the maximum range.
- 1NT opening bids are 15-17 and are based on high card points (HCP).
- 2NT opening bids are 20-21 HCP.
- Overcalls are allowed with as few as 10 total points with an upper limit of 17 total points.
- Each of the first three series books contains a bonus chapter, which the teacher may wish to incorporate into class time.
- Strong 2♣ bids are used along with weak two- bids.

The goal of this update is to enable the reader to learn basic bridge or to review and improve bridge techniques in a logical and progressive fashion. More importantly, the reader will have fun while learning the fundamental concepts of modern bridge bidding, play and defense which will be beneficial for a lifetime.

A NOTE TO THE READER

This is the last text of the ACBL Bridge Series. Some of you, who are reading this text, may have just finished the rest of the series, while some of you may have a significant amount of duplicate bridge experience. Those of you with some duplicate experience will recognize the competitive nature of bidding in a duplicate environment. This text will try to accommodate the real duplicate world – a world where opening bids can be based upon hands with 12 points (or fewer than 12 points).

Bridge is about different styles, different treatments of bids and different uses of conventions. It is up to you and your partner to decide how you would like to put your partnership's bidding style together. But, the bottom line remains the same – if you have 25 points in the combined hands, you want to make sure you are in a major suit game or 3NT.

This text is written assuming the opener can have a 12-point hand. When opener can have a hand with fewer than 13 points, it means that the ranges for responder's bids must be adjusted. For example, a limit bid must be adjusted from 10-11 points to 11-12 points. These adjustments have been made in the text. If your partnership still requires 13 points to open, please use the ranges that have been used in the first three texts of the ACBL Bridge Series. Remember, in learning conventions, it is the underlying theory that you need to understand as you add them to your bidding arsenal.

CHAPTER 1
The Negative Double

THE NEGATIVE DOUBLE

The double was introduced into the game as a deterrent to overbidding. The penalty double increases the score for the defending side if the contract is defeated and for the declaring side if the contract is made. Even before the days of contract bridge, however, players started putting the double to other uses. The informatory double, now known as the takeout double, is the oldest bidding convention, dating from about 1912. This use of the double is so common that most players today don't even think of it as a convention.

The double is such a flexible call — taking up no room in the auction — that many partnerships put it to a number of uses, the least common of which is for a penalty.

The Negative Double

Suppose West opens the bidding 1 ♦ , and this is East's hand:

East (Responder)

♠ 7 3 2
♥ A J 8 4
♦ 9 5
♣ K J 10 6

East plans to respond 1 ♥, looking for an eight-card fit in a major suit. If West doesn't support hearts, some other suitable contract can be reached. If West rebids 1NT, for example, East can pass, comfortable in the knowledge that the partnership doesn't have enough strength for game and doesn't have a major-suit fit.

What happens, however, if North overcalls West's opening bid with 1 ♠? This bid interferes with East's planned response. With 9 high-card points, there isn't enough strength to introduce a new suit at the two level. 1NT doesn't feel like a good choice with no strength in the opponent's suit. Even if West has something in spades, South's opening lead will probably trap West's high cards. Another possibility is to pass, but this wouldn't give West any indication of East's strength and desire to compete for the contract.

About the time the Russians launched their first satellite into orbit, the famous partnership of Alvin Roth and Tobias Stone introduced a new idea into tournament bridge that dealt with exactly this type of problem — they named it Sputnik. Adopting an idea originally introduced by Lou Scharf of New York, the Roth–Stone bidding system redefined the meaning of a double by responder after a 1♠ overcall as a takeout double, rather than a penalty double. Over time, the Sputnik double has evolved into the modern-day concept of the negative double.

DEFINITION OF THE NEGATIVE DOUBLE

The theory behind the negative double is similar to that for the takeout double. It's rare to want to double an opponent's one-level or two-level bid for penalty, so the double can be put to better use.

Responder's double of an opponent's low-level overcall is for takeout showing:

- Support for the unbid suits.
- Enough strength to compete.

Let's look at the first hand again. The auction would now start like this:

WEST	NORTH	**EAST**	SOUTH
1♦	1♠	Double	

East's double of North's 1♠ overcall would tell West that East has support for the unbid suits — hearts and clubs — and enough strength for the partnership to compete to at least the two level.

Ideally, the negative double shows four-card support for both unbid suits. In practice, however, responder may use it on a hand that doesn't fit the ideal pattern.

Support for the Unbid Majors

Responder should have at least four-card support for an unbid major suit to use a negative double. This is invariably the case when there is one unbid major suit.

WEST	NORTH	**EAST**	SOUTH
1♦	1♥	?	

♠ A 9 6 3
♥ J 7 2   *7 prs*
♦ 8 4
♣ Q 10 5 4

Double. With four-card support for the unbid suits, this is an <u>ideal negative double</u>. Bidding 1♠ tends to promise a five-card suit, since a double can be used to look for a 4–4 fit.

♠ 9 6
♥ J 7 2
♦ 8 4 3
♣ A Q 10 5 4

Pass. A double would promise four-card support for spades, the unbid major. Although East has support for clubs, West is much more likely to pick spades. The hand isn't strong enough to bid 2♣, a new suit at the two level, and any other bid is unappealing. Passing doesn't end the auction. There may be an opportunity to show the clubs later.

WEST	NORTH	**EAST**	SOUTH
1♣	1♦	?	

♠ Q 9 4 3
♥ K J 7 2
♦ 8 5 3
♣ J 4

Double. With four-card support for both of the unbid majors, East would like to find an eight-card major-suit fit. If the partnership uses a five-card-major bidding style, it's quite possible West has one four-card major suit, and maybe both. If North hadn't interfered, East would have responded 1♥, searching for an eight-card fit up the line.

♠ 7 4
♥ A J 8 2
♦ 9 6 3 2
♣ Q 4 3

1♥. East has support for hearts, but not spades. A negative double is likely to get the partnership into trouble if West bids spades. Although a response of 1♥ <u>usually shows a five-card</u> suit when the partnership plays negative doubles, sometimes there are exceptions at the one level. In this sequence, 1♥ shows at least four hearts.

WEST	NORTH	**EAST**	SOUTH
1♦	2♣	?	

♠ Q 10 7 5	Double. There isn't enough strength to bid 2♥.
♥ K J 9 6 4	The negative double shows support for both major
♦ Q 3	suits. It allows East to enter the auction.
♣ 8 2	

There may be some hands that don't quite meet the requirements.

♠ K J 9	Double. It would be ideal to have four-card sup-
♥ A J 7 2	port for both majors. This hand doesn't quite fit
♦ 8 5 3	the requirements for a negative double, but it is
♣ 9 7 3	probably the best option. If West bids hearts, an
	eight-card fit is found. If West bids spades, the

partnership plays in a seven-card fit, but the high cards should compensate. The alternative is to pass and risk being shut out of the auction.

Support for Unbid Minors

The negative double should, but not always, show support for any unbid minor suit, too.

WEST	NORTH	**EAST**	SOUTH
1♥	1♠	?	

♠ 10 4	Double. There isn't enough strength to introduce
♥ 9 6	a new suit at the two level. The negative double
♦ Q J 8 4 2	tells West that East has enough to compete and has
♣ K Q 7 3	support for both of the unbid suits.

WEST	NORTH	**EAST**	SOUTH
1♦	1♥	?	

♠ A 9 6 3	Double. East has support for both the unbid major
♥ J 7 2	suit, spades, and the unbid minor suit, clubs. East
♦ 8 4	will be comfortable if West picks either suit.
♣ Q 10 5 4	

Here is an application of the negative double where East, the responder, doesn't have support for the unbid minor but has a bid available if West, the opener, bids the minor suit.

♠ A 9 6 3
♥ J 7 2
♦ Q 10 5 4
♣ 8 4

Double. West assumes that East has support for both spades and clubs, but that's all right. If West bids spades, an eight-card fit is found. If West bids clubs, East can give preference back to diamonds, showing spades and diamonds, rather than spades and clubs.

Five-Card or Longer Suits

With a five-card or longer unbid suit, responder should bid the suit. The negative double was primarily designed to uncover a 4–4 major-suit fit.

WEST	NORTH	**EAST**	SOUTH
1♦	1♥	?	

♠ A 9 6 4 3
♥ J 7
♦ 8 4
♣ Q 10 5 4

Respond 1♠. With a five-card or longer major suit, a natural response is best. There is enough strength to bid a new suit at the one level, so East shows the spades. West will expect at least a five-card spade suit, since a negative double could be used with only four cards in the unbid major.

♠ A 9 6 3
♥ 7
♦ 8 4
♣ A Q J 10 4 2

Respond 2♣. With enough strength to bid a new suit at the two level, start with the longest suit first and bid 2♣, planning to show the spades later. A negative double would tell partner about the four-card spade suit, but makes it difficult to let partner know about the excellent club suit and the extra strength.

WEST	NORTH	**EAST**	SOUTH
1♠	2♦	?	

♠ J 4
♥ A K J 7 2
♦ 8 5 3
♣ K 9 7

Bid 2 ♥. With a five-card suit and enough strength to bid a new suit at the two level, don't use a negative double. Make the natural response.

There are exceptions. If responder doesn't have enough strength to introduce a new suit at the two level, for example, responder can start by using the negative double holding a five-card or longer suit.

♠ J 4
♥ Q J 10 5 3 2
♦ 8 5
♣ K 7 3

Double. East doesn't have enough strength to introduce a new suit at the two level. To compete, start with a negative double. West will assume a four-card heart suit and is likely to rebid in a minor suit. Then East bids hearts. This will tell West about a five card or longer heart suit, and not enough strength to bid a new suit at the two level.

STRENGTH SHOWN BY A NEGATIVE DOUBLE

There is no upper limit to the strength shown by the negative double. It shows at least enough strength to compete to the level at which opener will be forced to rebid, but it may show a much stronger hand. Opener will initially assume that responder has only enough to compete. With a stronger hand, the doubler plans to bid again after hearing opener's rebid.

Consider the following hands for East as responder after the auction starts:

WEST	NORTH	**EAST**	SOUTH
1♣	1♥	?	

♠ K J 7 3
♥ 10 2
♦ Q 10 5 3 2
♣ 6 2

Double. With support for both unbid suits, East can compete with a negative double with as few as 6 or 7 points. If West has four spades, the partnership won't need to go beyond the one level to find its fit.

♠ A Q 9 4
♥ A 3
♦ K J 8 3
♣ 7 4 2

Double. With 14 HCPs, East has enough to take the partnership to the game level. The first priority is to look for a major-suit fit. By making a negative double, East will find out if West has four spades or four diamonds. Then East can put the partnership in the appropriate game contract.

♠ J 8 3 2
♥ Q 6 2
♦ J 7 4 2
♣ 8 3

Pass. East doesn't have enough to respond to the opening bid, and the opponent's overcall has done nothing to change the situation. East doesn't have enough to compete, even at the one level.

What would East call if the auction starts like this?

WEST	NORTH	**EAST**	SOUTH
1♠	2♦	?	

♠ 9 4
♥ K 10 6 3
♦ J 7 2
♣ A J 8 4

Double. With support for the unbid suits, most players would risk competing at the two level. Even if West has a minimum-strength hand, the risk of getting too high isn't that great. If West rebids 2♥, 2♠, 2NT, or 3♣, East intends to pass and the partnership should be in a reasonable contract. East–West's bidding may also have the effect of pushing North–South to a higher level than they planned.

♠ K 6
♥ A Q 8 3
♦ J 10 7 3
♣ K 7 2

Double. East is strong enough to take the partnership to the game level but wants to explore for the best contract. A bid of 2♥ at this point is forcing but would promise a five-card or longer suit. The best way to find out whether West has four hearts is to start with a negative double. If West bids hearts, East can take the partnership to game in that suit. East doesn't have four-card support for clubs, but if West bids clubs, East has enough strength to put the partnership in 3NT.

♠ J 5
♥ K J 8 2
♦ 9 7 2
♣ A Q 10 6

Double. With 11 high-card points, East has a hand of invitational strength. To check for a fit in hearts or clubs, East makes a negative double, intending to make an invitational rebid at the next opportunity. For example, if West rebids 2 ♥, East can then raise to 3 ♥.

♠ Q 4
♥ A J 10 8 4
♦ 6 3
♣ K 7 4 2

2 ♥. The negative double is primarily designed to find a 4–4 major-suit fit. With enough strength to bid a new suit at the two level, East should bid hearts to show a five-card or longer suit.

THE LEVEL THROUGH WHICH THE NEGATIVE DOUBLE APPLIES

The partnership needs to agree on the level through which the negative double applies. Some partnerships prefer to play the negative double only after a 1 ♠ overcall. Others use it through overcalls up to 4 ♦ or even higher. It's important that the partnership agree on which double of an opponent's overcall is for penalty and which is for takeout.

Most partnerships play negative doubles through 2 ♠. If partner opens the bidding in a suit at the one level and the next opponent makes a natural-suit overcall up to and including 2 ♠, responder's double is for takeout. If the opponent makes an overcall higher than 2 ♠, responder's double is for penalty.

WEST	NORTH	**EAST**	SOUTH
1 ♣	2 ♠	?	

♠ 5 4 2
♥ K 9 8 3
♦ K J 7 4
♣ 9 5

Pass. With only 7 points, East doesn't have enough to compete to the three level. A negative double could get the partnership into trouble if West has a minimum-strength hand. With a strong hand, West can bid again.

♠ 9 4
♥ K J 7 2
♦ A 9 8 4 2
♣ Q 3

Double. With 11 points — 10 HCPs plus 1 for the five-card suit — East is willing to compete to the three level. A negative double is a better choice than 3 ♦. It is the appropriate call to describe East's hand — enough strength to compete to the three level and support for the unbid suits.

♠ 8 3
♥ K J 10 8 7 2
♦ K 7
♣ 10 4 3

Double. East doesn't have enough strength to make a forcing response of 3 ♥, but would like to compete in hearts. The partnership could have a 10-card heart fit that might get lost in the auction if East passes. The best approach is to start with a negative double, planning to bid the hearts next. For example, if West rebids 2NT, 3 ♣ or 3 ♦, East can bid 3 ♥, showing a five-card or longer suit — likely six or more at this level — without the strength to bid 3 ♥ right away. This could get the partnership overboard, but most players would be willing to take the gamble.

NEGATIVE OR PENALTY?

It's important to make the distinction between a negative double and a penalty double. The standard agreement is that a negative double applies only if the opening bid is one of a suit.

Without a specific partnership agreement to the contrary, responder's double is for penalty in the following situations:

- After a 1NT opening bid by partner followed by an over-call.

- If an opponent overcalls in notrump.

- If an opponent makes a conventional overcall, such as a Michaels cuebid.

- After an opening bid at the two level or higher.

Here are some examples if the partnership has agreed to play negative doubles through 2 ♠:

WEST	NORTH	**EAST**	SOUTH
1♥	2♠	Double	

East's double would be a negative double. East presumably has support for both minor suits.

WEST	NORTH	**EAST**	SOUTH
1♠	3♥	Double	

East's double in this auction would be for penalty unless the partnership has agreed to play negative doubles through a higher level than 2♠. Most partnerships would actually treat East's double as "penalty-oriented" rather than 100% for penalty. With a hand that is unsuitable to defend 3♥ doubled — a very long spade suit, a second five-card or longer suit or a hand with slam potential — West can take the double out to try for a better result.

WEST	NORTH	**EAST**	SOUTH
1♦	1NT	Double	

The double of a 1NT overcall is treated as a penalty double. There are three unbid suits, and if East has support for all of them and the strength to compete, it's doubtful that North can make 1NT.

WEST	NORTH	**EAST**	SOUTH
1NT	2♥	Double	

East's double is a penalty double in most partnerships, although the partnership could have a specific agreement to play negative doubles in this situation.

WEST	NORTH	**EAST**	SOUTH
2♥	2♠	Double	

Whether West's opening bid is a weak two-bid or a strong two-bid, East's double in this situation is normally played as a penalty double.

WEST	NORTH	**EAST**	SOUTH
1♦	2♦	Double	

East should discover the meaning of North's 2♦ overcall before making a call. Even if 2♦ is a natural bid that shows diamonds rather than some form of conventional bid for takeout, East's double would be for penalty rather than takeout.

OPENER'S REBID AFTER A NEGATIVE DOUBLE

When responder makes a negative double, opener presumes responder has enough strength to compete and has support for the unbid suits, especially any unbid major.

- With a minimum-strength hand, opener chooses a rebid at the cheapest available level. Opener may pass if the next opponent bids or redoubles after the negative double.

- With a medium-strength hand, opener jumps a level or bids, even if there is further competition.

- With a maximum-strength hand, opener gets the partnership to the game level, cuebidding the opponent's suit if in doubt about the best contract.

Responding to a Low-Level Negative Double

Responder's negative double is for takeout. If the next opponent passes, opener rarely converts the double into a penalty double by passing.

WEST	NORTH	EAST	SOUTH
1 ♦	1 ♠	Double	Pass
?			

♠ J 4 2
♥ Q J 6 3
♦ A J 9 5
♣ A 6

Rebid 2 ♥. East has promised at least four cards in hearts and the strength to compete at the two level. With a minimum-strength hand, West bids at the cheapest available level. Bidding 2 ♥ in this sequence isn't a reverse. It's as though East had bid 1 ♥ and West is raising to the two level with a minimum-strength hand.

♠ J 4
♥ A J 9 3
♦ A Q J 7 3
♣ K 5

Rebid 3 ♥. With a medium-strength hand, West shows extra values with a jump. Again, it's as though East bid 1 ♥ and West jumps to the three level to invite East to bid game.

♠ J 3
♥ K Q 10 8
♦ A K J 7
♣ K Q 5

Rebid 4 ♥. With a maximum-strength hand, West puts the partnership at the game level in the known eight-card fit.

♠ 10 2
♥ K 5
♦ K J 7 5 3
♣ A J 8 3

Rebid 2 ♣. East has theoretically shown support for both of the unbid suits. It will be up to East to bid again without support for clubs. East might rebid 2 ♦ or bid 2 ♥ with five or more cards in that suit and not enough strength to respond 2 ♥ initially.

♠ A J 5
♥ Q 4
♦ A J 8 7 3
♣ J 9 5

Rebid 1NT. With a balanced hand, strength in the opponent's suit and no fit with either of the suits suggested by East, 1NT is West's most descriptive rebid.

♠ A Q 5
♥ 6 2
♦ A K J 10 7 3
♣ K 5

Rebid 3NT. East is showing cards in clubs and hearts, and this is a maximum-strength hand with strength in the opponent's suit. 3NT appears to be the best game contract.

♠ 8 4 3
♥ A Q 7
♦ K Q 6 2
♣ Q 8 3

Rebid 2 ♥. This is an awkward hand to bid. A rebid of 1NT isn't appealing, because there is no strength in the opponent's suit. Rebidding diamonds with a four-card suit isn't attractive, since East may not have support for that suit. Instead, West picks one of East's suits. The three hearts are strong enough to treat them as a four-card suit. West hopes 2 ♥ will be a reasonable contract if everyone passes.

Responding to a Negative Double at the Two Level

The higher the level of interference, the more opportunity to defeat the opponent's contract, especially since responder will tend to have a stronger hand to make a negative double at a high level. The negative double is still meant as a takeout double, however, so opener should bid something. Only with considerable strength in the opponent's suit should opener consider passing.

WEST	NORTH	EAST	SOUTH
1♣	2♠	Double	Pass
?			

♠ K J
♥ 10 8 6 3
♦ K 8 2
♣ A Q 9 4

Rebid 3♥. With a minimum-strength opening bid, West's rebid is at the cheapest available level and puts the partnership in its eight-card fit. West is not promising extra strength. East needs enough strength to warrant competing to this level.

♠ Q 10 7 4
♥ 4 2
♦ K 8 3
♣ A K J 5

Rebid 2NT. Although West has length and strength in the opponent's suit, the negative double should not be turned into a penalty double. East's double is for takeout. Without knowing East's exact hand, West's choice to defend rather than to bid could be dangerous. This hand is described with a notrump rebid.

♠ 9 3
♥ A Q 8 2
♦ K 5
♣ A Q J 7 5

Rebid 4♥. With a medium-strength hand, a jump shows extra strength. In this situation, the jump is to the game level. That's all right. East has enough strength to compete to the three level, and West has something extra.

♠ 3
♥ A K 10 5
♦ Q J 5
♣ A K J 8 3

Rebid 3♠ (cuebid). With a maximum-strength hand, go to at least the game level. There may be a slam if East has a little extra. The cuebid of the opponent's suit is the strongest bid West can make. It commits the partnership to game and shows interest in slam.

♠ A K J 8
♥ 4
♦ 8 6 3
♣ A K 8 4 2

Pass. Although a negative double is rarely passed, there's always an exception. This looks like the type of hand with which opener's side can extract a large enough penalty to compensate for any contract opener's side might make. Time to defend.

Opener's Rebid when there Is Further Competition

If opener's right-hand opponent bids after responder's negative double, opener no longer has to bid. Responder is interested in competing for the contract, however, so opener should take this into account.

WEST	NORTH	EAST	SOUTH
1 ♦	1 ♥	Double	2 ♥
?			

♠ K J
♥ J 8 2
♦ A J 9 8 4
♣ Q 8 3

Pass. After South's raise, West no longer has to bid, and with this hand, that's a good thing.

♠ K 10 8 3
♥ J 5
♦ A Q 9 7 3
♣ K 3

Rebid 2♠. Although West doesn't have to bid, East has shown the strength to compete and support for spades. West would rather play partscore in 2♠ than defend 2♥ with these cards. Bidding at the cheapest available level doesn't promise extra values. With a stronger hand, West could have jumped.

♠ K 6
♥ Q 8 2
♦ A Q 8 4
♣ Q 9 6 3

Pass. If South hadn't bid 2♥, West would have bid 2♣, since East is showing support for both of the unbid suits. West would have to bid 3♣, but West has a minimum hand. With extra values, East can always bid later.

RESPONDER'S REBID AFTER A NEGATIVE DOUBLE

Responder's negative double shows the strength to compete at the required level.

- With nothing extra, responder passes opener's minimum rebid. Responder can give a simple preference to opener's original suit or bid a new suit without a jump.

- With an invitational-strength hand of 11 or 12 points,* responder can bid again. A raise of opener's second suit, a jump preference of opener's first suit and 2NT are all invitational bids.

- With 13 or more points, responder should get the partnership to the game level. If responder still isn't sure about the best contract after hearing opener's rebid, responder can cuebid the opponent's suit. The cuebid is forcing to the game level.

Here are examples of East's rebid as responder after the auction has started:

WEST	NORTH	**EAST**	SOUTH
1♦	1♠	Double	Pass
2♣	Pass	?	

♠ Q 5 4
♥ A 10 7 3
♦ 8 6
♣ Q 10 8 2

Pass. With a minimum for the negative double, East has no reason to bid any further.

♠ Q 5 4
♥ A 10 7 3
♦ Q 10 8 2
♣ 8 6

Bid 2♦. East hoped the negative double would uncover a fit in hearts. West has picked the other unbid suit, so East should give preference to West's original suit. Since East didn't jump, West won't expect anything extra and will assume a hand with four hearts plus diamond support — exactly what East has.

♠ 9 5
♥ A J 10 8 4 3
♦ 10 7
♣ J 6 2

Bid 2♥. This sequence shows a hand with five or more hearts, but not enough strength to bid 2♥ directly over the overcall. With a minimum-strength hand, West will pass after this sequence and leave East to play in partscore.

♠ 8 6 2
♥ A Q 9 4
♦ Q 5
♣ K 10 8 7

Bid 3♣. With an invitational-strength hand of 11 points,* East is strong enough to invite game.

*Partnerships will be opening 12 point hands at this level of experience.

♠ A J 4
♥ K J 10 6
♦ Q 9 3
♣ 8 4 2

Bid 2NT. East hoped West had a four-card heart suit. That's not the case, but there is enough for another bid. 2NT is invitational, showing 11 or 12 points and some strength in the opponent's suit.

♠ J 9 3
♥ A Q J 7
♦ Q 4
♣ A 10 7 4

Bid 2♠ (cuebid). Although an eight-card fit in clubs has been found, the best contract isn't yet clear. The partnership belongs at the game level, but that could be in 5♣ or in 3NT. East shouldn't bid 3NT without a sure trick in spades, but West may have something in spades and be able to bid notrump. East will know better what to do after hearing West's next bid.

Responder's Action when the Opponents Compete Further

If the opponents compete further after the negative double, responder can double again to show extra strength. The second double isn't strictly for penalty, although opener may choose to defend with no better spot.

Here are examples of East's rebid as responder when the opponents compete further after the double:

WEST	NORTH	**EAST**	SOUTH
1♦	1♠	Double	2♠
Pass	Pass	?	

♠ J 8 2
♥ Q J 7 3
♦ 9 4
♣ K 10 9 5

Pass. East was willing to compete to the two level if West had a fit with one of the unbid suits, but there's a limit to how much East can do with this 7-point hand. West didn't bid over South's raise and figures to have a minimum-strength hand.

♠ 5 4
♥ K 10 8 5
♦ A 9 6 3 2
♣ J 5

Bid 3♦. East was intending to give a simple preference to 2♦ if West didn't show a fit for hearts. Bidding at the three level isn't ideal, but East doesn't want to let the opponents buy the contract without showing West the fine support for diamonds. West won't expect too much in this competitive situation. With an invitational-strength hand, East could jump to 4♦.

♠ Q 9
♥ K Q 7 2
♦ 6 4 2
♣ A J 7 3

Double. With 12 HCPs, East was intending to make an invitational* raise after hearing West's rebid. The opponents' bidding has silenced West, but East has too much to let the opponents buy the contract in 2♠. The second double isn't for penalty. It shows extra strength. West will still expect East to have a hand oriented toward the unbid suits. It will be up to West to decide whether to bid or defend after learning that East still wants to compete.

♠ 7
♥ Q J 7 3
♦ Q 5
♣ K J 10 8 5 4

Bid 3♣. East was hoping to find a heart fit with the double, but still has enough to show the club suit at the three level. The bid is invitational. With a stronger hand, East would have bid 2♣ originally rather than make a negative double. West may still have a fit for hearts, but not enough strength to show it after South's raise. If that's the case, West will now have the opportunity to bid 3♥.

DOUBLING FOR PENALTIES WHEN PLAYING NEGATIVE DOUBLES

This is East's hand in the following auction. West opens the bidding 1♥, and North overcalls 2♦:

♠ 9 6 3
♥ 4
♦ A Q 10 7 3
♣ K Q 5 2

WEST	NORTH	**EAST**	SOUTH
1♥	2♦	?	

Now what? East would like to double the opponent's overcall for penalty. Playing negative doubles, however, a double would be for takeout. If East doubles, West will probably rebid hearts or choose spades as the trump suit, neither of which is very attractive. East could bid notrump, but that would let North escape a penalty, and with no fit with West's suit, the partnership could get to an unmakeable contract. This is a disadvantage of playing the negative double. The low-level penalty double is no longer available.

*Partner may have a 12 point opener.

To overcome this disadvantage, East, the responder, passes. West, the opener, usually will make another call after an overcall followed by two passes. With shortness in the opponent's suit, West should double, even with a minimum-strength hand.

This agreement allows East to defend for penalty by passing with the above hand. Assuming South also passes, West should now double with shortness in diamonds. West's double is referred to as a reopening double or a balancing double. When North passes, East passes again, converting West's double into a penalty double.

A complete deal and auction might be something like this:

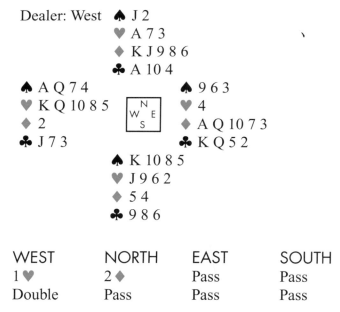

Dealer: West ♠ J 2
♥ A 7 3
♦ K J 9 8 6
♣ A 10 4

♠ A Q 7 4   ♠ 9 6 3
♥ K Q 10 8 5   N   ♥ 4
♦ 2   W   E   ♦ A Q 10 7 3
♣ J 7 3   S   ♣ K Q 5 2

♠ K 10 8 5
♥ J 9 6 2
♦ 5 4
♣ 9 8 6

WEST	NORTH	EAST	SOUTH
1 ♥	2 ♦	Pass	Pass
Double	Pass	Pass	Pass

Many players would overcall with North's hand. When East and South pass, the bidding comes back to West. With a minimum-strength opening bid and shortness in diamonds, West should reopen the bidding with a double. From West's point of view, this is a takeout double, showing a willingness to compete further, but it also allows for the possibility — as in this case — that responder has length in diamonds and wants to defend. After North passes, East's pass converts the double into a penalty double.

This sequence has an advantage over the immediate penalty double. North doesn't know that East will pass West's reopening double. When East does pass, it's too late for North to try to find another place to play the hand. If East had doubled for penalty right away, North would get another chance to bid and might be able to find a better contract.

It's usually safe for West to reopen with a double on this type of auction, even with a hand of minimum strength and shortness in diamonds. Once East and South have passed, it's quite likely that this is the layout. With a lot of strength or a good fit for diamonds — or both — South would have bid. When South passes, the inference is that East probably has some strength, some length in diamonds, or both. If it turns out that East doesn't have the type of hand to defend 2♦ for penalty, East can bid something.

Keep the same hand for West and change the other three hands.

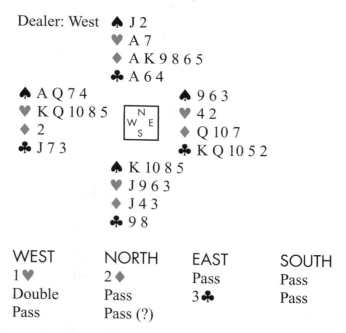

Dealer: West

	North		
	♠ J 2		
	♥ A 7		
	♦ A K 9 8 6 5		
	♣ A 6 4		

West		East	
♠ A Q 7 4		♠ 9 6 3	
♥ K Q 10 8 5		♥ 4 2	
♦ 2		♦ Q 10 7	
♣ J 7 3		♣ K Q 10 5 2	

	South		
	♠ K 10 8 5		
	♥ J 9 6 3		
	♦ J 4 3		
	♣ 9 8		

WEST	NORTH	EAST	SOUTH
1♥	2♦	Pass	Pass
Double	Pass	3♣	Pass
Pass	Pass (?)		

On this layout, North has a stronger hand for the overcall. With scattered values, East can't make a negative double without four-card support for spades. East and South pass. When West reopens, East doesn't have enough length or strength in diamonds to convert the double into a penalty double. Instead, East takes the double out to 3♣. East may make this contract if left to play there, or East may be defeated only one trick. Alternatively, North–South might bid on to 3♦. East–West can defend 3♦ and will probably defeat it by one trick.

East–West have to cooperate to get the best result. If South raised diamonds immediately or made some other bid, West would pass with a minimum hand.

With length in the overcaller's suit — three or more cards — opener shouldn't reopen the bidding with a minimum hand. It becomes unlikely that partner also has length and strength in the opponent's suit and is waiting to defend for penalty. Additionally, since partner didn't make a negative double, it would appear that partner isn't interested in competing. For example, consider this layout and auction:

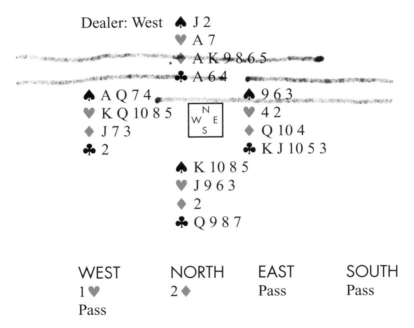

Dealer: West
♠ J 2
♥ A 7
♦ A K 9 8 6 5
♣ A 6 4

♠ A Q 7 4
♥ K Q 10 8 5
♦ J 7 3
♣ 2

♠ 9 6 3
♥ 4 2
♦ Q 10 4
♣ K J 10 5 3

♠ K 10 8 5
♥ J 9 6 3
♦ 2
♣ Q 9 8 7

WEST	NORTH	EAST	SOUTH
1♥	2♦	Pass	Pass
Pass			

If West were to reopen the bidding with a double in this situation, the partnership is likely to get a poor result. East doesn't have enough to leave the double in for penalty, and whatever East now bids will lead to a poor contract.

SUMMARY

When partner opens the bidding in a suit at the one level and right-hand opponent (RHO) overcalls in a suit, most partnerships use the negative double.

Negative Double

Responder's double of an opponent's suit overcall up to and including 2♠ — or higher, if agreed by the partnership — is for takeout, rather than penalty. There's no upper limit to the strength shown by the double, but opener assumes responder has 10 or fewer points unless responder bids again. Ideally, the negative double shows:

- **Support:** Four-card or longer support for the unbid major suit; support for an unbid minor suit, unless responder has something else to bid if opener rebids the minor suit.

- **Strength:** A negative double of a one-level overcall promises at least 6 total points. A negative double of a two-level overcall promises at least 8 total points.

With a five-card or longer suit, responder bids the suit rather than doubling. If responder doesn't have enough strength to introduce the suit at the required level, responder starts with a negative double, planning to bid the suit at the next opportunity.

Opener's Rebid after a Negative Double

- With a minimum-strength hand, opener chooses a rebid at the cheapest available level. Opener can pass if the next opponent competes after the negative double.

- With a medium-strength hand, opener jumps a level or bids even if the next opponent competes after the negative double.

- With a maximum-strength hand, opener gets the partnership to the game level, cuebidding the opponent's suit if in doubt about the best contract.

Note: Opener rarely passes to convert the double into a penalty double unless opener holds considerable strength in the opponent's suit. Responder's double is meant for takeout.

Responder's Rebid after Making a Negative Double

- With nothing extra, responder passes opener's minimum rebid. A simple preference of opener's original suit or the bid of a new suit without a jump doesn't show extra strength. Responder is still limited to about 10 points.

- With an invitational-strength hand of 11 or 12 points,* responder can bid again. A raise of opener's second suit, a jump preference of opener's first suit and 2NT are invitational bids.

- With 13 or more points, responder gets the partnership to the game level. If still uncertain about the best contract after opener's rebid, responder can cuebid the opponent's suit, which is forcing to the game level.

Doubling for Penalty when Using the Negative Double

When there is an overcall followed by two passes, opener reopens the bidding with shortness in the opponent's suit, even with a minimum-strength hand. This is a takeout double, but responder can now pass for penalty with length and strength in the opponent's suit.

*Assuming opener can bid with 12 points.

Note: The following exercises illustrate the methods outlined in the summary.

Exercise One — The Negative Double

What would East respond with each of the following hands after the auction starts?

WEST	NORTH	EAST	SOUTH
1♣	1♠	?	

1) ♠ 9 8 2
♥ Q J 6 5
♦ K Q 10 6
♣ 10 5

2) ♠ J 8
♥ K 10 8 4
♦ 7 3
♣ K J 8 5 2

3) ♠ K J 2
♥ 10 4 2
♦ A J 6 5
♣ 9 6 3

4) ♠ 9 5
♥ A Q J 8 3
♦ A Q 6 2
♣ 10 4

5) ♠ 7 4
♥ K J 10 8 7 6
♦ Q J 2
♣ 7 5

6) ♠ K J 10 8 7 3
♥ 7 3
♦ A 8 2
♣ 9 4

Exercise Two — Opener's Rebid after a Negative Double

What does West call with each of the following hands after the auction begins?

WEST	NORTH	EAST	SOUTH
1♠	2♦	Double	Pass
?			

1) ♠ A Q J 8 5
♥ 10 8 4 3
♦ A J 5
♣ 3

2) ♠ A 10 8 6 3
♥ A 7
♦ 6 4
♣ K Q 8 3

3) ♠ A K 10 9 8 6
♥ Q 4
♦ K 7 2
♣ 10 5

4) ♠ K Q 9 7 5
♥ J 5
♦ A Q 8
♣ Q 9 3

5) ♠ A K 7 5 4
♥ K Q 9 6
♦ J 3
♣ K 5

6) ♠ A K 8 6 2
♥ 4
♦ K Q J 9 7
♣ 6 3

Exercise One *Answer* — The Negative Double

1) Double. With support for both unbid suits and enough strength to compete, this is an ideal hand for a negative double.

2) Double. Although East doesn't have support for diamonds, East can support clubs if West picks diamonds and not hearts.

3) 1NT. East doesn't have four-card support for hearts, but East does have another bid available to compete for the contract.

4) 2♥. There's no need for a negative double, since East has enough strength to bid a new suit at the two level.

5) Double. East doesn't have enough strength to bid 2♥ directly, but East would like to compete in that suit. West will assume that East's double shows support for both hearts and diamonds. If West doesn't bid hearts, East can bid them later to describe this type of hand — a competitive hand with a five-card or longer heart suit.

6) Pass. A double would be for takeout. East's best chance to get a good score is to pass and hope that West can reopen the bidding with a double. East will then pass for penalty.

Exercise Two *Answer* — Opener's Rebid after a Negative Double

1) 2♥. East has indicated support for hearts and clubs. With a minimum-strength opening, West puts the partnership in its eight-card heart fit at the cheapest available level.

2) 3♣. East has indicated support for hearts and clubs. West puts the partnership in its club fit.

3) 2♠. With no fit for either hearts or clubs, West rebids the six-card major suit.

4) 2NT. West doesn't have a fit for either hearts or clubs, but does have a balanced hand with strength in the opponent's suit. Bidding notrump at the cheapest available level shows a minimum-strength balanced hand.

5) 3♥. East's negative double promises four hearts, so East–West have a fit. With a medium-strength hand, West jumps a level to invite East to bid game with a little extra. A rebid of 2♥ would show a minimum-strength hand.

6) Pass. West wouldn't usually convert East's takeout (negative) double into a penalty double, but this would be the exception.

Exercise Three — Responder's Rebid after a Negative Double

What does East call with each of the following hands after the auction has started?

WEST	NORTH	**EAST**	SOUTH
1♣	1♠	Double	Pass
2♥	Pass	?	

1) ♠ 8 4
   ♥ K J 8 3
   ♦ Q 10 7 5
   ♣ Q 9 2

2) ♠ A 4
   ♥ K 10 7 5
   ♦ K 10 8 6
   ♣ J 4 2

3) ♠ 10 6 2
   ♥ Q 10 8 4
   ♦ A Q 7 5
   ♣ A J

Exercise Three *Answer* — Responder's Rebid after a
                                  Negative Double

1) Pass. East has already described this hand with the double. West's minimum rebid doesn't show interest in reaching a game contract.

2) 3 ♥. Although West is showing a minimum opening with the non-jump rebid, East has enough to invite partner to bid game. If the opponents didn't interfere, the auction might have started 1 ♣–1 ♥; 2 ♥–3 ♥.

3) 4 ♥. East has enough strength to put the partnership in game now that the heart fit has been uncovered.

Exercise Four — More about Negative Doubles

What does East call with each of the hands after these auctions?

	WEST	NORTH	**EAST**	SOUTH	
1)	1♠	2♣	Double	Pass	♠ 9 6
	2♦	Pass	?		♥ A J 10 8 7 3
					♦ 9 5
					♣ Q 4 3

	WEST	NORTH	**EAST**	SOUTH	
2)	1♣	1♠	Double	Pass	♠ 9 4 3
	2♦	Pass	?		♥ K J 8 3
					♦ 10 5
					♣ A J 6 5

	WEST	NORTH	**EAST**	SOUTH	
3)			1♥	3♣	♠ Q 6 2
	Double	Pass	?		♥ A Q 9 8 4
					♦ A J 8 5
					♣ 5

	WEST	NORTH	**EAST**	SOUTH	
4)		Pass	1♠	2♦	♠ K Q 10 8 2
	Pass	Pass	?		♥ A J 7 4
					♦ 5
					♣ K 8 3

	WEST	NORTH	**EAST**	SOUTH	
5)		Pass	1♦	2♠	♠ Q 3
	Double	Pass	3♣	Pass	♥ 8 6
	3♥	Pass	?		♦ K Q 8 6 3
					♣ A Q 9 7

	WEST	NORTH	**EAST**	SOUTH	
6)			1NT	2♥	♠ A Q 7 3
	Double	Pass	?		♥ 10 4
					♦ K Q 9 4
					♣ K J 5

	WEST	NORTH	**EAST**	SOUTH	
7)			1♠	1NT	♠ K Q 8 6 3
	Double	Pass	?		♥ A J 8 4
					♦ 9 5
					♣ K 4

	WEST	NORTH	**EAST**	SOUTH	
8)			2♥	2♠	♠ 4
	Double	Pass	?		♥ K Q 10 8 7 6
					♦ K 9 5
					♣ 8 7 5

Exercise Four *Answer* — More about Negative Doubles

1) 2♥. East made a negative double in order to compete, but wasn't strong enough to bid a new suit at the two level. Now East can finish describing this hand to partner (West).

2) 3♣. East's negative double showed support for both hearts and diamonds. Now that West has bid diamonds, rather than hearts, East needs to give preference to West's original suit.

3) Pass. Assuming the partnership has agreed to play negative doubles through the 2♠ level, West's double of the 3♣ overcall is for penalty. East has no reason to disturb the contract.

4) Double. With shortness in the opponent's suit, East should reopen with a double, even with a minimum-strength opening bid. It's quite possible West has length and strength in diamonds and wants to penalize the overcall. If that's the case, West will pass the reopening double. If not, West will bid something.

5) Pass. West's negative double presumedly showed support for both hearts and clubs. Now that East has picked clubs, West's correction to 3♥ shows a hand with a long heart suit that was too weak to bid 3♥ directly over the overcall. If that's the case, East shouldn't bid any more.

6) Pass. The standard agreement is that responder's double is for penalty after a 1NT opening bid. Negative doubles apply only after an opening bid of one of a suit.

7) Pass. The double of a notrump overcall is for penalty. It's not a negative double.

8) Pass. Negative doubles are only used after opening suit bids at the one level. West's double is for penalty. East has already described this hand with the weak two-bid.

Bid and Play — Support for the Unbid Suits

(E–Z Deal Cards: #1, Deal 1 — Dealer, North)

Suggested Bidding

WEST	NORTH	EAST	SOUTH
	1♣	1♠	Double
Pass	2♥	Pass	Pass
Pass			

North opens the bidding 1♣. With a good five-card suit, East overcalls 1♠. South has enough to compete over 1♠, but isn't strong enough to bid a new suit at the two level. A response of 1NT is unappealing with no strength in spades. South solves the dilemma by making a negative double.

With two low cards in partner's suit, West can't raise partner's overcall, and 1NT is unattractive with no strength in clubs or hearts and only 6 points. West passes. Based on South's negative double, North now bids 2♥ to put the partnership in its eight-card fit and to show a minimum-strength hand at the same time. East has nothing more to say, and South doesn't have an invitational-strength hand, so the auction finishes in a contract of 2♥.

Dealer: North
Vul: None

♠ A 9 3
♥ Q 6 4 2
♦ J 5
♣ A Q 10 7

♠ 7 4
♥ 10 9 7
♦ A Q 8 4
♣ 6 5 4 2

N
W   E
S

♠ K Q J 6 2
♥ K 5
♦ 10 7 2
♣ K 9 3

♠ 10 8 5
♥ A J 8 3
♦ K 9 6 3
♣ J 8

Suggested Opening Lead

East is on lead and starts with the ♠K, top of a sequence.

Suggested Play

Declarer, North, has two spade losers, a potential heart loser even if trumps divide 3–2, two diamond losers and one club loser. There are several possibilities for eliminating one or more of the losers.

If West has the ♣K, North can hope to avoid a club loser by taking a successful finesse. North can also try to eliminate one of the diamond losers by leading toward dummy's ♦K, hoping East holds the ♦A. If both of these finesses lose — as they do on the actual lie of the cards — declarer will have to try to avoid losing a trump trick.

The play in the heart suit is interesting, because declarer is missing the ♥K, ♥10 and ♥9. Declarer can hope that East holds the ♥K, but if North leads the ♥Q, East will cover with the ♥K — covering an honor with an honor. Declarer can win this trick with the ♥A and take a second trick with the ♥J, but unless West started with exactly the doubleton ♥10 and ♥9, the defenders will still have a heart winner.

Declarer's best play, after winning a trick with the ♠A, is to play a low heart and finesse dummy's ♥J. When this wins, declarer plays dummy's ♥A, hoping East started with a doubleton ♥K. On the actual deal, East's ♥K falls under the ♥A, and declarer can draw West's remaining trump with the ♥Q. Even though both the diamond and club finesses lose, North still makes the contract — losing two spades, two diamonds and one club, but no hearts.

Suggested Defense

It appears that the defenders can do little to defeat the contract if declarer handles the trump suit correctly. They will get two spade tricks, two diamond tricks and a club trick. If North leads the ♥Q, East should cover with the ♥K to promote a winner in West's hand.

West actually has an opportunity to defeat the contract by giving declarer a losing option. If North correctly leads a low heart to dummy's ♥J, West should play the ♥9 (or ♥10). This is likely to create the illusion in declarer's mind that West started with a doubleton ♥10 and ♥9. Declarer might decide to come back to the North hand to lead the ♥Q expecting that, after East covers with the king and the ace is played from dummy, the remaining high heart will appear from West's hand. Then declarer would be able to draw the remaining trump with dummy's ♥8 and avoid the loss of a heart trick in that manner.

If West finds this clever play and declarer falls into the trap, this will become a memorable hand for the defenders.

Bid and Play — Looking for a Four-Card Major

(E–Z Deal Cards: #1, Deal 2 — Dealer, East)

Suggested Bidding

WEST	NORTH	EAST	SOUTH
		1♦	2♣
Double	Pass	2♠	Pass
4♠	Pass	Pass	Pass

East opens the bidding 1♦, and South overcalls 2♣. West has enough strength to put the partnership at the game level, but doesn't yet know where the partnership belongs. West can use a negative double to discover whether opener has a four-card major suit. When East shows the spade suit, West puts the partnership in the appropriate game contract.

Dealer: East
Vul: N–S

♠ 10 8 4 2
♥ 9 8 3
♦ Q 9 6 2
♣ 10 6

♠ K J 7 5
♥ A Q J 6
♦ J 8 4
♣ Q 7

♠ A Q 9 3
♥ K 5
♦ A 10 7 3
♣ 8 4 3

♠ 6
♥ 10 7 4 2
♦ K 5
♣ A K J 9 5 2

Suggested Opening Lead

South is on lead and could start with the ♣A, top of a broken sequence — or the ♣K if the partnership leads the king from ace–king.

Suggested Play

Declarer, East, starts with three diamond losers and three club losers. Two of the diamond losers can be discarded on the extra heart winners in dummy, and one of the club losers can be ruffed in the dummy.

Declarer must be careful to avoid losing a trump trick. Although the trump suit appears to be solid, North's four-card trump holding can prove dangerous. Suppose South takes the ♣A, ♣K and leads a third round of clubs. Since South overcalled in clubs, East must be careful to ruff this trick with a high trump, rather than a low trump. Otherwise, North will overruff.

Having overcome this hurdle, declarer should start drawing trumps by playing a low spade to the ♠A and then a low spade back to dummy's remaining high trump. If the trumps divided 3–2, declarer could then draw the last trump and take the remaining winners to make the contract. When North turns up with four trumps, declarer must lead dummy's remaining low trump and take a finesse against North's ♠10. Declarer can then draw the last trump and take the winners.

If declarer ruffs the third round of clubs with the ♠J and then plays the ♠K and a spade to the ♠/Q, the contract is in trouble. Declarer can't immediately get back to dummy to take a spade finesse without blocking the heart suit. If declarer tries to take the heart winners before drawing the last trump, North will ruff the fourth round, and declarer will be left with two diamond losers. Declarer must play the spade suit carefully to avoid these complications.

Suggested Defense

The defenders can make things difficult for declarer by starting with three rounds of clubs. North should encourage partner to continue leading clubs by making a high-low signal in the suit, the ♣10 followed by the ♣6. South should recognize that North has no clubs left after the first two rounds and lead another club, hoping that partner can overruff the dummy. If North held the ♠9 instead of the ♠2, this defense would be successful even if declarer ruffed with a high trump, since it would promote a trump trick in the North hand. Even on the actual lie of the cards, the third round of clubs creates a potential problem for declarer.

It won't do South any good to switch to another suit after playing the two top clubs. Declarer can win in the East hand and ruff a club anyway. If South switches after the first round of clubs, the play gets more complicated, but declarer can still make the contract after discovering the bad trump break.

Bid and Play — Penalty Doubles and Negative Doubles

(E–Z Deal Cards: #1, Deal 3 — Dealer, South)

Suggested Bidding

WEST	NORTH	EAST	SOUTH
			1 ♥
2 ♦	Pass	Pass	Double
Pass	Pass	Pass	

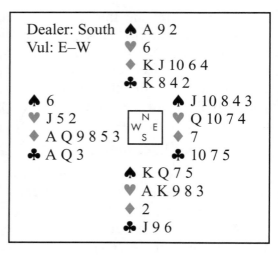

Dealer: South   ♠ A 9 2
Vul: E–W   ♥ 6
   ♦ K J 10 6 4
   ♣ K 8 4 2

♠ 6   ♠ J 10 8 4 3
♥ J 5 2   ♥ Q 10 7 4
♦ A Q 9 8 5 3   ♦ 7
♣ A Q 3   ♣ 10 7 5

♠ K Q 7 5
♥ A K 9 8 3
♦ 2
♣ J 9 6

After South opens the bidding 1 ♥, West overcalls 2 ♦. North would like to double this for penalty, but a double at this point would be negative, for takeout. North has to pass. When East passes, the bidding comes back to South. With shortness in diamonds, South should reopen with a double despite holding a minimum-strength hand. This allows for the possibility that North wants to penalize the opponent's contract, as in the actual layout. Otherwise, North can return to hearts or pick another contract. North is happy to pass and convert the reopening double into a penalty double.

East–West can't get out of trouble by playing the S.O.S. redouble (next chapter). Even if East redoubles, the partnership doesn't have a safe landing spot. East–West would probably wind up in worse trouble.

Suggested Opening Lead

North should lead the singleton in partner's suit, hoping to establish tricks in that suit, or to get ruffs, or both.

Suggested Play

This isn't a good deal for West, the declarer. West has one spade loser, two heart losers, four trump losers — due to the unfavorable split — and two club losers. There's not much declarer can do except hope to find an extra trick or two.

The defenders are likely to start by winning two high hearts and playing a third round for North to ruff. North may then lead the ♠A and another spade, which declarer can ruff. West should be aware from the auction that North has most of the missing trumps, so playing the ♦A and another diamond is unlikely to do much good. West should play a low diamond, letting North win the trick and putting North back on lead. If North leads another spade, declarer can ruff this and lead another low diamond. North wins but now has to lead a diamond or a club, which will help declarer. West may be able to take five or six tricks, not enough to make the contract.

Suggested Defense

The defenders should have an easy time defeating the doubled contract of 2♦. It's mostly a question of whether they collect 500, 800 or 1100 points.

After winning the first two tricks with the ♥A and ♥K, South should lead the ♥9, a high heart, for partner to ruff. This is a suit preference signal for the higher-ranking of the two logical suits, spade and clubs. After ruffing this trick, North should switch to spades, rather than clubs. With complete confidence in partner, North could lead a low spade. Now South can win the trick and lead a diamond or a club through declarer's strength. In practice, North will probably lead the ♠A and another spade, which declarer will ruff. The defenders should still get three more trump tricks and at least one club trick, for a penalty of 800 points. That's much more than the value of any game contract in their direction.

Bid and Play — Make the Best Bid Possible

(E–Z Deal Cards: #1, Deal 4 — Dealer, West)

Suggested Bidding

WEST	NORTH	EAST	SOUTH
Pass	1♦	1♠	Double
Pass	2♣	Pass	2♥
Pass	Pass	Pass	

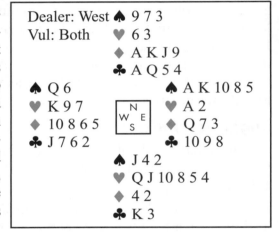

Dealer: West ♠ 9 7 3
Vul: Both   ♥ 6 3
             ♦ A K J 9
             ♣ A Q 5 4

♠ Q 6   ♠ A K 10 8 5
♥ K 9 7   ♥ A 2
♦ 10 8 6 5   ♦ Q 7 3
♣ J 7 6 2   ♣ 10 9 8

             ♠ J 4 2
             ♥ Q J 10 8 5 4
             ♦ 4 2
             ♣ K 3

With two four-card minors, North opens the higher-ranking, diamonds. East overcalls 1♠. That creates a challenge for South, who doesn't have enough to bid a new suit at the two level. An immediate 2♥ would be forcing and the partnership would probably get too high. Instead, South starts with a negative double, planning to bid hearts at the next opportunity.

West might venture 1NT but is more likely to pass opposite a one-level overcall. North, expecting partner to have support for both unbid suits, bids 2♣. Being vulnerable and not hearing any support from partner, East has done enough.

South now bids 2♥. This shows a five-card or longer heart suit with too little strength to freely bid 2♥ on the previous round. North can pass, leaving the partnership in its best contract.

Suggested Opening Lead

West is on lead and would start with the ♠Q, top of the doubleton in partner's suit.

Suggested Play

South has three immediate spade losers and two top heart losers. With no losers in diamonds or clubs, South's only concern is avoiding a third trump loser. To minimize that possibility, South should plan to lead trumps from dummy at every opportunity after gaining the lead. As discussed below, even that might not be good enough.

Suggested Defense

Excellent defense will defeat the 2♥ contract. When West leads the ♠Q, East can play an encouraging ♠10. West leads another spade, and East takes the ♠K and ♠A. West will discard a low club or a low diamond.

If East leads a fourth round of spades, declarer could discard a loser from one hand and ruff in the other — a ruff and a sluff. On this deal, however, East doesn't have anything to lose by leading another spade. Looking at dummy, East can see that the defenders are unlikely to get any tricks in diamonds or clubs, so the only hope is the trump suit. By leading another spade, East might be able to promote an extra trump winner for the defense.

If East does lead a fourth round of spades, the defense isn't over. Declarer is aware that West is out of spades and will ruff with the ♥10 (or ♥J or ♥Q) to prevent West from ruffing with the ♥9. If West overruffs with the ♥K, declarer will win the race. Whatever suit West returns, declarer can win in dummy and lead a trump. If East wins the ♥A and leads another spade, declarer can ruff high with the ♥J and draw the defender's remaining trumps with the ♥Q.

Instead, West must discard a club or a diamond when declarer ruffs with the ♥10, resisting the temptation to overruff with the ♥K. There's no harm in discarding, since the ♥K will always get a trick later. Declarer can cross to dummy and lead a heart, but East could win the ♥A and lead a fifth round of spades. Again, if declarer ruffs high with the ♥J, West must again discard and resist the temptation to overruff. Now West's ♥K and ♥9 will take two tricks, since the only high heart declarer has left is the ♥Q.

Even if East ducks the first heart led from dummy, declarer will have to play the ♥J to force out West's ♥K. Declarer wins West's return in dummy and leads a second round of hearts, which East wins with the ♥A. Again, East leads the last spade. With only the ♥Q left, declarer has no winning option. If declarer ruffs low, West overruffs with the ♥9. If declarer ruffs with the ♥Q, West's ♥9 is promoted into a trick.

CHAPTER 2
Other Doubles

OTHER DOUBLES

The double is a versatile call that can be put to many uses other than penalty. In order to use the double for more than one purpose, both partners must understand what the double means in each bidding situation.

When a double is used at some point in the auction, it's important that both partners agree on whether the double is for penalty, for takeout or is somewhere in between: cooperative or optional — giving partner the choice of leaving the double in for penalty or taking it out. There are different situations and many types of doubles, so the partnership needs general guidelines.

Doubles Which Are Primarily for Takeout

Some doubles are clearly intended for takeout. Partner is expected to bid, unless the intervening opponent bids or redoubles.

THE CLASSIC TAKEOUT DOUBLE

When an opponent opens the bidding with a natural bid in a suit, a double of a partscore contract at the first opportunity is for takeout unless partner has already doubled or overcalled. If partner has already doubled or overcalled, then a double is for penalty unless the partnership has another agreement.   *3RD DBL IS PENALTY*

West					East
♠ Q 8 6	WEST	NORTH	EAST	SOUTH	♠ 7 3
♥ J 6 5 3	Pass	1♠	**Dbl**	Pass	♥ A Q 8 4
♦ Q 10 8 3	2♥	Pass	Pass	Pass	♦ K 9 5
♣ 9 6					♣ K Q 8 3

East's double of North's opening suit bid is for takeout, showing support for the unbid suits. With a weak hand, West bids a suit at the cheapest available level. With a choice of suits, West picks the unbid major because it is worth more, and East will usually have four cards in the unbid major. Support for the unbid minors may be a little more suspect. Having described the hand with a takeout double, East has nothing further to add when West doesn't show an interest in game.

The double of a preemptive opening bid is for takeout. Consider this example:

West		East
♠ K Q 7 3		♠ J 10 6 2
♥ 3		♥ Q 9 4
♦ A 9 7 6		♦ K J 10 2
♣ K J 4 3		♣ A 5

WEST	NORTH	EAST	SOUTH
			3♥
Dbl	Pass	4♠	Pass
Pass	Pass		

The higher the level, the stronger West should be to bring the partnership into the auction. Nonetheless, the player with the right distribution should stretch to compete in order to avoid being shut out of the auction by the opponent's preempt. East should rarely leave partner's takeout double in for penalty, even at a high level. With 11 HCPs, East has enough to jump to game, expecting a good hand from partner for a takeout double at the three level. If East doesn't bid game, East–West will miss game, because West won't bid again for fear East has been forced to respond with very few points.

In the next auction, North and South bid two suits, so the double shows the two unbid suits.

West		East
♠ 10 8 6 2		♠ A J 9 3
♥ J 9		♥ 7 5
♦ A 10 7 4		♦ J 6 5
♣ K 8 2		♣ A Q J 4

WEST	NORTH	EAST	SOUTH
			1♦
Pass	1♥	Dbl	2♥
2♠	Pass	Pass	Pass

East's double is for takeout, showing support for spades and clubs. Once South bids, West doesn't have to bid, but with 8 points, West should compete for the contract.

A passed hand can make a takeout double as seen in the following example:

West		East
♠ 9		♠ K J 8 7
♥ K 10 7 5		♥ Q J 6 2
♦ Q 10 9 6		♦ A 8 5
♣ A 8 6 3		♣ 10 7

WEST	NORTH	EAST	SOUTH
Pass	1♠	Pass	1NT
Dbl	Pass	2♥	Pass
Pass	Pass		

Although West passed originally, West can still make a takeout double. If East had overcalled or doubled, however, West's double would be for penalty, unless the partnership has some other agreement. The double of South's 1NT response shows support for the unbid suits — clubs, diamonds and hearts.

East, even with 11 HCPs, doesn't jump in response to the takeout double. From West's initial pass, East knows the partnership is only competing for a partscore.

The double of a 2NT response is for takeout.

West					East
♠ 10 6 2	WEST	NORTH	EAST	SOUTH	♠ A Q 8 5
♥ Q 9 7 5				1 ♥	♥ —
♦ 8 2	Pass	2NT	**Dbl**	4 ♥	♦ K 10 9 7 3
♣ Q 10 7 5	Pass	Pass	Pass		♣ K J 6 4

East's double of North's 2NT response is a takeout double for the unbid suits. It would be unusual for East to want to make a takeout double after North's natural 2NT response, since North–South presumably have the balance of strength. It would be more common if North–South are using Jacoby 2NT and the 2NT response shows a fit for hearts.

A takeout double can also be used to show a hand too strong for a simple overcall — about 17 or more HCP.

West					East
♠ Q 8 2	WEST	NORTH	EAST	SOUTH	♠ A K J 9 7 5
♥ 9 6 2		1 ♥	**Dbl**	Pass	♥ K 7
♦ K J 8 5 2	2 ♦	Pass	2 ♠	Pass	♦ Q 7
♣ 8 3	3 ♠	Pass	4 ♠	Pass	♣ K Q 7
	Pass	Pass			

West responds under the assumption that East has a standard takeout double. When East bids again, West invites to game. If East overcalled 1 ♠, West might have passed, and the reasonable game contract would be missed.

In the balancing position — where the opening bid has been followed by two passes — the doubler is given some latitude.

West				East
♠ 9 5				♠ A 8 4
♥ K Q 7 3				♥ 6 5
♦ Q 9 5				♦ K J 10 7 3
♣ K 10 6 5				♣ Q J 7

WEST	NORTH	EAST	SOUTH
	1♠	Pass	Pass
Dbl	Pass	3♦	Pass
Pass	Pass		

A balancing takeout double by West can be made with less than the values required by East in the direct position — immediately following the opening bid. West may stretch to enter the auction, because there is an inference from South's pass that East holds some values. Nonetheless, West could have full values, so East should not be too cautious in responding.

With game invitational values, East can jump a level. West passes with a below average takeout double. Exactly how light West may be to double in this position is a matter of partnership style, but most partnerships allow as few as 9 or 10 high-card points. *← IN BALANCING SEAT*

If West had passed originally, it would be obvious that West didn't have a hand worth an opening bid. East would take that into account and bid only 2♦, since the partnership can't have game-going values.

THE BALANCING DOUBLE

The previous example might be considered a form of balancing double, since the logic of the situation dictates that West should take some action to prevent the opponents from buying the contract too cheaply. West, however, could still have the full values for a takeout double in the above auction. A more typical situation in which a takeout double is made with less than the values for an opening bid is the following:

West				East
♠ Q 10 8 2				♠ A J 6 3
♥ J 3				♥ 10 4
♦ K 9 6 5				♦ A 10 3
♣ K J 3				♣ 10 9 5 2

WEST	NORTH	EAST	SOUTH
			1♥
Pass	2♥	Pass	Pass
Dbl	Pass	2♠	Pass
Pass	3♥	Pass	Pass
Pass			

At one time, West's double was treated as a penalty double, since West had the opportunity to make a takeout double on the first round of bidding.

Today, most partnerships treat West's double as takeout. The opponents have found a fit and stopped in partscore. West knows that partner has some strength and takes a balancing action. The idea is to try to find a playable partscore contract or perhaps to push the opponents to a higher level than they planned. Once East–West find their eight-card spade fit, the opponents go one level higher to play in their trump suit. East doesn't bid any more, knowing that partner didn't have enough strength to make a takeout double on the first round. East–West hope they can defeat 3 ♥.

The partnership needs to be clear on the ground rules for this type of double. There are similar sounding auctions where the double may or may not be for takeout. These are discussed later in the chapter.

RESPONDER'S TAKEOUT (NEGATIVE) DOUBLE

As discussed in the previous chapter, the partnership may agree to play the negative double. After an opening bid of one-of-a-suit, responder's double of a natural overcall in a suit up to and including 2 ♠ (or higher if that is the partnership agreement) is for takeout.

West
♠ K 9 2
♥ K J 8 5
♦ A Q 9 6
♣ 7 4

WEST	NORTH	EAST	SOUTH
1 ♦	1 ♠	**Dbl**	Pass
2 ♥	Pass	Pass	Pass

East
♠ 8 4 3
♥ Q 10 7 3
♦ 10 8
♣ A Q 6 5

North's overcall prevents East from responding 1 ♥. East uses the negative double to show the values to compete and to show support for the unbid suits, hearts and clubs. In effect, the end result is as though North had passed, East had responded 1 ♥ and West had raised to 2 ♥.

OPENER'S TAKEOUT DOUBLE

The opening bidder can make a takeout double if the opponents compete in a suit and partner passes. Opener's double of a partscore contract would be for takeout.

West	WEST	NORTH	EAST	SOUTH	East
♠ A Q 9 2	1♦	1♥	Pass	2♥	♠ 7 4 3
♥ 6	**Dbl**	Pass	3♣	Pass	♥ J 10 7 5
♦ A K 9 5	Pass	Pass			♦ 10 3
♣ K J 10 5					♣ Q 9 6 4

After West opens the bidding, North–South compete in the auction. West's double is for takeout, showing a strong hand with shortness in the opponents' suit.

West	WEST	NORTH	EAST	SOUTH	East
♠ 5 4	1♥	Pass	Pass	1♠	♠ Q 10 8 2
♥ A Q J 8 4	**Dbl**	Pass	2♥	Pass	♥ 10 7 3
♦ K Q 7	Pass	Pass			♦ J 8 6 4
♣ A Q 10					♣ 8 2

Despite East's pass of the opening bid, West wants to compete when South enters the auction with an overcall. West makes a takeout double, showing support for the unbid suits. East has to choose between bidding diamonds and supporting hearts. Knowing West holds five hearts for the opening bid, East makes a suitable decision.

West	WEST	NORTH	EAST	SOUTH	East
♠ A K 9 4 3	1♠	2♦	Pass	Pass	♠ 6
♥ Q 8 6 2	**Dbl**	Pass	Pass	Pass	♥ K 10 5
♦ 4					♦ K Q 10 8 3
♣ A 8 3					♣ J 9 7 2

If the partnership plays the negative double, opener should reopen the bidding with a takeout double when short in the opponent's suit, after an overcall followed by two passes. The double serves a dual purpose. East may pass with length and strength in the opponent's suit, converting the takeout double into a penalty double. Otherwise, East takes the double out. West doesn't need extra strength to make a takeout double in this situation because of the way the negative double works. If the partnership does not play the negative double, West would need extra values to make a takeout double.

OVERCALLER'S TAKEOUT DOUBLE

It is also possible to make a takeout double after making an overcall.

West			East
♠ 7 4			♠ A K J 8 5
♥ J 8 6 3			♥ 4
♦ Q 4			♦ A J 8 2
♣ Q J 8 4 2			♣ K 10 7

WEST	NORTH	EAST	SOUTH
Pass	1 ♥	1 ♠	2 ♥
Pass	Pass	**Dbl**	Pass
3 ♣	Pass	Pass	Pass

East overcalls with a good five-card suit. When the bidding comes back around, East wants to compete further. East's double is for takeout and shows a strong hand that wasn't ideal for an initial takeout double. West shouldn't expect four-card support for the unbid suits. Without a reasonable suit to bid, West could return to East's overcalled suit.

COOPERATIVE, COMPETITIVE, AND OPTIONAL DOUBLES

Many doubles fall somewhere between takeout and penalty. These go by various names depending on the exact partnership agreements — cooperative, competitive and optional. They are takeout doubles that give partner the option of passing for penalty because the doubler has additional strength. In deciding whether a cooperative double should be left in for penalty or taken out, it's important to consider the level of the auction, whether or not the opponents have found a fit and the position of the doubler.

The Level

The higher the level at which a double is made, the fewer tricks are needed to defeat the contract. Defending for penalty is much more appealing when the opponents are at the four level or higher.

The Importance of Fit

If the opponents have found a suitable trump fit, avoid defending a partscore for penalty with no length or strength in the opponents' suit, unless there are considerable extra values. The trump suit is very powerful, especially when combined with shortness in other suits. Declarer can often make a lot of tricks with very few high cards when distribution is taken into account. Don't be too eager to double for penalty just because the partnership appears to have the majority of the high-card strength.

In addition, when one side has an eight-card or longer trump fit, the other side will usually have a fit of its own. Look to play in the partnership's best trump fit. If one side has a fit in two suits, the other side will invariably have an eight-card or longer fit.

On the other hand, if the opponents have not found a fit, then defending for penalty becomes more appealing. The largest penalties are usually obtained when the opponents have a misfit. If that appears to be the situation, be more willing to defend.

Over or Under

Suppose the opponents have reached a heart contract and one defender holds ♥ K J 9. The defensive prospects depend on whether the defender is sitting over (behind or to the left) or under (before or to the right) the opponent who likely has the length and strength in the suit.

Consider these two layouts:

1)	NORTH	2)	NORTH
	♥ 8 6 3		♥ 8 6 3
WEST ■ EAST		WEST ■ EAST	
♥ K J 9 ♥ 4 2		♥ 4 2 ♥ K J 9	
	SOUTH		SOUTH
	♥ A Q 10 7 5		♥ A Q 10 7 5

If South has bid hearts, the West position is over the heart bidder and will likely get two heart tricks on defense as in the first layout. If the ♥ K J 9 is held by East under the heart bidder, there may not be any tricks if declarer can reach the North hand twice to take finesses, as in the second example.

Defending in the first situation is better than in the second, so be aware of the position at the table when considering whether to take a double out or leave it in for penalty. Of course, it's not always clear how the opponents' high cards are located. North could hold the ♥ A or ♥ Q or both. The auction, however, will usually give some indication.

Cooperative (Competitive, Optional) Doubles in Action

Here are examples of doubles that are cooperative in nature — partner may leave the double in for penalty or take it out. These doubles typically occur after the first round of bidding.

The double can be made by the responder.

West			East
♠ Q 3			♠ A 4
♥ J 8 3			♥ K Q 9 7 2
♦ A 10 9 7 4			♦ 6 5
♣ K Q 5			♣ J 8 7 2

WEST	NORTH	EAST	SOUTH
1♦	Pass	1♥	1♠
Pass	2♠	**Dbl**	Pass
3♥	Pass	Pass	Pass

After West's opening bid and East's initial response, South comes into the bidding with an overcall. With a minimum-strength hand for the opening bid, West passes. (Some partnerships would have West double now. This would be a support double showing three-card heart support. You can read more about support doubles beginning on page 344.) North raises partner's overcall to the two level, giving East a tough decision. With an invitational-strength hand — 10 HCPs plus 1 for the five-card suit — East doesn't want to leave the opponents in their 2 ♠ partscore, but doesn't have a good bid at this point. East doubles. Since the opponents have found a fit in spades and are only at the two level, this is a cooperative double rather than a penalty double. East wants partner to take some action. With a minimum hand and poor defense against the opponents' contract, West belatedly shows heart support. East–West reach their best partscore despite North–South's interference.

Here's another example:

West					East
♠ A K 8 4 3					♠ J 5
♥ Q 2					♥ J 9 3
♦ 7 2					♦ A Q J 4 3
♣ A 10 8 5					♣ K 9 2

WEST	NORTH	EAST	SOUTH
1♠	2♥	3♦	4♥
Pass	Pass	**Dbl**	Pass
Pass	Pass		

After West's opening bid and North's overcall, East shows the diamond suit. South jumps to game and the bidding comes back to East, whose double at this point doesn't show a lot of hearts. East is merely saying, "I think we have the majority of strength, and I don't want to let the opponents take the contract away from us undoubled." At this level, West decides that it will be easier to take four or more tricks on defense than to try for ten or more on offense. So West passes and converts the optional double into a penalty double.

A double can be made after an original negative double.

West					East
♠ Q 8 5					♠ 7 6
♥ K 7 4 3					♥ A Q J 5
♦ 7 2					♦ K J 9 6
♣ A K J 6					♣ 8 4 2

WEST	NORTH	EAST	SOUTH
1♣	1♠	Dbl	2♠
Pass	Pass	**Dbl**	Pass
3♥	Pass	Pass	Pass

East's first double is for take out, a negative double. South raises the overcall, and West no longer has to bid with a minimum opening. When the bidding comes back around, East doubles again to show extra values. Since the opponents have found a fit, East's double is cooperative in nature. West has to decide what to do. Knowing the partnership has an eight-card heart fit, West chooses to bid rather than risk defending at such a low level. East–West might defeat the 2♠ contract, but they might not. It's usually best to bid when both sides have a fit.

At times the first double is made after the opponents get to game.

West					East
♠ Q 9 7 6 5 3					♠ A K 4
♥ J 4					♥ 8
♦ Q 9 3					♦ A K J 5
♣ 6 5					♣ K 9 7 4 2

WEST	NORTH	EAST	SOUTH
			1♥
Pass	4♥	**Dbl**	Pass
4♠	Pass	Pass	Pass

The auction is already at the game level by the time East has an opportunity to bid. Although doubles at the game level or higher are typically for penalty, a double in this situation is really optional, or cooperative. With both North and South showing length in hearts, East can't be expected to have many tricks in the trump suit, sitting under the opening bidder. Instead, East's double is strength-showing, and it's up to West to decide whether to leave the double in for penalty or take it out. With little defensive strength but good playing potential, West elects to remove the double by bidding 4♠. West is expecting that some of East's strength will be in the spade suit.

The situation would be similar if South had opened the bidding 4♥ and both West and North passed. East's double would be more of a balancing double, promising strength, but not a lot of hearts.

DELAYED TAKEOUT DOUBLE

A takeout double after the first opportunity to double sends a slightly different message.

West		WEST	NORTH	EAST	SOUTH		East
♠ K 7 6 4					1♣		♠ Q J 5 3
♥ 5		Pass	1♥	Pass	2♥		♥ K 8 4 2
♦ K J 9 3		**Dbl**	Pass	2♠	Pass		♦ 10 7 6
♣ A K J 5		Pass	Pass				♣ 6 2

Without support for hearts, West can't make a takeout double initially. Once the opponents have found their heart fit, West would like to compete for the contract in one of the other suits. West's delayed double shows support for the unbid suits — spades and diamonds — but also for clubs, South's suit. With a two-suited hand of spades and diamonds, West would probably have overcalled one of the suits. Although West's double is for takeout, the fact that West has some length and strength in opener's first bid suit increases the likelihood that East might want to defend for penalty with a good holding in hearts. East has a fit for spades and not enough strength or length in hearts to consider passing the double.

DOUBLES THAT ARE PRIMARILY FOR PENALTY

A double that isn't for takeout and isn't cooperative is meant for penalty. Partner does have the option of taking the double out with exceptional distribution or undisclosed values, but that's the exception. Experienced partnerships sometimes have other conventional agreements, but these are outside the scope of standard practice.

Here are examples of penalty doubles. West's belated double is for penalty.

West					East
♠ 2					♠ 9 7 6 4 3
♥ Q J 10 8 6					♥ —
♦ A Q 6					♦ 9 8 4 2
♣ A 8 7 3					♣ J 10 4 2

WEST	NORTH	EAST	SOUTH
			1♥
Pass	2♥	Pass	4♥
Dbl	Pass	Pass	Pass

The opponents are now in a game contract, and West had an opportunity to make a takeout double on the first round and didn't. It's not a good idea to make a penalty double when it might help declarer make the contract by figuring out how the missing cards lie. West, however, feels that there's not much declarer will be able to do to overcome the unlucky trump division.

A direct double of an opening notrump bid is for penalty — assuming the partnership doesn't use a conventional defense to the opponents' 1NT opening.

West					East
♠ Q 7 5 2					♠ A 6
♥ J 6 4 2					♥ K 10 3
♦ 8 2					♦ K Q J 10 5
♣ 10 5 4					♣ K J 3

WEST	NORTH	EAST	SOUTH
Pass	1NT	**Dbl**	Pass
Pass	Pass		

A direct double of an opening notrump bid usually promises at least the upper range of the strength shown by the opponent's bid. If North–South are using a range of 15 to 17 points, for example, East would have 16 or more points.

Be careful about doubling an opening 1NT bid for penalty without a good suit to lead. This can make the contract difficult to defeat, since partner will have very few points. With scattered values, it's usually best to pass and defend quietly, even with a lot of points.

The double of an opponent's overcall after partner opens the bidding 1NT is for penalty, unless the partnership has some other agreement.

West					East
♠ A 10 7 3					♠ K 5 2
♥ J 4					♥ Q 10 8 2
♦ A K J 5					♦ 4 3
♣ K 9 5					♣ Q J 7 2

WEST	NORTH	EAST	SOUTH
1NT	2♥	**Dbl**	Pass
Pass	Pass		

After West opens 1NT and North overcalls 2♥, East's double is for penalty, not takeout.

Assume East–West have agreed to play negative doubles through 2♠ only.

West					East
♠ 6					♠ K 10 8 2
♥ Q 9 3					♥ A K 8 2
♦ A K 8 7 3					♦ 6 5
♣ K J 8 4					♣ Q 6 2

WEST	NORTH	EAST	SOUTH
1♦	3♠	**Dbl**	Pass
Pass	Pass		

East's double of North's 3♠ bid is for penalty. With a normal opening bid, West has no reason to overrule partner's decision. Had North overcalled 1♠ or 2♠, a double by East would be for takeout.

A double of a notrump overcall is for penalty.

West					East
♠ 6					♠ K 10 8 2
♥ Q 9 3					♥ J 8 4 2
♦ A K 8 7 3					♦ J 6 5
♣ K J 8 4					♣ A 6

WEST	NORTH	EAST	SOUTH
1♦	1NT	**Dbl**	Pass
Pass	Pass		

East's double of North's 1NT overcall is for penalty. With West having opened the bidding and East holding a reasonably balanced hand and 9 points or more, it's unlikely North will be able to take seven tricks in a notrump contract.

Double by either partner of an opponent's opening notrump bid or notrump overcall is for penalty.

West	WEST	NORTH	EAST	SOUTH	East
♠ A 7 3	1♥	1NT	Pass	Pass	♠ J 9 4 2
♥ K Q J 10 8	**Dbl**	Pass	Pass	Pass	♥ 7 5
♦ A 5					♦ Q 7 6 3
♣ A J 5					♣ 10 8 2

West's reopening double in this situation is for penalty, not takeout. West is showing a better hand than North and is willing to defend, even though East hasn't promised any strength.

If the partnership has found a fit, the double of the opponent's bid is for penalty.

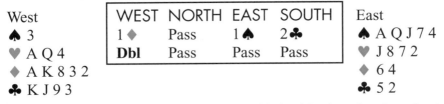

West	WEST	NORTH	EAST	SOUTH	East
♠ A 6	1♥	Pass	3♥	4♣	♠ K Q 8 2
♥ A Q 8 4 3	**Dbl**	Pass	Pass	Pass	♥ K J 7 2
♦ 9 2					♦ Q 10 5
♣ Q J 9 3					♣ 4 2

West's double is for penalty. East–West have already found a suitable trump fit.

With only one unbid suit, a double is for penalty.

West	WEST	NORTH	EAST	SOUTH	East
♠ 3	1♦	Pass	1♠	2♣	♠ A Q J 7 4
♥ A Q 4	**Dbl**	Pass	Pass	Pass	♥ J 8 7 2
♦ A K 8 3 2					♦ 6 4
♣ K J 9 3					♣ 5 2

Some partnerships use a *support double* in this situation (see the Appendix). Without any special agreement, West is saying that South has made a mistake coming into the auction.

A double can be for penalty when the opponents are at the game level.

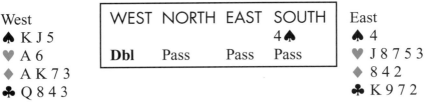

West	WEST	NORTH	EAST	SOUTH	East
♠ K J 5				4♠	♠ 4
♥ A 6	**Dbl**	Pass	Pass	Pass	♥ J 8 7 5 3
♦ A K 7 3					♦ 8 4 2
♣ Q 8 4 3					♣ K 9 7 2

With the long spade suit in South's hand, West expects to get tricks with both the ♠K and ♠J. If North had opened the bidding 4♠ and East and South had passed, West's double would be more cooperative in nature, since West would be under the spade bidder.

A double is for penalty when partner has already bid, unless the partnership has other agreements.

West		East
♠ A K J 8 6		♠ 5
♥ 5		♥ Q J 10 7
♦ J 7 5 2		♦ A K 6
♣ A 6 5		♣ J 10 8 3 2

WEST	NORTH	EAST	SOUTH
			1♥
1♠	3♥	Dbl	Pass
Pass	Pass		

East's double is for penalty, because West has already bid. East's double would also be for penalty if West had made a takeout double rather than overcalled. This situation is rare, since doubling the opponents' partscore contract for penalty when they have found a fit is usually dangerous. Some partnerships prefer to put the double to other uses in this situation. (See *responsive doubles* in the Appendix.)

In the following example, the opponents have not found a fit.

West		East
♠ A Q J 8 2		♠ 4
♥ 5		♥ Q 10 8 7 3
♦ A K 3		♦ 7 6 4 2
♣ K 7 4 2		♣ J 10 5

WEST	NORTH	EAST	SOUTH
			1♠
Pass	1NT	Pass	2♠
Dbl	Pass	Pass	Pass

West's double sounds similar to the balancing double discussed previously. It looks as though the opponents are about to settle in a partscore in spades. Most partnerships, however, would play West's double for penalty. North–South have not found a fit. North may be quite short in spades. West had a chance to make a takeout double on the first round of the auction and didn't. In addition, West is not in the balancing position. If West passed, East would still have an opportunity to balance.

Double of a Conventional (Artificial) Bid

If an opponent makes a conventional (artificial) call, a double is penalty-oriented, unless the partnership has discussed some other specific defense to the convention. In practice, it is highly unlikely that the opponents are planning to play in a suit they have bid conventionally, so the double really suggests that partner take some subsequent action. This is easier to follow through some examples.

West					East
♠ K 2	WEST	NORTH	EAST	SOUTH	♠ 7 3
♥ A Q 10 8 5 3			Pass	1♠	♥ K 6 2
♦ K Q 4	2♥	3♥	Dbl	3♠	♦ 8 6 5 2
♣ J 4	Pass	4♠	Pass	Pass	♣ Q 8 6 3
	Pass				

North's 3♥ bid is conventional, showing support for South's spade suit. East's double merely says, "I have some strength in hearts, partner." East's double may help West decide whether or not to bid higher, or it may help West find the best opening lead.

West					East
♠ 6	WEST	NORTH	EAST	SOUTH	♠ K J 10 8 3
♥ Q 9 3	1♦	2♦	Dbl	2♥	♥ K 10 2
♦ A K 8 7 3	Dbl	Pass	Pass	2♠	♦ 6 5
♣ K J 8 4	Pass	Pass	Dbl	Pass	♣ A 6 2
	Pass	Pass			

North's 2♦ overall is conventional, showing both major suits. East's first double is penalty-oriented, showing a willingness to defend. East isn't expecting North–South to play in 2♦, since diamonds is West's suit. When South chooses hearts as a trump suit, West makes a penalty double, with the knowledge that partner is likely to have some length in the heart suit to have suggested defending. When the bidding comes around again, South tries 2♠. West, holding a singleton spade, isn't as eager to double that contract for penalty and passes the decision to partner. East doubles for penalty.

In the next example, North's 2♣ is the Stayman convention in response to South's opening bid of 1NT, asking opener to bid a four-card major suit.

West					East
♠ Q 9 5 3	WEST	NORTH	EAST	SOUTH	♠ J 7 2
♥ J 7 3				1NT	♥ 8 6
♦ K 10 7 6	Pass	2♣	Dbl	2♥	♦ 9 5 3
♣ 6 3	Pass	4♥	Pass	Pass	♣ A K J 10 4
	Pass				

East's double shows strength in clubs, but isn't for takeout. Since it's unlikely the opponents will want to play with clubs as trump, East's primary purpose in doubling is to help partner with the opening lead. If the opponents arrive in 3NT or some other contract, East is suggesting that a club lead may be the best start for the defense. This is sometimes referred to as a *lead-directing double*. Occasionally, partner might enter the auction with a good fit for the suit being shown.

The situation would be similar if North had responded to South's 1NT with a conventional 2 ♥ as a Jacoby transfer to 2 ♠. A double by East would show strength in hearts. It would be different if North responded with a natural 2 ♥ bid. Then a double by East would be for takeout.

Some partnerships have special agreements about doubles of responses to a 1NT opening bid. For example, if the 1NT opening is a weak notrump, such as 12 to 14 points, some players use the double of any response as a general strength-showing bid, rather than showing a specific suit. This requires some discussion beforehand to make sure both partners are in agreement about the meaning of the double in various situations.

THE LEAD-DIRECTING DOUBLE

The last auction (see page 55) shows an example of a lead-directing double — a double which may help partner find the best opening lead on defense. Such doubles occur in a variety of different formats.

Double of a Conventional Bid

Without specific agreements to the contrary, a double of an opponent's conventional bid shows strength in that suit. At a low level, the doubler will usually have enough length in the suit that the opponents won't want to play in the doubled contract. With a fit, partner may occasionally be influenced into competing in that suit, but the initial purpose is to tell partner the suit you'd like led on defense. At a higher level, the double of the conventional bid is almost always lead-directing and may be based on only one or two high cards in the suit.

Here are two examples:

West			East
♠ Q 10 3			♠ 9 4
♥ K 8 3			♥ A Q J 9 5
♦ A 9 4 3			♦ K 8 6 2
♣ K 8 5			♣ 10 7

WEST	NORTH	EAST	SOUTH
	Pass	Pass	1NT
Pass	2♥	**Dbl**	2♠
3♥	3♠	Pass	Pass
Pass			

North's 2♥ response is announced as a Jacoby transfer bid, asking opener to bid spades, so East's double shows length and strength in hearts. This influences West to compete to 3♥ after South accepts the transfer, pushing North–South to the three level, perhaps high enough that East–West can defeat the contract.

West			East
♠ 10 9 8 5 2			♠ 7 6 3
♥ 6 3			♥ 8 4 2
♦ 10 6 5 3			♦ K Q 7
♣ 9 4			♣ A 6 3 2

WEST	NORTH	EAST	SOUTH
	Pass	Pass	1♥
Pass	2♣	Pass	3♥
Pass	4♥	Pass	4NT
Pass	5♦	**Dbl**	6♥
Pass	Pass	Pass	

With interest in reaching a slam, South uses the Blackwood convention. North's response of 5♦ is conventional, showing one ace. East uses this opportunity to double, asking partner to lead a diamond. East hopes to establish a diamond winner while the ♣A is still an entry. Without the double, West might lead another suit.

It's important that both partners listen carefully to an auction such as this. If East's diamonds and spades were exchanged, East would pass over North's conventional 5♦ response. West should take this silence into account when deciding what to lead. By inference, West should lead a spade, since East had an opportunity to double diamonds but failed to do so. This concept is not easy, but it is a step on the path to becoming a better defender.

The Lightner Double

If the opponents voluntarily bid to a slam contract, they are unlikely to be defeated by more than one trick. There's little to be gained by doubling them — you're already getting a fine result if they go down.

Theodore Lightner, a top player from the early days of contract bridge, invented a better use for the double. He suggested that if the player not on lead doubled a voluntarily bid slam, then the double would request the opening leader to make an unusual lead, one which might result in the defeat of the contract.

A Lightner double asks partner not to lead a trump and not to make the standard lead of a suit bid by the defenders or an unbid suit. It usually asks for the lead of a side suit bid by the opponents. The doubler may be able to ruff that suit or have two tricks to take if that suit is led. If the opening leader is in doubt as to which suit to lead, the first suit bid by dummy is usually considered to be the most likely one being requested by partner. But the opening leader is expected to use good judgment. Here is an example in a complete deal:

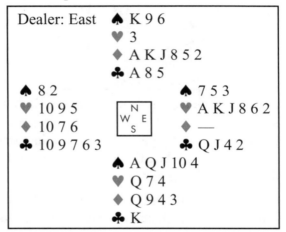

WEST	NORTH	EAST	SOUTH
		1 ♥	1 ♠
Pass	2 ♦	Pass	3 ♦
Pass	4NT	Pass	5 ♦
Pass	6 ♠	**Dbl**	Pass
Pass	Pass		

After East opens the bidding 1 ♥, North–South get to slam. East makes a Lightner double, asking for an unusual lead. Without the double, West would probably have led a heart — partner's suit — or a club — the unbid suit. After the double, West makes the unusual lead of a diamond, the side suit bid and raised by the opponents. East ruffs and takes a trick with the ♥ A to defeat the contract. If West leads anything but a diamond, declarer will make the contract.

Perhaps North shouldn't have shown the diamond suit on this auction. If North had immediately bid slam, East might still double for an unusual lead, but West would have to guess whether to lead a diamond or a club. West might pick the longer suit, clubs, hoping that was the suit partner could ruff. South would take all of the tricks after a club lead.

The Lightner double is rare, but it can be useful when the right situation arises.

Other Lead-Directing Doubles

The principle of the Lightner double calling for an unusual lead has been extended to other doubles. The most frequent use is when the opponents have freely bid to 3NT, and the player who is not on lead doubles. Conventionally, this double asks partner to lead from one of the following suits, in order of priority:

- suit bid by the opening leader.
- A suit bid by the doubler.
- Dummy's first-bid suit, if it has not been rebid.

If neither side has bid a suit during the auction, the double shows a solid suit. If the opening leader can find the lead of that suit, the contract should be defeated. With nothing to go on, the opening leader will tend to lead a short major suit, hoping that's the right one.

Here are a couple of examples:

West	WEST	NORTH	EAST	SOUTH	East
♠ Q J 9 8 5				1♦	♠ 2
♥ 6 3	Pass	1♥	Pass	1NT	♥ K Q J 10 8
♦ 10 6 5	Pass	3NT	**Dbl**	Pass	♦ A 7 4
♣ 8 4 2	Pass	Pass			♣ J 10 9 3

East's double of 3NT asks West to find an unusual lead. Since neither West nor East has bid a suit, the next priority is dummy's first-bid suit.

West should lead a heart. East hopes to establish four heart winners with the ♦ A as an entry. If East doesn't double, West will make the standard lead of a spade. Declarer will then be able to drive out East's ♦ A before the defenders can establish enough winners to defeat the contract.

West					East
♠ 6 4					♠ A K Q J 10
♥ 10 9 7 3					♥ 8 4 2
♦ Q 8 4 2					♦ 7 6
♣ J 8 6					♣ 10 7 3

WEST	NORTH	EAST	SOUTH
			1NT
Pass	3NT	**Dbl**	Pass
Pass	Pass		

Knowing it's highly unlikely partner will lead a spade against the opponents' 3NT contract, East makes a lead-directing double. West isn't sure which solid suit East has, but it doesn't figure to be clubs or diamonds, since West has honors in both of those suits. West picks the shorter major and leads a spade. If West had guessed wrong, the opponents would make their doubled contract, probably with an overtrick or two. That's the chance East takes by making a conventional double.

THE REDOUBLE

The redouble is a call that is used infrequently. It can be made whenever an opponent doubles and there has been no intervening bid. Remember that pass is a call but not a bid.

For example:

WEST	NORTH	**EAST**	SOUTH
1 ♥	Double	?	

East can redouble, or West can redouble if East and South pass. South can't redouble partner's double. If East or South make a call other than pass, then West can't redouble. Three passes following a redouble ends the auction. The effect of the redouble is to increase the penalty if the contract is defeated and increase the trick score and bonuses for overtricks if the contract is made. There is a bonus of 100 points for making a redoubled contract.

A redouble is rarely used to increase the score when one side has been doubled for penalty. The loss for declarer's side will be large if the contract is defeated, and declarer's side will usually get an excellent result if the doubled contract is made. By far the more common use of the redouble is following a takeout double.

Redouble after a Takeout Double

When an opponent makes a takeout double, most players use the redouble to let partner know that the hand belongs to their side. Typically, when partner's opening suit bid at the one level is doubled, a redouble shows a hand of 10 or more points, but it doesn't tell opener what to do next with all of this combined strength. The redoubler could be planning to double the opponents' contract for penalty; the redoubler could be intending to show support for opener's suit; the redoubler could be planning to bid a new suit or notrump. The redoubler intends to describe the exact nature of the hand during the next round of bidding.

Not knowing which type of hand responder has for the redouble, opener will usually pass until responder has had an opportunity to describe the hand. Opener does have the option of doubling, if the next opponent bids, or bidding immediately with a weak distributional hand unsuitable for defending.

Here are examples of how the auction might proceed after a redouble.

West	WEST	NORTH	EAST	SOUTH	East
♠ 8 5	1 ♥	Double	**Redbl**	Pass	♠ K J 10 7
♥ A K J 8 5	Pass	1 ♠	Double	Pass	♥ 4 2
♦ A 9	Pass	Pass			♦ Q J 5 2
♣ Q 10 6 2					♣ A 7 5

After North doubles, East, holding 11 HCPs, redoubles. South no longer has to respond to the takeout double and passes with nothing to say. West passes to await a further description of the redoubler's hand. North now has to bid or let East–West play in 1 ♥ redoubled, which would often be made with overtricks for a large score. North tries 1 ♠. With good defensive prospects and shortness in West's suit, East doubles for penalty. With a sound opening bid and a hand suitable for defending, West is happy to respect partner's decision.

If South, rather than North, had bid 1♠ or 2♦, West would have passed to see what East was planning to do. If South had bid 2♣, West could double. That would let partner know West was willing to defend, especially if East could take care of any other suit the opponents might choose to bid.

West		East
♠ 8 5		♠ K 10 7
♥ A K J 8 5		♥ 10 2
♦ A 9		♦ Q 5 2
♣ Q 10 6 2		♣ A K 9 7 5

WEST	NORTH	EAST	SOUTH
1♥	Double	**Redbl**	1♠
Pass	Pass	2♣	Pass
3♣	Pass	3NT	Pass
Pass	Pass		

With a hand worth 13 points — 12 HCPs plus 1 point for the five-card suit — East announces that the East–West partnership holds the majority of strength by redoubling. When South bids 1♠, West passes the auction to partner. East doesn't have the right type of hand to double 1♠. Instead, East bids a new suit. This new-suit bid is forcing, since East has already promised 10 or more points. West raises, and the partnership reaches an excellent game contract.

West		East
♠ 8 5		♠ A 10 6 4
♥ A K J 8 5		♥ Q 9 2
♦ A 9		♦ 8 5 4
♣ Q 10 6 2		♣ K J 5

WEST	NORTH	EAST	SOUTH
1♥	Double	**Redbl**	2♦
Pass	Pass	2♥	Pass
4♥	Pass	Pass	Pass

East has 10 HCPs and three-card support for partner's suit. East starts with a redouble and shows support when the bidding comes around again. Having redoubled, East needs to bid only 2♥ on the second round, showing a limit raise with three-card support. With 13 or more points, East would most likely jump to 4♥ at this point.

West		East
♠ J		♠ K 10 4 3
♥ 6 5		♥ Q 10 4
♦ A J 8 7 3		♦ 9 2
♣ K Q 9 4 3		♣ A J 8 2

WEST	NORTH	EAST	SOUTH
1♦	Double	**Redbl**	1♥
2♣	2♥	3♣	Pass
Pass	Pass		

With a minimum-opening bid and a distributional hand, West bids a second suit rather than pass the decision to the redoubler. West isn't willing to defend a low-level doubled partscore. When North raises to 2 ♥, East shows support for opener's second suit and a hand of invitational strength by competing to 3♣. West passes, and the partnership rests in partscore.

The redouble can be used in a similar manner after other opening bids.

West	WEST	NORTH	EAST	SOUTH	East
♠ A K J 8 6 2	2♠	Double	**Redbl**	3♣	♠ 10
♥ 9 4	Pass	Pass	Double	Pass	♥ A Q J 5 2
♦ 7 6 3	Pass	Pass			♦ K 10 4
♣ 10 3					♣ A J 9 2

West opens with a weak two-bid, and North doubles for takeout. East's redouble says the hand belongs to East–West, so West is happy to defend when East doubles the opponents' contract.

When Responder Doesn't Redouble

An advantage of using the redouble with 10 or more points, after partner's one-level opening bid is doubled for takeout, is that the meanings of any other calls are changed. For example, with no interference, a response in a new suit at the two level shows at least 10 or more points. After a takeout double, responder can bid a new suit at the two level with fewer than 10 points, since a redouble shows 10 or more.

Most partnerships use the following agreements after a takeout double:

1) A redouble shows 10 or more points with interest in doubling the opponents for penalty. Responder usually won't have a fit with opener's suit. (See 6 below).

2) A new suit bid at the one level shows 6 or more points and is still forcing. Responder can have 10 or more points, but decide it's more important to bid naturally than to redouble and try to penalize the opponents.

3) A new suit bid at the two level, however, isn't forcing and shows a five-card or longer suit with fewer than 10 points. With 10 or more points, responder redoubles rather than bid a new suit at the two level.

4) A jump in a new suit is weak and non-forcing. It shows a good six-card or longer suit with fewer than 10 points. With 10 or more points, responder redoubles first and then bids the suit.

5) A jump raise to the three level in opener's suit shows four-card or longer support and is weak — fewer than 10 points. This type of raise preempts the bidding room of the opponents.

6) A jump to 2NT shows four-card or longer support for opener's suit and 10 or more points, and the bid is referred to as Truscott, Jordan or Dormer. This text will use "Jordan."

7) All other bids retain their usual meaning.

Here are examples of this approach after the auction has started:

WEST	NORTH	**EAST**	SOUTH
1 ♦	Double	?	

♠ Q 3
♥ K Q 10 8 5
♦ K 6 2
♣ 9 5 4

Respond 1 ♥. Although there are 10 HCPs, showing the heart suit might be difficult if East starts with a redouble. The opponents might bid and raise spades, for example. Most partnerships treat a one-level response as though the double hadn't occurred. The bid of a new suit at the one level shows 6 or more points and is forcing.

♠ 9 3
♥ 8 4 2
♦ Q 9
♣ K J 10 8 7 5

Respond 2♣. The bid of a new suit at the two level isn't forcing. It shows a good five-card or longer suit and fewer than 10 points. With 10 or more points, East would start with a redouble. The takeout double has actually made it easier for East to describe this hand. If North had passed, East would have to respond 1NT.

♠ Q J 10 9 7 6   Jump to 2♠. It's impractical to use the standard
♥ 4   meaning for a jump shift after a takeout double.
♦ J 8 3   It's rare to have a very strong hand, and East could
♣ 10 8 3   always start with a redouble if that's the case. Instead, most partnerships treat a jump in a new suit as a weak bid, showing a good six-card or longer suit.

♠ 6 2   Jump raise to 3♦. Most players find that making
♥ 7 3   a preemptive jump raise to the three level with this
♦ K J 8 7 5   type of hand is effective. There is no need to use
♣ J 10 8 4   the jump as a limit raise, since with 10 or more points East could redouble or use 2NT as a limit raise. (See next example.)

♠ 10 9 5   Jump to 2NT (or redouble). Most partnerships
♥ K 4   use the Jordan 2NT following a takeout double
♦ A J 8 6 3   of either a major suit or a minor suit. If East re-
♣ Q 8 3   doubles, showing support later may be difficult if the opponents compete to a high level. 2NT also has the advantage of making it more difficult for South to enter the auction. If the partnership doesn't use this convention, East would start with a redouble.

♠ Q J 4   Respond 1NT. A response of 1NT keeps its usual
♥ K 7 3   meaning. After a takeout double, responder will
♦ Q 9 4   tend to have a hand closer to the top of the range for
♣ J 10 8 3   a 1NT response. With a bare minimum, responder doesn't have to bid over the takeout double.

The S.O.S. Redouble

If the partnership has been doubled for penalty in a low-level contract, redoubling is generally impractical. Declarer's side will get a good score if the doubled contract is made, and the penalty will be much greater if the redoubled contract can't be made. In this situation, many partnerships use the redouble as a request for partner to pick another contract. This is commonly referred to as an *S.O.S. redouble* — "Partner, please rescue me from this doubled contract!" — or as a *Kock-Werner redouble*, after the Swedish pair that invented the convention.

It's important that both partners are clear on when the redouble is for rescue and when it's strength-showing.

Here are sample auctions:

West		East
♠ A Q 9 8 3		♠ —
♥ J 4		♥ Q 10 8 7 6
♦ K 5		♦ J 9 3
♣ Q 7 6 2		♣ 10 9 8 5 4

WEST	NORTH	EAST	SOUTH
			1 ♦
1 ♠	Pass	Pass	Double
Pass	Pass	**Redbl**	Pass
2 ♣	2 ♦	Pass	Pass
Pass			

After West's 1 ♠ overcall, East passes, hoping that the partnership doesn't get into any more trouble. When South reopens with a double, however, and North passes for penalty, East knows the partnership is probably headed for a bad score. East makes an S.O.S. redouble, asking West to pick a better spot. Since East passed after the overcall, West recognizes that the redouble isn't strength-showing. West bids a second suit, and this proves to be a safe landing spot for the partnership. North–South don't want to defend 2 ♣ and bid on to their partscore in diamonds.

West		East
♠ A J 6 2		♠ 7 4 3
♥ Q 9 5		♥ 10 8 6 3 2
♦ A 8 3		♦ Q J 7 5
♣ Q 9 4		♣ 6

WEST	NORTH	EAST	SOUTH
1 ♣	Double	Pass	Pass
Redbl	Pass	1 ♥	Double
Pass	Pass	Pass	

West opens the bidding 1 ♣, and North makes a takeout double. After East passes, South leaves the double in for penalty by passing. West realizes that this probably isn't a good spot for the partnership and redoubles. East recognizes that this is for rescue, since opener could have passed and played in 1 ♣ doubled with a good hand. East picks hearts as trump. The contract of 1 ♥ is also doubled for penalty by North–South, but it should prove to be a better spot than 1 ♣ doubled.

West	WEST	NORTH	EAST	SOUTH	East
♠ A K J 10 7	1♠	Pass	Pass	Double	♠ 9 8 3
♥ K Q 9	**Redbl**	Pass	Pass	2♦	♥ J 3 2
♦ A 4	Pass	Pass	2♠	Pass	♦ 10 7 3
♣ J 5 2	Pass	Pass			♣ K 10 8 7

West's redouble isn't for rescue. South's double is for takeout, not for penalty, so West's redouble shows a strong hand. East can pass the redouble and see what the opponents do. When South bids 2♦, West can pass, having shown a good hand. When the auction comes back to East, East can belatedly raise partner's suit to the two level, showing a little something.

West	WEST	NORTH	EAST	SOUTH	East
♠ A Q J 8 6 2	1♠	Pass	3♠	Pass	♠ 10 9 7 4
♥ —	4♠	Double	Pass	Pass	♥ Q 10 3 2
♦ Q J 10 8 3	**Redbl**	Pass	Pass	Pass	♦ K 6
♣ Q 2					♣ A J 7

After West accepts East's invitational raise, North makes a penalty double. With a little surprise in store for the defenders — the void in hearts — West redoubles. This isn't an S.O.S. redouble, since the partnership has agreed on a trump suit and freely bid to the game level. East is content to pass the redouble.

SUMMARY

The partnership needs to be able to distinguish among the various types of doubles, such as takeout, negative, penalty, competitive and lead-directing. Some common guidelines:

Guidelines on Doubles

When the partnership opens the bidding:

- If partner opens one-of-a-suit and the next opponent makes a natural overcall in a suit, up to and including 2♠, double is for takeout — a negative double. Otherwise, double is for penalty.

- If partner opens 1NT and the next opponent makes a natural overcall in a suit, double is for penalty.

- If partner opens at the two level or higher and the next opponent overcalls, double is for penalty.

- If the partnership has not yet found a fit and there are exactly two unbid suits, opener's double is for takeout. Otherwise, opener's double is penalty-oriented.

When the opponents open the bidding:

- If an opponent opens the bidding in a suit below the game level, double is for takeout.

- If an opponent opens the bidding in notrump, double is penalty-oriented.

- Double of responder's first bid below the game level — a new suit, a raise (conventional or natural) or 1NT — is for takeout, if partner hasn't overcalled or doubled.

In general:

- Without specific agreements otherwise, the double of an opponent's conventional suit bid is penalty-oriented, showing strength in the bid suit. If the opponents are likely to play the eventual contract, the double is a lead-directing double.

- If the opponents appear to be stopping at the partscore level and have found a fit, a double is for takeout. If they haven't found a fit, the double is for penalty.
- A double at the game level or higher is penalty-oriented.

Responder's Actions after a Takeout Double

Most partnerships use the following agreements after opener's bid is doubled for takeout:

- A redouble shows 10 or more points with interest in doubling the opponents for penalty. Responder usually won't have a fit with opener's suit.
- A bid of a new suit at the one level shows 6 or more points and is forcing.
- A bid of a new suit at the two level is non-forcing and shows a five-card or longer suit with fewer than 10 points.
- A jump in a new suit is weak and non-forcing. It shows a good six-card or longer suit with fewer than 10 points.
- A jump raise to the three level in opener's suit shows four-card or longer support and is weak (preemptive).
- A jump to 2NT shows four-card or longer support for opener's suit and 10 or more points.

When your side has been doubled for penalty in a low-level suit contract, you can agree to use a redouble as a conventional S.O.S. redouble to ask partner to choose a better contract.

NOTE: See the Appendix (pages 342–346) for a discussion of these supplemental conventions and/or treatments.

Responsive Double
Maximal Double
Support Double
Lebensohl in Response to a
  Takeout Double of a Weak Two-Bid

Note: The following exercises illustrate the methods outlined in the summary.

Exercise One — More about Doubling

What call would East make with each of the following hands after the auction goes as indicated?

1)
WEST	NORTH	**EAST**	SOUTH
1NT	2♠	?	

♠ Q J 9 6
♥ 10 5
♦ A J 8 4
♣ J 10 3

2)
WEST	NORTH	**EAST**	SOUTH
2♦	2♠	?	

♠ J 9 4
♥ K Q 7 3
♦ 8 5
♣ K J 9 2

3)
WEST	NORTH	**EAST**	SOUTH
1♥	1♠	2♦	2♠
Pass	Pass	?	

♠ 9 5 3
♥ 10 7
♦ A K J 8 5
♣ K 8 4

4)
WEST	NORTH	**EAST**	SOUTH
	4♣	?	

♠ 7 3
♥ K Q 7 4
♦ A 8 5 2
♣ A J 9

5)
WEST	NORTH	**EAST**	SOUTH
			1♣
Pass	Pass	?	

♠ Q 8 5
♥ K 8 3
♦ A 8 5 2
♣ K Q 10

Exercise One *Answer* — More about Doubling

1) Double (Penalty). Opposite West's 1NT opening bid, East should be able to extract a large penalty. After West opens 1NT, a double of an overcall is for penalty.

2) Pass. A double would be for penalty after West's weak two-bid is overcalled. Double would not be negative in this situation.

3) Double (Cooperative). Since the opponents have found a fit, East's double isn't primarily for penalty. It shows enough strength to compete further for the auction. Double is flexible, since there isn't another bid that would be more descriptive at this point.

4) Pass. A double would be for takeout, not penalty. With a low doubleton in spades, this is not the right shape for a takeout double. East hopes West will reopen with a double.

5) 1NT. In the balancing seat, when you reopen with 1NT it shows approximately 11–15 HCP and a balanced hand, with at least one stopper in the opponent's suit.

Exercise Two — Yet More Doubles

What call would West make with each of the following hands after the auction goes as indicated?

	WEST	NORTH	EAST	SOUTH
1) ♠ 7 2		1NT	Double	Pass
♥ J 8 3				
♦ Q 10 8 4 3	?			
♣ J 7 4				

	WEST	NORTH	EAST	SOUTH
2) ♠ A J 8 3		NORTH	EAST	SOUTH
♥ 10 7 2				1NT
♦ K 8 4 3	Pass	2♣	Double	2♥
♣ 9 6	?			

	WEST	NORTH	EAST	SOUTH
3) ♠ J 7		NORTH	EAST	SOUTH
♥ A 6 3	Pass	1♠	Pass	2♠
♦ J 6 2	Pass	Pass	Double	Pass
♣ Q 9 7 6 2	?			

	WEST	NORTH	EAST	SOUTH
4) ♠ J 9 7 4		NORTH	EAST	SOUTH
♥ Q 6			1♦	1♥
♦ 8 6 2	Pass	3♥	Double	Pass
♣ J 10 7 5	?			

	WEST	NORTH	EAST	SOUTH
5) ♠ K 8 5		NORTH	EAST	SOUTH
♥ Q 9 6 3				1♠
♦ 10 4 2	Pass	1NT	Double	2♠
♣ K 9 4	?			

Exercise Two *Answer* — Yet More Doubles

1) Pass. East's double is for penalty. West has more than East could expect, so West's hand should be useful on defense.

2) Pass. East's double of the opponent's conventional Stayman response to 1NT shows length and strength in clubs. It is a suggestion that West lead a club against the opponents' final contract if South is declarer.

3) 3♣. The opponents have found a fit, so East is making a balancing double. West takes it out into the best suit. East should have at least three-card support for clubs, but doesn't have the strength for an immediate takeout double.

4) 3♠. East's double is for takeout, not penalty. The opponents have found a fit, and the double shows a strong opening bid with support for the unbid suits. West hopes that East will have four-card support for spades. With only three-card support, East should have extra strength to compensate.

5) 3♥. East's double of the 1NT response is a takeout double of spades. With 8 high-card points and a fit for East's likely four-card heart suit, West enters the auction.

Exercise Three — Lead-directing Doubles

What opening lead would East make with each of the following hands after the auction goes as shown?

1)

WEST	NORTH	**EAST**	SOUTH
	1NT	Pass	2♥ ‡
Double	2♠	Pass	3NT
Pass	Pass	Pass	

♠ J 10 9 4
♥ 9 4
♦ Q J 8 7 5
♣ 8 3

‡*Jacoby transfer*

2)

WEST	NORTH	**EAST**	SOUTH
	1NT	Pass	3NT
Double	Pass	Pass	Pass

♠ 6
♥ J 8 5 3
♦ Q J 8 3
♣ 10 9 6 2

3)

WEST	NORTH	**EAST**	SOUTH
	1♥	Pass	3♦
Pass	3♥	Pass	4NT
Pass	5♣	Pass	6♥
Double	Pass	Pass	Pass

♠ J 10 9 5
♥ 6 4
♦ 10 8 7 5 2
♣ 9 3

4)

WEST	NORTH	**EAST**	SOUTH
	1♥	1♠	2♣
Pass	2NT	Pass	3NT
Double	Pass	Pass	Pass

♠ K J 8 5 3
♥ K 7
♦ Q J 10 8 3
♣ 5

5)

WEST	NORTH	**EAST**	SOUTH
	1♠	Pass	3♠
Pass	4NT	Pass	5♥
Pass	5NT	Pass	6♣
Pass	6♠	Pass	Pass
Pass			

♠ K 5
♥ 10 8 7
♦ 8 7 3 2
♣ 9 5 4 3

Exercise Three *Answer* — Lead-directing Doubles

1) ♥9. West's double of the conventional 2♥ transfer bid asks East to lead a heart.

2) ♠6. West has made a lead-directing double of the opponents' 3NT contract, asking for an unusual lead. It looks as though West has a long and strong spade suit.

3) A diamond. West's Lightner double asks for an unusual lead. In this situation, it usually calls for the lead of dummy's first bid suit. West is likely to be void in diamonds and hoping to get a ruff to go along with a trick in another suit.

4) ♠5. West's unusual double asks East to lead a spade, even though West didn't support spades. West figures to have a doubleton ace or queen in East's suit, not enough to support, but enough to help out.

5) A diamond. There is no clear-cut opening lead. The only clue is that West had opportunities to double the conventional 5♥ response and the conventional 6♣ response to Blackwood. West didn't double either of those bids, so perhaps West's strength is in diamonds.

Exercise Four — All about Redoubles

What call does West make with each of the following hands, after the auction goes as indicated?

1) ♠ 6
   ♥ A Q 7 3
   ♦ K Q 9 8 4
   ♣ 10 6 2

WEST	NORTH	EAST	SOUTH
	Pass	1♠	Double
?			

2) ♠ J 7 2
   ♥ 6 4
   ♦ K J 10 9 7 3
   ♣ Q 5

WEST	NORTH	EAST	SOUTH
		1♥	Double
?			

3) ♠ K J 8 3
   ♥ 8 7
   ♦ A K 9 6 2
   ♣ Q 5

WEST	NORTH	EAST	SOUTH
1♦	Double	Redbl	1♥
?			

4) ♠ 9
   ♥ K 8 3
   ♦ A Q J 8 4
   ♣ K 7 4 2

WEST	NORTH	EAST	SOUTH
1♦	Double	2♠	Pass
?			

5) ♠ J 9 8 7 3
   ♥ 9 7 2
   ♦ 2
   ♣ Q 10 8 3

WEST	NORTH	EAST	SOUTH
		1♦	Double
Pass	Pass	Redbl	Pass
?			

Exercise Four *Answer* — All about Redoubles

1) Redouble. With 11 high-card points but no fit for East's suit, West starts with a redouble. If the opponents bid hearts or diamonds, West can double for penalty. If they bid clubs, West shows the diamond suit, unless East doubles first.

2) 2 ♦. This would be forcing without the interference. Over the takeout double, showing the diamond suit doesn't promise much strength. With 10 or more high-card points, West could redouble first and then bid diamonds.

3) Pass. East's redouble says the hand belongs to East–West, but it covers several possibilities. West wants to see what East plans to do next. East might want to double the opponents in 1 ♥ for penalty. If not, West will be well-placed to decide what to do after hearing East's next bid.

4) Pass. After the takeout double, the standard partnership agreement is that a jump in a new suit is weak, not strong. East probably has a good six-card or longer spade suit with very little outside. West should not get the partnership any higher.

5) 1 ♠. East's redouble is for rescue, an S.O.S. redouble. East would pass to play with diamonds as trump. West bids the longest suit and hopes to get the partnership out of trouble. East should have at least three-card support for spades.

Bid and Play — Opener Makes a Takeout Double

(E–Z Deal Cards: #2, Deal 1 — Dealer, North)

Suggested Bidding

WEST	NORTH	EAST	SOUTH
	Pass	1 ♥	1 ♠
Pass	2 ♠	Double	Pass
3 ♦	Pass	Pass	Pass

After North passes, East opens 1 ♥. South has a good five-card suit and overcalls 1 ♠. With only 2 high-card points and no support for partner's suit, West passes. North has enough to raise partner's overcall to the two level. This serves a dual purpose. If South has a strong overcall, the partnership can compete for the contract and may belong in game. If South has a light overcall, North's raise will make it more difficult for East–West to find their best spot.

```
Dealer: North    ♠ Q J 6 2
Vul: None        ♥ Q 9 7 3
                 ♦ 10 4
                 ♣ K 7 5
  ♠ 9 5 4                      ♠ 8
  ♥ 8 5          ┌─────┐       ♥ A K 10 4 2
  ♦ J 9 7 5 2    │N    │       ♦ K Q 8
  ♣ J 9 8        │W   E│       ♣ A Q 6 3
                 │  S  │
                 └─────┘
                 ♠ A K 10 7 3
                 ♥ J 6
                 ♦ A 6 3
                 ♣ 10 4 2
```

East has a strong hand — 18 HCPs plus 1 for the five-card suit. Even though West didn't bid after the 1 ♠ overcall, it's still possible that the hand belongs to East–West. East can compete with a double. Since the opponents have found a fit and are still at a low level, the double is for takeout, not penalty. East has already shown the five-card heart suit. The double shows support for the unbid suits, diamonds and clubs. It's a more flexible choice than bidding 3 ♣, which would keep diamonds out of the picture.

South doesn't have enough to go to the three level after a single raise from partner. Now West must bid something. Since East has promised support for diamonds, West bids diamonds at the three level, even with a weak five-card suit.

North might consider competing to the three level with a maximum raise and four-card support, but will probably pass. If North passes, East, who has already shown a strong hand with the opening bid and the subsequent double, passes also. Since West hasn't shown any strength, the partnership is probably high enough. The auction will end with West as declarer in a diamond partscore.

Suggested Opening Lead

North is on lead against 3 ♦ and would start with the ♠Q, top of touching honors in partner's suit.

Suggested Play

In 3 ♦, West has three spade losers, a diamond loser and a club loser. Unless the defenders lead diamonds right away, West should be able to ruff at least one of the spade losers in dummy. If the defenders never switch to trumps, West might get to ruff two spade losers in the dummy. Declarer hopes not to lose a trick to the ♦10, but will probably be okay, since North's ♦10 is doubleton.

Declarer also may be able to avoid a club loser by establishing an extra heart winner in dummy on which to discard a club. Since North has the ♣K, declarer won't have a club loser. With the lack of entries to the West hand, this may not be easy, but it is possible. Suppose the defenders take a spade winner and then lead the ♦A and another diamond to prevent declarer from ruffing two spade losers in dummy. Declarer wins the second diamond in dummy, plays the ♥A and ♥K and ruffs a heart. Declarer ruffs a spade loser in dummy, then ruffs another heart. Declarer draws the defenders' remaining trump and then takes the club finesse. Either a club loser or a spade loser can be discarded on dummy's heart winner. Declarer loses only three tricks.

Suggested Defense

As described above, declarer is likely to take 10 tricks in a diamond contract. There isn't much the defenders can do to prevent this, unless North finds an initial diamond lead. That will prevent declarer from ruffing any spade losers. Declarer can still take nine tricks by establishing an extra winner in hearts on which to discard one of the losers.

If North–South compete to 3 ♠, East–West should defeat that contract. East–West should get two heart tricks, one diamond trick and two club tricks.

Bid and Play — The Balancing Double

(E–Z Deal Cards: #2, Deal 2 — Dealer, East)

Suggested Bidding

WEST	NORTH	EAST	SOUTH
		1 ♥	Pass
2 ♥	Pass	Pass	Double
Pass	2 ♠	Pass	Pass
Pass			

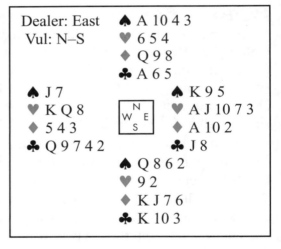

Dealer: East   ♠ A 10 4 3
Vul: N–S   ♥ 6 5 4
                ♦ Q 9 8
                ♣ A 6 5

♠ J 7   ♠ K 9 5
♥ K Q 8   ♥ A J 10 7 3
♦ 5 4 3   ♦ A 10 2
♣ Q 9 7 4 2   ♣ J 8

                ♠ Q 8 6 2
                ♥ 9 2
                ♦ K J 7 6
                ♣ K 10 3

East opens the bidding 1 ♥. With only 9 HCPs, South doesn't have enough to compete with a takeout double. North would expect a better hand, and the partnership might get too high. After South passes, West raises to 2 ♥ with three-card support and 8 HCPs.

With a balanced 10 points, North has nothing to say and passes. East has a minimum-strength opening bid and also passes. The auction comes back to South who is in the balancing, or reopening, position. South has the option of passing and letting East–West buy the contract for 2 ♥ or making a call that will keep the auction going.

Although South has only 9 HCPs, there is a strong inference that North–South have about half of the total strength on this deal. West has shown 6 to 10 points* with the raise to the two level, and East has shown a minimum-strength opening bid by passing the raise. North is marked

---

* Based on the partnership agreement that opener may have a 12-point hand.

with about 10 points. With support for all of the unbid suits, South can compete for the contract by making a takeout double. South's double is for takeout, since the opponents have found a fit and are at a low level.

When South doubles and West passes, North can bid 2 ♠. Although North has 10 HCPs, there's no need to jump. South didn't make a takeout double on the first round of bidding, so North can conclude that partner doesn't have a full opening bid with support for the unbid suits. South is competing for a partscore. North's 2 ♠ bid will end the auction.

Suggested Opening Lead

East doesn't have an attractive choice of opening leads. A trump lead or the ♣ J, maybe to get a ruff, are possibilities. East will probably choose the ♥ A, however, expecting to take tricks in the suit that East–West have bid and raised.

Suggested Play

Even if the missing spades divide 3–2, North has two potential spade losers, three heart losers, one diamond loser and one club loser. North can hope to avoid losing more than one trump trick by leading toward the ♠ Q, hoping East holds the ♠ K. One of the heart losers could be ruffed in the dummy. Another possibility is to try to establish an extra diamond winner on which to discard the club loser. That will work if the missing diamonds are divided 3–3 or the ♦ 10 falls.

Whatever North chooses to do should work. The defenders' trumps are divided 3–2 with East holding the ♠ K. Declarer can eventually ruff a heart loser in dummy. Declarer will also get to discard the club loser on South's fourth diamond, provided the defenders don't lead clubs early on. Only three tricks are lost, one spade, two hearts and one diamond.

Suggested Defense

The defenders cannot prevent declarer from taking at least eight tricks. By leading clubs early on, the defenders may be able to establish a club winner, or East may be able to get a club ruff. If they take their heart tricks early, however, West won't be able to regain the lead. West needs to play a third round of clubs before declarer can drive out East's ♦ A and establish an extra diamond winner.

East–West might do better to compete to 3 ♥. That contract will likely be defeated one trick. The defenders can get one spade trick, two diamonds and two clubs, if they are careful. Down one in 3 ♥ would be less than the value of the opponents' 2 ♠ contract.

The important point is for North–South to get a plus score, either by playing in 2 ♠ or by pushing East–West to 3 ♥. If North–South let East–West play in 2 ♥, East is likely to make that contract.

Bid and Play — The Lead-Directing Double

(E–Z Deal Cards: #2, Deal 3 — Dealer, South)

Suggested Bidding

WEST	NORTH	EAST	SOUTH
			1 ♦
Pass	1 ♠	Pass	1NT
Pass	3NT	Double	Pass
Pass	Pass		

With a balanced hand and 13 HCPs, South opens the bidding 1 ♦. West passes and North responds 1 ♠, looking for a major-suit fit. East has a nice hand, but a double at this point would be for takeout, asking West to choose clubs or hearts as a trump suit. So East passes. South rebids 1NT to show a minimum-strength balanced hand. With 13 HCPs, North raises to game in notrump.

Dealer: South   ♠ J 9 8 7
Vul: E–W   ♥ Q 6
  ♦ Q 6 5
  ♣ A K J 2

♠ 5 3 2   ♠ A K Q 10
♥ J 10 9 8   N   ♥ 5 4 2
♦ 9 7   W   E   ♦ A 8 3 2
♣ 10 8 6 5   S   ♣ 9 4

    ♠ 6 4
    ♥ A K 7 3
    ♦ K J 10 4
    ♣ Q 7 3

At this point, East should make a lead-directing double. East knows that with nothing better to go on, West is likely to lead one of the unbid suits. East would like West to lead a spade, dummy's first-bid suit. To alert West to make an unusual lead, East doubles. North–South have nothing further to say, so the double should end the auction.

Suggested Opening Lead

West's natural lead is the ♥ J, top of a sequence in one of the unbid suits. East's double, however, should steer West away from making the normal lead. Since neither East nor West bid a suit during the auction, the standard interpretation of East's unusual double is a request to lead dummy's first-bid suit. West should lead a spade.

Suggested Play

Declarer has seven sure tricks, three in hearts and four in clubs. If West doesn't lead a spade, South should plan to establish extra tricks in the diamond suit.

Declarer will make the contract if West leads something other than a spade. Suppose West leads a heart. Declarer wins and leads a diamond to drive out East's ♦ A. East can take three top spade tricks, but dummy's ♠ J will prevent the defenders from taking any more tricks.

If West leads a spade, declarer has no chance to make the contract. Declarer can try a low spade from dummy, hoping West holds the ♠ 10, but that doesn't work.

Suggested Defense

Everything depends on the opening lead. If West leads a spade, the defenders set the contract. If West leads anything else, declarer will take nine tricks.

The opportunity to make a lead-directing double doesn't occur often, but when it does, the partnership should use it. East should recognize that a spade lead will defeat the contract. Either the ♠ J will be in dummy and be trapped or it will be in one of the other hands and fall under the top three spade honors. Declarer is unlikely to hold four spades since South didn't raise North's suit during the auction. The only way to get West to lead North's suit is to double and hope West recognizes the situation.

Holding the ♦ A, East can visualize exactly how the spade lead will result in the defeat of the contract. Doubling would be more difficult if East held only the four spade tricks and did not hold an outside trick. Nonetheless, East should probably double anyway, hoping partner can come up with a trick somewhere after the spade lead. If not …

Bid and Play — Doubling for Penalty

(E–Z Deal Cards: #2, Deal 4 — Dealer, West)

Suggested Bidding

WEST	NORTH	EAST	SOUTH
Pass	1♠	Double	Redbl
Pass	Pass	2♣	Double
Pass	Pass	Pass	

After West passes, North opens the bidding 1♠. With an opening bid and support for all of the unbid suits, East makes a takeout double.

With 12 HCPs and no good fit with partner's suit, South starts with a redouble. This announces that the partnership holds the balance of power. West has no preference for any of the unbid suits and passes. It would not be a good idea for West to bid 1NT with such a weak hand and the knowledge that partner is short in spades.

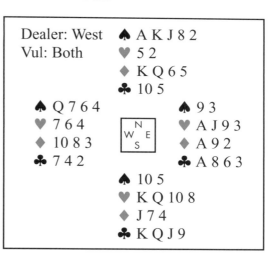

Dealer: West
Vul: Both

♠ A K J 8 2
♥ 5 2
♦ K Q 6 5
♣ 10 5

♠ Q 7 6 4
♥ 7 6 4
♦ 10 8 3
♣ 7 4 2

♠ 9 3
♥ A J 9 3
♦ A 9 2
♣ A 8 6 3

♠ 10 5
♥ K Q 10 8
♦ J 7 4
♣ K Q J 9

With a normal opening bid and a hand suitable for defending, North passes rather than bid a second suit. North waits to hear more about the nature of South's redouble. Getting no preference from partner, East bids 2♣, the cheapest available suit. With good defense against clubs, South makes a penalty double. West has nowhere to go and passes. North passes also, respecting partner's decision.

East might try to find a better spot but to no avail. South will double 2♥ for penalty. North will double 2♦ for penalty. East–West have no safe landing spot.

Suggested Opening Lead

If South is on lead against 2♣ doubled, South should start with the ♣K. It's generally a good idea to lead trumps against a low-level contract that has been doubled for penalty. The trump lead prevents declarer from taking tricks by ruffing with low trump cards.

Suggested Play

If East is declarer in a doubled partscore, taking more than the three aces will be difficult. Unless the defenders slip up, there's not much possibility for a fourth trick. East might get a trick with the ♥J, but is still down four.

Suggested Defense

North–South should have little difficulty collecting a penalty of at least 800 points (down three doubled and vulnerable). They might get 1100 or even 1400 with perfect defense.

North–South can make 3NT, but that is not nearly as good a result as defeating the opponents three or more tricks in a vulnerable, doubled contract. To get themselves in a position to collect a substantial penalty after East intervenes, they need to understand the mechanics of the re-double. Otherwise, East–West might escape.

East's takeout double is quite reasonable. East might be cautious once West passes initially, but most players would take a chance on a takeout double with the East cards. Unfortunately, it leads to a poor result on this deal.

CHAPTER 3
Overcalls

OVERCALLS

Once the opponents open the bidding, there are a number of ways to enter the auction. One is to use the takeout double. Another tactic is the natural overcall in a suit or notrump. In addition, there are a number of conventional (artificial) approaches that are popular among competitive bridge players. We'll look at natural overcalls in this chapter. We'll focus on two-suited overcalls in the next chapter.

SIMPLE OVERCALL IN A SUIT

When the opponents have opened the bidding, one way to enter the auction is to overcall in a suit at the cheapest available level — a simple overcall. A simple overcall tells partner something about the hand. The partnership may get to buy the contract. It may push the opponents too high in the auction. It may get the partnership off to a favorable lead on defense. Partner needs to know what to expect from a simple overcall and how to respond to it.

Requirements for a Simple Overcall

Most partnerships agree on a wide range of 8 to 16 HCP (10-17 total points) for a simple overcall. This allows the partnership to overcall at the one level with considerably less than the values required for an opening bid. An overcall at the two level or higher, however, will generally show at least the equivalent to an opening bid. The upper limit is less than that for opening bids, because with a strong hand of 17 or more HCP, there is the option of making a takeout double and then bidding the suit. Having an upper limit of 16 HCP means that partner doesn't have to stretch to respond to the overcall with fewer than 9 points for fear of missing a game contract.

Apart from the strength shown by the overcall, the other requirement is a good suit. This is usually interpreted as a five-card or longer suit, although an overcall at the one level can be made with a very strong four-card suit. A good suit is necessary because of the danger that the opponents might double for penalty. For example, if East opens the bidding and South makes a simple overcall, West has some information about East's hand and will be well prepared to double the overcall for penalties with some length and strength in the suit. If the partnership plays negative doubles, West will pass and later pass East's reopening double. The better the suit, the less likely the opener's side will want to double the overcall for penalty. Even if they hold the balance of strength, they will be more inclined to simply bid to their own contract. By promising a decent suit, the overcaller makes it easier for partner to compete and helps partner make the best opening lead on defense. The weaker the overcaller's hand is, the better the suit should be for an overcall.

One other factor to consider when overcalling is the vulnerability. Overcalling at unfavorable vulnerability — vulnerable against non-vulnerable — is most dangerous. Being defeated, especially doubled, could be expensive, and the overcaller may lose more points than the value of any contract the opponents could make. On the other hand, at favorable vulnerability — non-vulnerable against vulnerable — the non-opening side can compete more aggressively. Even doubled and defeated, the loss may be less than the value of some contract the opponents could have bid and made. At equal vulnerability — both sides non-vulnerable or both sides vulnerable — the non-opening side should try not to be too conservative or too aggressive.

What does West call on the following hands after South has opened the bidding:

WEST	NORTH	EAST	SOUTH
			1 ♥
?			

♠ A Q J 9 5   Overcall 1 ♠. Although West has only 8 high-card
♥ 8 3   points, this would be a reasonably safe overcall at
♦ J 10 7 5   any vulnerability. West has an excellent five-card
♣ 9 3   suit to show at the one level. An overcall may help
East compete for the contract, and if East is on opening lead, a spade lead is a good suggestion.

♠ 9 4   Overcall 2 ♦. This is a typical two-level overcall:
♥ 8 3   a good six-card suit and the values for an open-
♦ A K J 9 8 5   ing bid. Although it's possible that the opponents
♣ A 10 5   might double for penalty, it's unlikely.

♠ J 6 5
♥ Q 8 3
♦ A 8
♣ K J 7 4 2

Pass. This hand is full of warning signs. The suit isn't that good, and West would have to overcall at the two level. North could have a strong enough holding in the suit to want to defend for penalty, and West might take only a couple of tricks. If East is on opening lead, it's not clear that a club lead would be a good choice. Pass and await developments. The auction isn't over yet.

♠ Q J 6 3
♥ 8 4
♦ K J 6 5
♣ A J 8

Double. With no good suit but with enough strength to want to compete, this is a good hand for a takeout double. West lets East choose the suit.

♠ A K Q 10
♥ K 6 3 2
♦ 6 4
♣ 9 7 2

Overcall 1 ♠. Although an overcall generally shows a five-card or longer suit, this is an exception. The suit is excellent, and the hand is unsuitable for a takeout double (no good support for either minor suit). Most players would risk overcalling 1 ♠.

♠ A K J 9 3
♥ 10 2
♦ A K 7 4
♣ K 5

Double. With 18 high-card points, most partnerships — but not all — would consider this hand too strong for a simple overcall. Double first, intending to bid spades next. This would show a hand of 17 HCP or more, too strong for an overcall.

What does West call on the following hands after North opens and South responds:

WEST	NORTH	EAST	SOUTH
	1 ♦	Pass	1 ♠
?			

♠ K 4
♥ A Q J 9 8 3
♦ 7 4 2
♣ J 3

Overcall 2 ♥. There's more danger in entering the bidding after both opponents have exchanged information about their hands, but most players would overcall with West's hand. With a good six-card suit, it's unlikely that the opponents will double for penalty.

♠ 3
♥ K Q 10 2
♦ J 7
♣ A K 10 8 6 5

Double. Although there is a good suit to overcall, a heart fit might get lost after a 2♣ overcall. A takeout double shows support for both unbid suits, so it's the more flexible call.

♠ 10 8 2
♥ A J 8 7 3
♦ K 9 3
♣ Q 10

Pass. Entering the auction at any vulnerability is not a good idea. The possible benefits aren't worth the risk.

ADVANCING AFTER A ONE-LEVEL OVERCALL

Some partnerships use the same approach to respond to an overcall as to respond to an opening bid. Most partnerships, however, make several adjustments because of the lower range of strength promised by the overcall. A common set of agreements for the advancer — the responder to an overcall — is the following:

With support:

- A single raise shows three-card support and 8 or 9 points,.

- A jump raise is preemptive, showing four-card support and a weak hand, with 5 to 8 points.

- A raise to game can be made with the intention of making the contract. It is more frequently made as a weak preemptive bid with five-card or longer support, designed to make the auction more difficult for the opponents.

- With 10 or more points and support, the advancer starts with a cuebid of the opponent's suit. This is forcing for one round, showing interest in reaching a game contract if the overcaller has more than a minimum overcall. If opener makes a minimum rebid of the suit, the advancer can pass with 9 to 11 points, raise with 12 to 14 points, and bid game or cuebid again with 15 or more points.

Without support:

- The bid of a new suit at the cheapest level shows a good five-card or longer suit but is non-forcing.

- A jump in a new suit is invitational, showing a good six-card or longer suit and 11 to 13 points.

- 1NT is non-forcing, showing 8 to 11 points with some strength in the opponent's suit.

- 2NT is non-forcing, showing 12 to 15 points with some strength in the opponent's suit.

- 3NT shows 16 or more points with some strength in the opponent's suit.

- With a hand too strong to make a non-forcing bid or to jump in a new suit, the advancer starts with a cuebid of the opponent's suit. This is forcing, showing interest in reaching game. If partner makes a minimum rebid of the overcalled suit, the advancer's bid of a new suit is now forcing. The advancer can bid another suit or cuebid again to force partner to keep bidding.

What does West respond on the following hands after this auction?

WEST	NORTH	EAST	SOUTH
	1 ♦	1 ♥	Pass
?			

♠ A 7 4 ♥ K 8 3 ♦ 9 5 2 ♣ J 7 6 3	Raise to 2 ♥. East's overcall shows a five-card or longer suit, so only three-card support is needed to raise. Although a game contract is unlikely (the overcall has an upper limit of about 16 HCP), West should raise to make it more difficult for the opponents to re-enter the auction.

♠ 8 4
♥ Q J 8 3
♦ 7 3
♣ J 9 6 5 2

Jump to 3 ♥. Most partnerships use the jump raise of an overcall as a weak preemptive bid, designed to make the auction more difficult for the opponents. With a hand strong enough for a limit raise or better, West would start with a cuebid of the opponent's suit.

♠ A Q J 8 5
♥ 8 3
♦ 10 8 3
♣ K 9 2

Bid 1♠. Using standard methods, the bid of a new suit is non-forcing — unlike the response of a new suit to an opening bid. With a minimum-strength hand for the overcall, East doesn't need to bid again. Some players prefer to play that a new suit is forcing for one round — at least by an unpassed hand — but that requires discussion by the partnership.

♠ K 7 2
♥ 6 4
♦ J 3
♣ A Q J 8 6 3

Jump to 3♣. Since it's rare to hold a very strong hand when an opponent opens the bidding and partner has enough to overcall, there's no need for the jump shift to show a powerful hand. The jump shift can be used instead to show an invitational-strength hand with a good six-card or longer suit without support for partner's suit. With a stronger hand, West would start with a cuebid of 2♦. (As an alternative approach, see fit-showing jumps in the Appendix.)

♠ Q 10 7 4
♥ 6 5
♦ K Q 8 7
♣ Q 9 4

Bid 1NT. This shows 8 to 11 points and some strength in the opponent's suit. 1♠ would be non-forcing and would promise a five-card suit.

♠ A Q 9
♥ J 8
♦ K 10 9 5
♣ Q J 8 2

Jump to 2NT. This shows 12 to 15 points and is invitational. 2NT is not forcing, since East could have as few as 8 points. It's also a natural bid, even if the partnership uses Jacoby 2NT. (Jacoby 2NT is used to respond to an opening bid in a major suit, not to respond to an overcall.)

♠ A 8 5 2
♥ K 9 3
♦ 10 8
♣ K Q 6 2

Cuebid 2♦. A single raise shows 8 or 9 points and a jump raise is preemptive. With three-card support and 10 or more points, West starts by cuebidding the opponent's suit. That's the only forcing response at this point.

ADVANCING AFTER A TWO-LEVEL OVERCALL

When partner makes a two-level overcall, there is less bidding room for the advancer. The overcaller, however, will usually have the equivalent of an opening bid or better to enter the auction at the two level. The advancer's options are similar to those over a one-level overcall.

With support:

- A single raise shows three-card or longer support and shows 8 or 9 points.

- A jump raise is preemptive, showing four-card or longer support and a weak hand (5 to 8 points).

- With 10 or more points and support, the advancer starts with a cuebid of the opponent's suit. This is forcing for one round and shows interest in reaching game if partner has more than a minimum overcall. If opener makes a minimum rebid of the suit, the advancer can pass with 9 to 12 points. With 13 or more points, the advancer can bid game or cuebid again.

Without support:

- The bid of a new suit shows a good five-card or longer suit but is non-forcing.

- A jump in a new suit is forcing, showing a good six-card or longer suit and 11 or more points.

- 2NT is non-forcing and shows 9 to 11 points with some strength in the opponent's suit.

- 3NT shows 12 or more points with some strength in the opponent's suit.

What does West respond on the following hands after this auction?

WEST	NORTH	EAST	SOUTH
	1 ♠	2 ♦	Pass
?			

♠ Q 9 7 3
♥ K 8 5 3
♦ J 5
♣ J 9 4

Pass. Although East is showing a good hand with an overcall at the two level, there's no need to stretch to make a response. East probably has fewer than 17 points, so it's unlikely game will be missed.

♠ A J 8 3
♥ Q 8 2
♦ Q 6 4
♣ Q 10 7

Bid 2NT. After a two-level overcall, a response of 2NT is invitational and shows 9 to 11 points. With strength in the opponent's suit, 2NT is more descriptive than a raise to 3 ♦.

♠ 9 4
♥ A Q 10 9 4
♦ J 5 2
♣ K 8 2

Bid 2 ♥. This is an awkward hand. West is caught between raising partner's suit and showing a new suit. In standard methods, the response of 2 ♥ is non-forcing. In practice, with enough strength to overcall at the two level, partner will rarely pass in this situation. The alternative is to cuebid 2 ♠

or jump to 3 ♥, which takes up bidding room. Many players prefer to treat a new suit as forcing in this situation, but they would have to have an agreement with partner beforehand.

♠ A 6 4
♥ K 8 5 2
♦ A J 9 3
♣ J 4

Cuebid 2 ♠. With a fit with partner's suit and a hand too strong to raise to the three level, West cuebids the opponent's suit. This is forcing and should enable the partnership to find the best contract, probably in notrump or diamonds.

Overcaller's Rebid after a Cuebid

The cuebid of the opponent's suit covers a lot of ground. Since a jump raise shows a weak hand, the cuebid is used when the advancer (the responder to the overcall) has a fit with overcaller's suit and a hand of at least invitational strength, 10 or more points. Since a bid of a new suit is non-forcing, the cuebid is sometimes used with a good five-card or longer suit and 13 or more points. It also can be used as a general forcing bid with a strong hand without support for the overcaller, without a good suit and without enough strength in the opponent's suit to bid notrump.

The cuebid in response to an overcall is forcing unless the next hand bids or doubles. The advancer (cuebidder) doesn't promise another bid if the overcaller merely rebids the suit, but any other bid is forcing.

What does East rebid on the following hands after this auction?

WEST	NORTH	**EAST**	SOUTH
	1 ♦	1 ♠	Pass
2 ♦	Pass	?	

♠ A Q 10 9 5
♥ 8 4 3
♦ 10 7
♣ K 8 2

Rebid 2♠. With nothing extra for the overcall, East can rebid spades at the lowest possible level to show a minimum hand. West can pass this rebid with support for spades but only 10 to 12 points.

♠ K Q 9 8 5
♥ A J 8 3
♦ 7 4 2
♣ 5

Rebid 2♥. Although there is no extra strength, there's no harm in showing a second suit. This is a forcing bid, but West can always return to 2♠ with nothing extra, and East can pass.

♠ A Q J 8 5
♥ J 4
♦ K 10 4
♣ Q 10 2

Rebid 2NT. With extra strength for the one-level overcall, East can afford to bid 2NT to describe this hand. West is forced to bid again. The cuebid has shown a hand that is interested in reaching game, and East has shown more than a minimum hand for the overcall.

♠ A K J 9 8 4
♥ A J 3
♦ 9 4
♣ 10 7

Jump to 3♠. With an excellent hand for the one-level overcall, East can't afford to rebid 2♠, since West might pass. East jumps to show extra strength. Opposite West's cuebid, there should be enough combined strength for game.

The Rest of the Auction

Following an overcall, the auction can proceed in many directions.
Here are examples:

West
♠ 7 2
♥ A J 10 8 3
♦ 8 5
♣ K 9 6 4

WEST	NORTH	EAST	SOUTH
			1 ♦
1 ♥	Pass	2 ♦	Pass
2 ♥	Pass	Pass	Pass

East
♠ K Q 6 4
♥ K 6 5
♦ J 7 2
♣ Q 8 3

West makes a one-level overcall with a decent five-card suit, but only 8 high-card points. East has support for the overcalled suit, but is too strong for a raise to the two level. Since a jump to 3 ♥ would be preemptive, East starts with a cuebid. West rebids hearts at the lowest possible level to show a minimum. With nothing extra for the cuebid, East passes.

West
♠ J 8
♥ J 6 3
♦ A K 10 9 2
♣ 10 7 2

WEST	NORTH	EAST	SOUTH
			1 ♣
1 ♦	Pass	2 ♣	3 ♣
Pass	Pass	3 ♥	Pass
4 ♥	Pass	Pass	Pass

East
♠ 9 6 4
♥ A K Q 8 4
♦ Q 4 3
♣ A 8

After West's overcall, East is too strong to make a non-forcing bid of 1 ♥. Instead, East starts with a cuebid. West shows a minimum hand by passing when South competes with 3 ♣. East now shows the heart suit. The cuebid followed by the bid of a new suit is forcing, so West raises to game.

West
♠ J 8 5
♥ K 6
♦ A Q J 7 5 3
♣ Q 6

WEST	NORTH	EAST	SOUTH
			1 ♥
2 ♦	2 ♥	3 ♥	Pass
3NT	Pass	Pass	Pass

East
♠ Q 7 4
♥ J 7 2
♦ K 10 6
♣ A K 9 3

East is too strong to raise West's two-level overcall to 3 ♦, but can't bid notrump without some strength in the opponents' suit. East cuebids 3 ♥ to force partner to bid again. With a good suit and a high card in the opponents' suit, West tries 3NT. East is happy to accept partner's choice.

West	WEST	NORTH	EAST	SOUTH	East
♠ K 8 4				1♦	♠ A 3 2
♥ K J 10 8 5	1♥	1♠	2♦	Pass	♥ Q 9 3
♦ J 5	2♥	Pass	3♥	Pass	♦ 10 8 2
♣ 10 4 3	Pass	Pass			♣ A K 9 5

With support for partner's suit and 13 high-card points, East cuebids to show interest in game. West rebids 2♥ to show a minimum, but East gives it one more try by raising to the three level. West still hasn't found anything extra, so the partnership stops in partscore.

West	WEST	NORTH	EAST	SOUTH	East
♠ K Q 9 8 3		Pass	Pass	1♦	♠ A 7 5 2
♥ Q 8	1♠	2♦	3♠	Pass	♥ 9 7 3
♦ 9 3	Pass	Pass			♦ 10 8
♣ A 10 6 2					♣ J 9 5 3

With four-card support for partner's suit and a weak hand, West makes a preemptive jump raise of partner's overcall. With the strength for a limit raise or better, East could have cuebid 3♦, so West has no reason to bid any more. East–West won't make their 3♠ contract, but North–South could get a better score by playing in hearts or diamonds. East's jump has made it difficult for the opponents to find their best spot.

Jump Overcall in a Suit

An overcall one level higher than necessary is a *jump overcall*. This is commonly used to show a good six-card suit, but there are various possible agreements about the strength shown by the jump overcall. One possibility is to play strong jump overcalls, showing a hand of 17 or more points. A second possibility is to play intermediate jump overcalls, showing a hand of 11 to 16 points. By far the most popular style today, however, is to use weak (preemptive) jump overcalls, showing a hand similar to a weak two-bid of fewer than 13 total points.

What does East call on the following hands after this auction, when the partnership uses weak jump overcalls?

WEST	NORTH	**EAST**	SOUTH
	1♥	?	

♠ A K J 10 8 3
♥ 8
♦ 10 8 5
♣ 9 4 3

Jump to 2♠. East has the values for a weak two-bid. 2♠ describes a hand with a good six-card suit, but little else outside.

♠ 9
♥ 8 4
♦ J 6 4 2
♣ A Q J 10 9 7

Jump to 3♣. Most players would jump to 3♣ not vulnerable. It would be more dangerous when vulnerable. Some players would bid 3♣ if both sides were vulnerable, but few players would take the risk when their side is vulnerable and the opponents are not.

♠ K Q 9 7 6 3
♥ K 4
♦ 9 5 2
♣ A 7

Overcall 1♠. This hand is too strong for a preemptive jump overcall, so it falls into the category of a simple overcall.

♠ A K J 9 8 4
♥ 9 4
♦ A Q J
♣ Q 7

Double. This hand is too strong for either a weak jump overcall or a simple overcall. East starts with a takeout double, planning to bid spades at the next opportunity. This sequence of calls will describe a hand too strong to overcall at the one level.

♠ K Q 10 8 7 6 3
♥ 5
♦ J 4 2
♣ 9 6

Overcall 3♠. A double jump overcall — two levels higher than necessary — shows a weak hand with a good seven-card or longer suit. It's similar to an opening, preemptive bid at the three level. Some players might bid only 2♠, a weak jump overcall, especially if vulnerable, but West would expect only a six-card suit.

OVERCALLING THE OPPONENT'S 1NT OPENING

♠ A J 8 5 3
♥ K Q 6 2
♦ J 5 4
♣ 3

North opens 1NT, and this is East's hand. With the opponents using a range of 15 to 17 HCP for an opening 1NT bid, the auction starts:

WEST	NORTH	**EAST**	SOUTH
	1NT	?	

Playing standard methods, entering the auction is dangerous at this point. A double would be for penalty, and an overcall of 2♠ would be risky. South, knowing North has a balanced hand with 15 to 17 HCP, is in an excellent position to double for penalty, even without a strong spade holding. If South does double 2♠ for penalty, East won't know what to do. West might have a singleton spade and four or five hearts. Bidding 3♥, however, may get the partnership into further trouble.

Nonetheless, East would like to compete. If West has either major suit, there might be a partscore. The bidding might push the opponents too high or into the wrong contract. Even if the contract is defeated, the result may be better than the result from defending 1NT.

Experience has shown that competing against a 1NT opening bid is safest with a one-suited hand or a two-suited hand. With one long suit, competing is reasonably safe, since neither opponent is likely to have enough length or strength in the suit to justify a double for penalty. With a two-suited hand, the partnership may find a safe landing spot in one of the two suits — provided partner knows which two suits. With a balanced hand or a three-suited hand, staying out of the auction is usually wiser.

On the example hand, coming into the auction would be safer if East had a way of getting West to choose between spades and hearts. If West doesn't have much, the partnership can stop at the two level in its best fit. If West does have a good fit for one or both major suits, the partnership may be able to compete further, although game is unlikely when the opponents open 1NT.

The standard approach is to treat all overcalls of the opponent's 1NT opening as natural, catering to a one-suited hand but leaving the partnership to guess what to do with a two-suited hand. Many conventional methods have been developed to compete over the opponent's 1NT opening bid. Almost all of them are designed to allow the partnership to compete relatively safely with both one-suited and two-suited hands. Some of the conventions are straightforward; others can be quite complex. Each partnership has to decide whether there is enough to be gained to compensate for the additional memory work.

Below is an example of one of the conventions that can be used after an opponent's 1NT opening bid. It illustrates some things the partnership must discuss before using such a convention. There are examples of other common conventions in the Appendix.

Landy

? DONT

One of the easiest conventions to use over an opponent's 1NT opening bid was developed by Alvin Landy, the chief executive officer for the ACBL throughout most of the 50's and 60's. *Landy* uses an overcall of 2♣ as conventional, showing both major suits. All other bids are natural.

The basic convention is straightforward, but there's lots for the partnership to discuss before using it. For example, the partnership needs to agree on whether the convention is used only in the direct position — immediately over the 1NT opening bid — or also in the balancing position — following two passes.

For example:

WEST	NORTH	**EAST**	SOUTH
	1NT	Pass	Pass
2♣	Pass	?	

Most partnerships playing Landy would treat West's 2♣ bid as takeout for the majors, but it's best to discuss the situation beforehand.

The partnership should also discuss whether the convention is used whatever the range of the 1NT opening bid. Some players prefer to use different methods depending on whether the opponents are playing a strong 1NT — 15 or more points — or a weak 1NT — 14 or fewer points. Most partnerships use the same convention over all ranges of 1NT.

Another consideration is how to show a hand with a long club suit.

Most partnerships use a direct jump to 3♣ to show clubs. That's the one disadvantage of using Landy. You can't stop at the two level with a one-suited hand when the suit is clubs.

Here are examples of Landy after North opens 1NT. What call does East make with these hands?

♠ Q J 9 8 5
♥ A J 8 7 3
♦ 9 3
♣ 3

Overcall 2♣. This is a good hand for the Landy convention, as long as West has three cards in one of the major suits. Less strength is needed for East to enter the auction with two five-card suits. East should be a little more cautious when vulnerable, but most players would take a chance with this hand at any vulnerability.

♠ A Q 10 8
♥ K Q 9 7
♦ K 6 3
♣ 7 4

Overcall 2♣. The hand isn't very distributional, but the strength makes up for it. With any luck, an eight-card fit will be found. Even with a seven-card fit, West may be able to take enough tricks. The alternative for East is to pass and keep out of the auction. That's not competitive enough for most players.

♠ J 8 7 4 2
♥ K 9 7 3
♦ Q 4
♣ K 4

Pass. With neither good distribution nor extra strength, East stays out of the auction. Bidding may get East–West into trouble or may help declarer in the play if North–South buy the contract.

♠ 9 4
♥ K Q 10 9 6 4 3
♦ A 8 6
♣ 6

Overcall 2♥. Landy allows for a natural overcall with a one-suited hand. With clubs rather than hearts, East would bid 3♣.

♠ 8 7
♥ Q 9 7 5 3
♦ 4
♣ A K 10 8 6

Pass. This is an awkward hand for Landy. East can't overcall 2♣, since that's conventional and West is likely to bid spades. Jumping to 3♣ with a five-card suit and overcalling with a weak five-card heart suit are not good choices. It's best to pass and see what happens. To compete on this type of hand, look at some of the other conventions in the Appendix. Many conventions provide ways of handling all two-suited hands, not just those with the majors.

Advancing After Landy

When competing against an opponent's 1NT opening, the main objective is to enter the auction rather than to get to game. This is especially true when the opponents are using a *strong* notrump. If partner uses Landy, proceed cautiously, giving partner lots of leeway. Ideally, partner should have five cards in each major suit, but could have four cards in one or both suits. Partner's bid covers a wide range of strength, from a fairly weak distributional hand up to an opening bid or more. Although a reasonable hand is expected from partner when vulnerable, to consider inviting to the game level when non-vulnerable, the partnership needs a good fit and close to the values for an opening bid. Partner might have taken a chance in entering the auction. Don't spoil partner's effort by competing too high. If the opponents are using a *weak* notrump opening and partner uses Landy, responder can afford to be a little more aggressive, since there is more of a possibility that the partnership can make a game contract.

While there's no standard agreement on the responses to Landy, the following approach can be used:

- 2♥ or 2♠ is a simple preference to a major suit and shows no interest in game.

- Pass shows a weak hand with a long club suit and fewer than three cards in either major.

- 2♦ shows a weak hand with a long diamond suit and fewer than three cards in either major.

- 3NT, 4♥ or 4♠ is to play.

- 2NT is conventional and forcing for one round. It shows interest in game but no four-card fit for either major suit. It's the only forcing response and asks partner for a further description.

- 3♣ or 3♦ is invitational and shows a good six-card or longer suit.

- 3♥ or 3♠ is invitational with three-card or longer support.

Here are sample auctions using the above methods:

West		East
♠ Q J 9 8 5		♠ K 7 3
♥ A J 8 7 3		♥ 10 4
♦ 9 3		♦ A 8 6
♣ 3		♣ Q 10 8 6 2

WEST	NORTH	EAST	SOUTH
			1NT
2♣	Pass	2♠	Pass
Pass	Pass		

With three-card support for spades, East gives simple preference at the two level. East shouldn't consider passing 2♣, since West's bid doesn't promise any clubs at all. Bidding 2♠ is likely to put the partnership in an eight-card fit. With not much more strength than West is entitled to expect, East shouldn't venture beyond the two level. The partnership has done well to compete to a reasonable partscore.

West		East
♠ K J 10 6 2		♠ Q 3
♥ Q J 8 7		♥ K 10 9 4
♦ 7 2		♦ A 9 8 6 3
♣ K 5		♣ 6 3

WEST	NORTH	EAST	SOUTH
			1NT
2♣	Pass	3♥	Pass
Pass	Pass		

With an excellent fit with one of partner's suits and useful-looking high cards in the other suits, East's hand is worth an invitational jump. West doesn't have enough extra strength to accept partner's game try.

West		East
♠ K J 8 7 2		♠ A 9 5
♥ A Q 8 3		♥ K 6 4
♦ 9 4		♦ 10 7 5 2
♣ 9 6		♣ A K 8

WEST	NORTH	EAST	SOUTH
			1NT
2♣	Pass	2NT	Pass
3♠	Pass	4♠	Pass
Pass	Pass		

East has enough to take the partnership to game when partner comes in with the Landy bid. Rather than guess which major suit to bid, East bids a conventional forcing 2NT to get more information. West's 3♠ bid shows a five-card suit, and East puts the partnership in the best game. With only four cards in each major, West could have bid the better minor suit with a minimum or 3NT with a maximum.

West		East
♠ A J 10 7 2		♠ 3
♥ K 10 8 7 3		♥ 4 2
♦ 9		♦ K Q 10 8 6 3
♣ 8 6		♣ A 7 5 3

WEST	NORTH	EAST	SOUTH
	Pass	Pass	1NT
2♣	Pass	2♦	Pass
Pass	Pass		

Without a fit for either of partner's suits, East bids diamonds. West accepts partner's decision. The partnership may not be in a great contract, but it would be in a worse position if West had overcalled 2♠.

HANDLING THE OPPONENTS' OVERCALLS

The overcall needs to be seen from opener's point of view. Often it can be ignored and the natural bid made. Sometimes an opponent's interference leaves no choice but to pass and hope to get a chance to compete later in the auction. Although an opponent's overcall does take away some bidding room, it also presents two new options, the double and the cuebid. The use of the double, either as a penalty double or as a negative double, was discussed in Chapters 1 and 2. Let's consider how most partnerships make use of the cuebid.

Cuebid as a Limit Raise or Better

The usual agreement after an opponent makes an overcall directly over partner's opening bid is:

- A cuebid of the opponent's suit shows a fit with opener's suit and at least the strength for a limit raise.
- A jump raise of partner's suit is weak and preemptive.

To see how this works, what action would East take on the following hands after the auction begins:

WEST	NORTH	**EAST**	SOUTH
1♥	2♦	?	

♠ A 9 4
♥ K J 8 4
♦ 10 7
♣ Q J 6 2

Cuebid 3♦. If North had passed, a jump to 3♥ would be a limit raise. When North interferes, a jump to 3♥ becomes weak and preemptive. With a fit and the strength for a limit raise, East cuebids the opponent's suit. The 3 ♦ cuebid says nothing about East's holding in the diamond suit. With a minimum, West can rebid 3 ♥, and the partnership will rest in partscore. With enough to accept an invitation, West can bid 4 ♥.

♠ K 9 3 ♥ A Q 8 4 ♦ A 7 ♣ J 8 6 2	Cuebid 3 ♦. The cuebid promises only enough strength for a limit raise, but responder can have more. If West returns to 3 ♥ showing a minimum hand, East continues to game. A direct jump to 4 ♥ would be a weak, preemptive bid, similar to a jump to 4 ♥ without the interference.
♠ Q 9 3 ♥ Q 10 5 ♦ 7 2 ♣ K 8 6 4 3	Raise to 2 ♥. The opponent's 2 ♦ overcall doesn't prevent East from making a natural response.
♠ K 10 8 5 ♥ Q 3 ♦ 7 5 4 ♣ A 10 7 3	Double. As played by most partnerships, this is a negative double. It allows East to compete when the opponent's overcall has taken away East's natural response.
♠ 7 3 ♥ Q 10 8 5 ♦ 9 3 ♣ Q 8 4 3 2	Jump to 3 ♥. Most partnerships treat a jump in this situation as weak, showing a fit with West's opening suit but very little strength outside. The idea is to take bidding room away from the opponents while showing support for West's suit. With enough strength for a limit raise, East would cuebid.

SUMMARY

Requirements for an Overcall

A simple overcall in a suit tends to show:

- A good five-card or longer suit.
- 8 to 16 HCP (10 to 17 total points).
  At the two level or higher, the overcall should show at least the equivalent of an opening bid.

A jump overcall (weak) shows:

- A weak hand.
- A good six-card or longer suit.

Advancing After an Overcall

- A single raise of a one-level overcall shows three-card or longer support and 8 or 9 points. A single raise of a two-level overcall shows 8 to 10 points.

- A jump raise of an overcall is weak and preemptive, showing four-card support and a weak hand, with 5 to 8 points.

- The bid of a new suit shows a good five-card or longer suit, but is non-forcing.

- A jump in a new suit shows a good six-card or longer suit and 11 to 13 points. It's invitational over a one-level overcall, but forcing over a two-level overcall.

- A notrump response shows some strength in the opponent's suit, but isn't forcing. 1NT shows 8 to 11 points. 2NT shows 12 to 15 points over a one-level overcall and 9 to 11 points over a two-level overcall. 3NT shows 16 or more points over a one-level overcall and 12 or more over a two-level overcall.

- A cuebid of the opponent's suit is forcing for at least one round, showing an interest in reaching a game contract.

When an Opponent Makes a Simple Overcall

- A cuebid of the opponent's suit shows a fit with opener's suit and at least the strength for a limit raise.

- A jump raise of opener's suit in this situation is weak and preemptive, rather than invitational.

NOTE: See the Appendix (pages 347–352) for a discussion of these supplemental conventions and/or treatments.

Jump Cuebid in Response to an Overcall

Fit-Showing Jumps

Conventional Defenses to an Opponent's 1NT Opening Bid

>**Ripstra**
>
>**Becker**
>
>**Brozel**
>
>**DONT**
>
>**Cappelletti (Hamilton, Pottage)**
>
>**Astro**

Note: The following exercises illustrate the methods outlined in the summary.

Exercise One — Simple Overcall in a Suit

East–West are non-vulnerable. What would East call with the following hands in the given auction? Would East make the same call if East–West were vulnerable?

WEST	NORTH	**EAST**	SOUTH
	1♦	?	

1) ♠ A K J 9 2
   ♥ 7 3
   ♦ 10 8 4
   ♣ K 8 2

2) ♠ Q 8
   ♥ A 8 2
   ♦ Q 7 3
   ♣ Q J 7 6 3

3) ♠ 7 2
   ♥ K J 9 8 2
   ♦ K 10 5
   ♣ J 7 3

4) ♠ 10 3
   ♥ A K J 10
   ♦ K 8 6 2
   ♣ 10 6 5

5) ♠ A K 3
   ♥ A K Q 9 2
   ♦ 7 4
   ♣ K 8 4

6) ♠ K Q 9 7 3
   ♥ 5
   ♦ 3
   ♣ A Q J 9 7 5

Exercise One *Answer* — Simple Overcall in a Suit

1) Non-vul: 1♠. East has a good five-card suit and enough strength to make a one-level overcall.

   Vul: 1♠. Although East might not open the bidding with this hand, it's worth a one-level overcall even if East–West are vulnerable.

2) Non-vul: Pass. The club suit isn't good enough to risk a two-level overcall.

   Vul: Pass. If the club suit is not good enough to overcall non-vulnerable, overcalling would be even riskier when vulnerable.

3) Non-vul: 1♥ or Pass. This is the minimum for a one-level overcall. The suit is reasonable and so East might risk entering the auction. If West would expect a better hand, it may be safer to pass.

   Vul: Pass. The stakes increase when vulnerable. To overcall with this hand, even at the one level, would be extremely risky.

4) Non-vul: 1♥. This four-card suit feels like a five-card suit, so it's reasonable to overcall with this hand. East wants West to lead a heart if they defend.

   Vul: 1♥. With a good suit, the risk of being doubled decreases. The ♦K figures to be favorably placed to take a trick, so it's worth risking an overcall on this hand when vulnerable.

5) Non-vul: Double. This hand is too strong for a one-level overcall. East starts with a takeout double, planning to bid hearts next. This series of calls shows a hand too strong for a simple overcall.

   Vul: Double. The vulnerability isn't a factor with a hand like this.

6) Non-vul: 2♣. East starts with the longer suit and plans to bid, and perhaps rebid, the spades at the next opportunity. West will know that the clubs are longer than the spades and can select the best trump suit accordingly.

   Vul: 2♣. The vulnerability has no effect on the choice of calls with this hand.

Exercise Two — Advancing After a Simple Overcall

What would West call with each of the following hands after this auction?

WEST	NORTH	EAST	SOUTH
	1♣	1♥	Pass
?			

1) ♠ 6 3
   ♥ J 7 4
   ♦ K 9 8 5 3
   ♣ A 8 3

2) ♠ 7 2
   ♥ K 9 7 3
   ♦ Q 10 7 6 2
   ♣ 9 5

3) ♠ K 10
   ♥ K J 8
   ♦ A 8 7 5
   ♣ 10 8 3 2

4) ♠ K Q 10 8 5
   ♥ 6 2
   ♦ A 8 7 3
   ♣ 8 7

5) ♠ Q 3 2
   ♥ A 8
   ♦ A K Q 7 5
   ♣ 6 5 4

6) ♠ Q 8 4
   ♥ J 6
   ♦ A J 10 3
   ♣ K Q 10 3

Exercise Two *Answer* — Advancing After a Simple Overcall

1) 2♥. East could have a very good hand for the overcall. Raising keeps alive the possibility of reaching game. If East has a minimum hand for the overcall, East–West may not make 2♥, but West's raise might make it more difficult for the opponents to find their best spot.

2) 3♥. A jump raise of East's overcall is weak and preemptive, showing four-card support and a weak hand. With a limit raise or better, West would start by cuebidding 2♣, the opponent's suit.

3) 2♣. The cuebid of North's suit followed by a raise of East's suit shows the strength for a limit raise. The hand is too strong to raise to 2♥, and an immediate jump to 3♥ would show a weak hand. East might pass a new-suit bid, and East–West would miss the heart fit.

4) 1♠. Without enough support to raise East right away, West bids a new (good) suit. This bid is not forcing, and East can pass with a minimum overcall. If East has a good hand, however, the partnership can find its best spot.

5) 2♣. Playing standard methods, a response of 2♦ would not be forcing. West starts with a cuebid, planning to show the diamond suit at the next opportunity. This style can be awkward on a hand like this one. Some partnerships prefer to treat a new suit response to an overcall as a forcing bid, which would work better on this hand.

6) 2NT. West shows a balanced hand with 12 to 15 points and strength in North's suit. It isn't forcing in response to an overcall. East can pass with a minimum overcall. With a hand worth an opening bid or better, East can bid game.

Exercise Three — Jump Overcalls in a Suit

What call would East make with each of the following hands after this auction?

WEST	NORTH	EAST	SOUTH
	1♥	?	

1) ♠ K Q J 9 7 6
   ♥ 7
   ♦ 10 9 7 3
   ♣ 6 4

2) ♠ A Q J 8 7 3
   ♥ K 8 2
   ♦ A 4
   ♣ 7 3

3) ♠ K Q 10 9 7 6 3
   ♥ 8
   ♦ 7
   ♣ 9 6 5 2

Exercise Four — Handling an Opponent's Overcall

What call would East make with each of the following hands after this auction?

WEST	NORTH	EAST	SOUTH
1♠	2♥	?	

1) ♠ K 8 7
   ♥ 10 8 4 3
   ♦ A 9 8 5
   ♣ 9 2

2) ♠ Q 10 7 3
   ♥ J 8
   ♦ K Q 9 7
   ♣ K 8 2

3) ♠ K 9 7 4
   ♥ 10 7
   ♦ 5 2
   ♣ Q J 8 3 2

4) ♠ A J 8 4
   ♥ 9 3
   ♦ A K 4
   ♣ Q 7 6 2

5) ♠ Q J 9 7 4
   ♥ 3
   ♦ Q 10 8 6 4
   ♣ 10 3

6) ♠ 10 7
   ♥ 9 6 5
   ♦ A J 9 3
   ♣ K Q 8 5

Exercise Three *Answer* — Jump Overcalls in a Suit

1) 2♠. With a good six-card suit and little else, this is a good hand for a weak jump overcall. The weak jump overcall is similar to an opening weak two-bid. East makes the auction difficult for the opponents, while describing the hand to West.

2) 1♠. This hand is too strong for a weak jump overcall. East makes a simple overcall at the one level. If the partnership used intermediate jump overcalls, rather than weak jump overcalls, this hand would qualify as a 2♠ bid.

3) 3♠. With a good seven-card suit and a weak hand, East makes a preemptive jump overcall at the three level. This is similar to an opening 3♠ bid. Most players would take the same action whether vulnerable or non-vulnerable. Jumping to only 2♠ wouldn't be unreasonable, however, if East–West were vulnerable against non vulnerable.

Exercise Four *Answer* — Handling an Opponent's Overcall

1) 2♠. The opponent's overcall doesn't prevent East from showing support for spades.

2) Cuebid 3♥. A jump to 3♠ would be preemptive after North's overcall. A cuebid shows support for West's spades and the strength for at least a limit raise. It isn't forcing to game. If West rebids 3♠, showing a minimum, East can pass.

3) 3♠. The jump to 3♠ is a weak, preemptive action after an opponent's overcall. It shows a weak hand with four-card support.

4) Cuebid 3♥. The cuebid of the opponent's suit shows a limit raise or better. On this hand, East will continue to game even if West rebids only 3♠. An immediate jump to 4♠ would be preemptive, and a slam might be missed if West has a good hand.

5) 4♠. This is a weak, preemptive raise, and the same bid would apply if North hadn't overcalled.

6) Double. This is a negative double, showing support for the unbid suits and enough strength to compete for the contract.

Bid and Play — When in Doubt, Pass

(E–Z Deal Cards: #3, Deal 1 — Dealer, North)

Suggested Bidding

WEST	NORTH	EAST	SOUTH
	1♣	2♠	Pass (?)
Pass	Pass (?)		

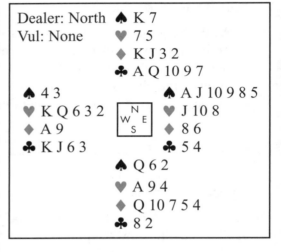

Dealer: North
Vul: None

♠ K 7
♥ 7 5
♦ K J 3 2
♣ A Q 10 9 7

♠ 4 3
♥ K Q 6 3 2
♦ A 9
♣ K J 6 3

♠ A J 10 9 8 5
♥ J 10 8
♦ 8 6
♣ 5 4

♠ Q 6 2
♥ A 9 4
♦ Q 10 7 5 4
♣ 8 2

North starts the bidding in the longest suit. With a good six-card spade suit and a weak hand, East makes a preemptive jump overcall of 2♠.

East's 2♠ bid makes the auction difficult for the opponents. South doesn't have enough to bid 3♦, and with only three-card support for hearts, the hand is unsuitable for a negative double. South might try 2NT, but that's a little ambitious with only 8 HCPs and a dubious spade stopper. South's best choice is to pass and hope to show some values later in the auction.

Although West has the values for an opening bid, East has described a weak hand that is useful only with spades as the trump suit. West passes. The partnership is probably high enough already.

North has a difficult choice of calls when the auction comes back around. With only a doubleton heart, North's hand is unsuitable for a reopening double, and the ♠K is of dubious value. North should probably pass and choose to defend.

In an experienced partnership, North might be able to reopen with an "unusual" 2NT, looking for a minor-suit fit. In most partnerships, however, this bid would be interpreted as natural and could give South a misleading picture of North's strength.

If East's 2♠ bid does buy the contract, East–West will have effectively "stolen" the contract. North–South can take 10 tricks in diamonds.

Suggested Opening Lead

South is on lead against 2♠ and would start with the ♣8, top of the doubleton in partner's suit.

Suggested Play

East has two potential spade losers, one heart loser, one diamond loser and two club losers. East could hope that South has either the ♣A or the ♣Q, but the auction and South's opening lead make that seem unlikely. If the defenders don't switch to diamonds soon enough, East may be able to discard the diamond loser on an extra heart winner in dummy.

East's best chance to avoid two spade losers is to take repeated finesses through North. That should work if North has the ♠K, or the ♠Q or both. Dummy has one entry with the ♦A, and declarer can create a second entry in the heart suit.

Suggested Defense

Perfect defense will defeat 2♠. Suppose South leads a club. The ♣J is played from dummy, and North wins the ♣Q. North, hoping to get a ruff, can lead a heart. South, taking the inference that East isn't likely to have a four-card heart suit for the 2♠ bid (which would give North a singleton heart), can let declarer win this trick. If declarer now takes a spade finesse, losing to South's ♠Q, South can play the ♥A and another heart to give North a ruff with the ♠K. North can now switch to a diamond to knock out dummy's ♦A, before East is able to discard the diamond loser. The defenders will take six tricks.

That defense, however, is double dummy, and it won't often be found even by experienced defenders. It is more likely that North will win the first trick with the ♣Q, play the ♣A and lead a third round of clubs. Declarer can now make the contract in a couple of ways. Declarer can discard the diamond loser on the third round of clubs, letting South ruff. On gaining the lead, declarer can simply play the ♠A and another spade. Declarer loses two clubs, two spade tricks and the ♥A. East could also ruff the third round of clubs with the ♠8. Whether or not South overruffs, declarer can take eight tricks.

In summary, 2♠ is a good spot for East–West. If North–South manage to find their diamond fit, the only losers are one spade, one heart and one diamond, since the club finesse is successful. In fact, if East–West don't lead hearts soon enough, the heart loser might disappear.

The play is interesting if North–South reach a notrump contract. If South is declarer and West leads a spade, declarer should play North's ♠K on the first trick — or duck the first trick completely — to prevent East from establishing the spade suit and keeping a spade entry. East–West can counter this play by leading hearts to establish enough winners in that suit before the ♦A is knocked out. If North is declarer in a notrump contract, East will have to lead a heart right away to prevent declarer from taking at least nine tricks.

Bid and Play — Cuebids Get the Message Across

(E–Z Deal Cards: #3, Deal 2 — Dealer, East)

Suggested Bidding

WEST	NORTH	EAST	SOUTH
		1 ♦	1 ♠
Pass	2 ♦	Pass	2 ♠
Pass	Pass	Pass	

East opens the bidding 1 ♦. South overcalls 1 ♠ to show a good five-card suit. West doesn't have enough to make a negative double and passes. North has too much for a simple raise to 2 ♠, but a jump to 3 ♠ would be weak and preemptive and show four-card support — and might get the partnership too high if South has a minimum overcall. Instead, North cuebids 2 ♦, showing an interest

```
Dealer: East    ♠ K 8 2
Vul: N–S        ♥ A 4 2
                ♦ Q 7 6 3
                ♣ Q 7 3

♠ J 9 6                    ♠ 4 3
♥ K 9 5 3      N           ♥ Q 10 7
♦ J 4        W   E         ♦ A K 10 9 2
♣ 10 6 4 2     S           ♣ A 9 5

                ♠ A Q 10 7 5
                ♥ J 8 6
                ♦ 8 5
                ♣ K J 8
```

in reaching game. After East passes, South rebids 2 ♠ to show a minimum hand for the overcall with no interest in getting to game. North has no reason to overrule partner's decision and, having shown support with the cuebid, passes to leave the partnership in partscore.

Without the use of the cuebid, there's a reasonable chance that North–South would get too high. The cuebid allows North to try for game without getting beyond the two level when South has less than an opening bid.

Suggested Opening Lead

West is on lead and would probably start with the ♦ J, top of a doubleton in partner's suit.

Suggested Play

Declarer has two heart losers, two diamond losers, and one club loser. To make the contract, declarer must avoid losing a trump trick. That won't be a problem if the suit is divided 3–2 and South can gain the lead to draw trumps, but there is a complication. After winning two diamond tricks, East may lead a third round of diamonds. If South ruffs with a low trump, West can overruff. If South ruffs with a high trump, the ♠A or ♠Q, West will eventually take a trick with the ♠J.

South might try ruffing the third round of diamonds with the ♠10, hoping West doesn't have the ♠J, but that doesn't work. On the surface, it seems that South must lose a trump trick if East plays another winning diamond after winning the first two tricks. South still has two heart losers and one club loser — that's one too many.

There is a way to make the contract. Suppose West wins the first trick with the ♦J and continues with a second diamond, which East wins with the ♦9. East now leads the ♦K. Since ruffing either high or low won't work, South shouldn't ruff at all! Instead, South should discard a heart. South planned on two heart losers anyway, and this is as good a time as any. If East continues by leading the ♦A, again South can't win by ruffing either high or low. So, South discards another heart. In effect, South has exchanged the two heart losers for two extra diamond losers.

The advantage of discarding the heart losers is that South can now avoid a trump loser. If East leads anything except another diamond, South can draw trumps after gaining the lead. If East leads a fifth round of diamonds, South can discard a club and West is helpless. If West doesn't ruff, declarer wins the trick by ruffing in dummy and can then draw trumps. If West ruffs, declarer overruffs in the dummy and can draw West's two remaining trumps. All declarer loses are four diamond tricks and the ♣A.

The tactic of throwing a loser on a losing trick is referred to as discarding a loser on a loser. South doesn't mind losing two extra diamond tricks while discarding hearts, since the two heart tricks would have been lost anyway. By exchanging the losers, however, declarer avoids the loss of a trump trick.

Suggested Defense

As can be seen from the above discussion, the best defense is for East to continue leading diamond winners. If declarer ruffs, West can overruff and the contract is defeated. The defenders will eventually take two heart tricks and a club trick to go along with the two diamond tricks and the trump trick.

If South does discard two hearts on the third and fourth rounds of diamonds, East's best defense is to lead a fifth round of diamonds — perhaps after taking the ♣A somewhere along the way. West can ruff the fifth round of diamonds with the ♠9, forcing declarer to overruff with dummy's ♠K to win the trick. Declarer can escape without a trump loser at this point by playing the ♠A and ♠Q, but doesn't know for certain that the remaining trumps divide 2–2. Declarer might decide to finesse the ♠10, hoping East started with the ♠J. West will then get an unexpected trick with the ♠J to defeat the contract.

Bid and Play — Using Landy

(E–Z Deal Cards: #3, Deal 3 — Dealer, South)

Suggested Bidding

WEST	NORTH	EAST	SOUTH
			Pass
Pass	1NT	2♣	Pass
2♥	Pass	Pass	Pass

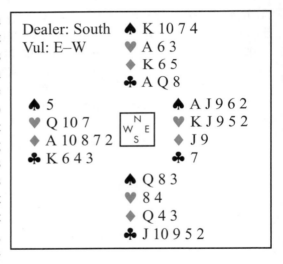

Dealer: South   ♠ K 10 7 4
Vul: E–W   ♥ A 6 3
            ♦ K 6 5
            ♣ A Q 8

♠ 5   ♠ A J 9 6 2
♥ Q 10 7   ♥ K J 9 5 2
♦ A 10 8 7 2   ♦ J 9
♣ K 6 4 3   ♣ 7

            ♠ Q 8 3
            ♥ 8 4
            ♦ Q 4 3
            ♣ J 10 9 5 2

After two passes, North opens the bidding 1NT. East would like to compete, but it is dangerous to enter the auction over 1NT. If East picks the wrong suit, the partnership might get into trouble if West doesn't have a fit. Having a two-suited hand provides some safety, since partner is likely to have a fit for at least one of the suits. If East–West use the Landy convention, East can overcall 2♣, showing both major suits.

South doesn't have enough to say anything over East's intervention. South's clubs aren't strong enough to double the conventional bid for penalty. West's diamonds aren't good enough to suggest that suit as trump. East has shown both major suits and could be very short in diamonds. Since East has asked West to pick a major, West should bid 2♥, which will probably end the auction.

Suggested Opening Lead

North has a difficult choice of opening leads. Knowing West prefers hearts to spades, North might choose to lead a trump, trying to prevent West from ruffing spades. North might lead a low heart, in case South holds some help in the suit. On regaining the lead, North will be in a position to play the ♥A and another heart.

Suggested Play

If North does lead a low heart at trick one, West needs to plan the play carefully. From West's perspective, there are only six winners: four hearts, the ♠A and the ♦A. West might consider ruffing club losers in the dummy, but the defenders will regain the lead and play two more rounds of trumps. A better plan is to try to establish the diamond suit.

Declarer wins the first heart in dummy (East) and leads the ♦J. If South plays a low diamond, declarer can finesse, losing to North's ♦K. If North then leads the ♥A and another heart, declarer can again win in dummy and lead the ♦9, overtaking with the ♦10 to repeat the finesse. With the favorable lie of the diamonds, this will give declarer four diamond tricks. Combined with four tricks from the heart suit and the ♠A, declarer will make the contract with an overtrick. If South covers the ♦J with the ♦Q, West can win the ♦A and then drive out North's ♦K. If North leads more hearts, declarer can win in the West hand and take the diamond winners. Again, declarer takes at least nine tricks.

Declarer should avoid being too eager to ruff any of East's spades. The defenders could then prevent West from getting four tricks from the diamond suit, because of entry problems.

Suggested Defense

If declarer does go about establishing tricks in the diamond suit, there isn't much the defenders can do. If declarer ruffs a spade in the West hand, the defenders can hold declarer to eight tricks. The defenders can lead trumps to prevent declarer from ruffing a second spade. If South covers the ♦J when it is led from dummy, West won't have enough entries to get four tricks from the suit. Declarer will still be able to establish dummy's fifth spade as a trick and take eight tricks.

East–West do well to get into the auction, since they can take at least eight tricks with hearts as trump. If East passes 1NT and that ends the auction, East will have to guess to lead a heart and not a spade. If East leads a spade against 1NT, declarer can make the contract.

If East overcalls 2♠, the auction will probably end there. East can be defeated in that contract, losing three spade tricks, one heart, one diamond, and one club.

Bid and Play — Dealing with Interference

(E–Z Deal Cards: #3, Deal 4 — Dealer, West)

Suggested Bidding

WEST	NORTH	EAST	SOUTH
Pass	1 ♥	2 ♦	3 ♦
Pass	3 ♥	Pass	Pass
Pass			

North opens 1 ♥ and East has enough to overcall 2 ♦. If East had passed, South would have made a limit raise to 3 ♥. After the interference, the usual agreement is that a jump raise is weak and preemptive. To show the strength for a limit raise or better, South starts with a cuebid of 3 ♦.

West passes and the auction comes back to North. With a minimum opening bid, North returns to 3 ♥, rejecting South's invitation.

```
Dealer: West    ♠ K 5
Vul: Both       ♥ A Q 8 6 2
                ♦ J 7 4
                ♣ K 5 2
♠ Q 10 7 6 3          ♠ J 8
♥ J 9 4          N    ♥ 10
♦ 9 2         W     E ♦ A K 10 8 6 3
♣ J 10 8         S   ♣ A 9 7 3
                ♠ A 9 4 2
                ♥ K 7 5 3
                ♦ Q 5
                ♣ Q 6 4
```

East has already described the hand with the overcall and, with no support from West, bidding any more would be dangerous. South should also pass. South has only enough strength for a limit raise and North has declined the invitation by rebidding 3 ♥. South's pass should end the auction.

Suggested Opening Lead

East is on lead against 3 ♥ and would start with the ♦A, top of touching honors — or the ♦K if the partnership leads the king from this combination.

Suggested Play

Assuming the missing hearts aren't divided 4–0, there are no heart losers, three diamond losers, and two club losers. After the opening lead, declarer can establish a winner in the diamond suit. Given East's overcall, however, there is some danger that West will be able to ruff declarer's diamond winner.

Suppose East plays the ♦ A and the ♦ K and then leads a third round of diamonds. If declarer ruffs with a low heart, West may overruff. There are still two potential club losers, so the contract might be defeated. Declarer could ruff the third round of diamonds with the ♥ K, but that might promote a trump winner for the defenders unless the missing hearts are divided 2–2.

Declarer's best play is to discard a club from dummy on the third round of diamonds. West can ruff this trick, but now declarer can avoid losing two club tricks. The third round of clubs can be ruffed in dummy after trumps have been drawn. Declarer loses two diamond tricks, a ruff, and one club trick.

Suggested Defense

On the lead of the ♦ A, West should play the ♦ 9 as an encouraging signal. East can continue with the ♦ K and a third round of diamonds. As noted above, if declarer ruffs with dummy's ♥ K, West will eventually get a trick with the ♥ J.

If declarer ruffs with a low heart, West can overruff. Now the defenders must be careful to get both of their club tricks. If West leads back the ♣ J, for example, and declarer plays a low club, East must avoid the temptation to play the ♣ A. That would give declarer two club tricks with the ♣ K and ♣ Q. Instead, East should play low, letting dummy's ♣ Q win the trick. Now declarer's ♣ K is trapped and the defense will eventually get two club tricks, defeating the contract.

CHAPTER 4
Two-Suited Overcalls

TWO-SUITED OVERCALLS

A competitive auction can make exchanging information challenging, but there are also advantages when the opponents enter the bidding. While a takeout double shows support for three suits at once, sometimes there is an opportunity to show a two-suited hand.

DIRECT CUEBIDS

After an opening bid at the one level in a suit, the opponents of the opening bidder rarely want to declare in the same suit. After an opening bid of 1 ♥, for example, an overcall of 2 ♥ to describe a hand with a long heart suit is impractical. If the player next to bid wants to declare with that suit as trump, the best thing to do is to pass and wait for a possible chance to double the opponents for penalty.

The direct overcall, or cuebid, of the opponent's suit was once used to show a hand too strong for even a takeout double — the type of hand suited for a strong two-bid.

For example, suppose North opens 1 ♥ and this is East's hand:

♠ A K J 9 7 5   North's bid of 1 ♥ creates a problem. East planned
♥ A 3   to open the bidding 2 ♠, playing strong two-bids,
♦ A K Q 4   or 2 ♣, playing weak two-bids. The hand is much
♣ 2   too strong to overcall 1 ♠, and even playing inter-
                       mediate jump overcalls, the hand is too strong to
overcall 2 ♠. A jump to 4 ♠ would risk missing a slam — and the hand might belong in diamonds if West has a singleton spade and four or more diamonds. Playing strong cuebids, East would bid the opponent's suit, 2 ♥, with this type of hand. West would know East wanted to be in a game and would simply start off by bidding a long suit. Then East would bid the spade suit to show this type of hand. Since East started with a cuebid, West would keep the bidding going until at least the game level is reached.

This type of hand is quite rare when the opponents open the bidding, so most players prefer to make a more practical use of the direct cuebid.

MICHAELS CUEBID

An overcall shows a one-suited hand; a takeout double shows support for the other three suits. A direct cuebid can be used to show a two-suited hand. This popular approach is referred to as the *Michaels cuebid*. This convention was named after Mike Michaels, a friend of Charles Goren, who used to teach and write about bridge in Miami, Florida.

It works like this:

- If the opening bid is 1♣ or 1♦, a direct cuebid of the opponent's suit shows at least five cards in each major suit.

- If the opening bid is 1♥ or 1♠, a direct cuebid of the opponent's suit shows at least five cards in the other major and five cards in an unspecified minor suit. Advancer (responder) can bid 2NT to ask for partner's minor.

The most common agreement on the strength for a Michaels cuebid is that it shows either a weak hand, with less than the values for an opening bid, or a very strong hand of about 17 or more points. Most of the strength should be concentrated in two suits. Holding a hand of 12 to 16 high-card points, make a simple overcall in the higher-ranking suit, planning to show the other suit at the next opportunity. Not all partnerships have this agreement, however, and some use the Michaels cuebid convention with any range of strength.

Here are examples of overcalls playing the Michaels cuebid. What call does East make?

WEST	NORTH	**EAST**	SOUTH
	1♣	?	

♠ K Q 9 5 3
♥ A J 10 8 4
♦ 7
♣ 9 4

Cuebid 2♣. A 1♠ overcall, the higher-ranking of East's two five-card suits, is a choice, but if the opponents were to bid to the three level or four level, deciding about whether to risk showing the heart suit would be difficult . The partnership might get too high. On the other hand, if West doesn't like spades, there may be a good fit in hearts. The Michaels cuebid (2♣) shows both suits right away. West will know East has at least five cards in each major suit and can choose one. Even if West has only three cards in one of the major suits, there will be an eight-card fit, and East–West should be able to make a partscore at the two level.

♠ Q J 9 6 5
♥ K 10 9 7 6 3
♦ 4
♣ 5

Cuebid 2♣. The Michaels cuebid doesn't promise much strength, only the required distribution. Without this convention, it would be difficult to enter the auction with either hearts or spades. Showing both suits at once is relatively safe, since West is likely to have a fit with one of the suits. Bidding will also take bidding room away from the opponents.

♠ K J 8 7 5
♥ K Q 9 3
♦ 8
♣ 7 4 2

Overcall 1♠. A Michaels cuebid shows at least five cards in each major. Some partnerships would use the convention on this type of hand, but it's not standard practice.

♠ A K J 8 7
♥ A K Q 9 8 4
♦ —
♣ 4 3

Cuebid 2♣. A Michaels cuebid can be used with a very strong hand. After determining which major suit West prefers, East would take this hand to at least game, perhaps cuebidding again along the way to get more information from West.

♠ K Q 10 8 4
♥ 5
♦ K J 10 8 3
♣ 9 6

Overcall 1♠. A cuebid of a minor suit shows both major suits, not a major and a minor.

WEST	NORTH	**EAST**	SOUTH
	1♥	?	

♠ K J 10 8 5
♥ 3
♦ K J 10 8 3 2
♣ 9

Cuebid 2♥. Deciding which suit to overcall is a tough choice without a conventional bid available. Should East bid the longer suit, diamonds, at the two level? Or, should East mention spades first, staying at the one level, but perhaps ending in the wrong trump suit? Playing the Michaels cuebid, a 2♥ cuebid shows at least five spades — the other major — and five cards in a minor suit.

With three or more spades, West can choose that suit. Without support for spades, West can bid 2NT, asking for the minor suit. East would rebid 3 ♦ and hope that will be the best partscore.

♠ K Q 8 6 3	Overcall 1 ♠. The Michaels cuebid is usually used
♥ 3	with either a weak hand or a very strong hand. With
♦ K 4	something in between, falling back on standard
♣ A Q 8 6 5	methods is usually best. Some players would use
	the Michaels cuebid with this hand, but it's not rec-
	ommended without having discussed with partner
	how the auction will continue after the cuebid.

♠ Q 9 7 6 3	Pass. This hand has the right shape to use the
♥ Q 6	Michaels cuebid, but neither of the suits is worth
♦ J 9 7 4 2	showing, let alone both. Bidding is more likely to
♣ K	help the opponents.

Advancing After a Michaels Cuebid

When partner makes a Michaels cuebid over a minor suit, visualize partner's hand as having two decent five-card major suits with the strength to compete but less than the values for an opening bid. If the next opponent passes, bid something — to avoid playing in the opponent's trump suit!

WEST	NORTH	EAST	SOUTH
	1 ♣	2 ♣	Pass
?			

Only three-card support for one of East's suits is needed to have an eight-card fit. The usual approach is the following:

- A preference to 2 ♥ or 2 ♠ shows no interest in game.
- A jump to 3 ♥ or 3 ♠ is weak and preemptive.
- A jump to 4 ♥ or 4 ♠ is to play. It could be weak and preemptive or be bid with the intention of making the contract.
- A further cuebid of North's suit is forcing for one round and shows at least game-invitational values. With a minimum for the Michaels cuebid — 5 to 8 high-card points — East bids 3 ♥. Any other rebid shows a reasonable hand according to the vulnerability.

- 2NT is natural and invitational, and 3NT is to play. Both bids are infrequent, given the nature of East's hand.
- A bid of the unbid minor suit is to play.

Here are examples of responding to a Michaels cuebid after the auction shown. What does West call on the following hands?

WEST	NORTH	EAST	SOUTH
	1♣	2♣	Pass
?			

♠ 8 4
♥ Q 7 3
♦ K J 8 7 3
♣ J 9 4

Bid 2♥. East's cuebid shows five cards in each major suit. With two spades and three hearts, West prefers hearts to spades. Since East has at least five hearts, there is an eight-card fit. West should avoid 2♦, even though diamonds is West's best suit. East is unlikely to hold many diamonds.

♠ Q J 7 4
♥ 9 5
♦ J 8 7 5
♣ Q 6 5

Jump to 3♠. With a good fit with one of East's suits and a weak hand, the jump to the three level is a preemptive action. Hopefully it will keep the opponents out of their best contract. If they double for penalty, there is a nine-card fit.

♠ K Q 7 5
♥ Q 8
♦ A 8 7 4
♣ 10 7 2

Jump to 4♠. The Michaels cuebid doesn't promise an opening bid, but East should have two good five-card suits, something like: ♠A 10 9 6 3 ♥K J 7 5 4 ♦9 3 ♣8. With a good fit with both of East's suits and an outside ace, the hands fit together and a game contract should be reasonable.

♠ K 8 3
♥ J 9 7 6 3
♦ 10 8 4
♣ J 9

Jump to 4♥. West doesn't expect to take 10 tricks. The objective is to make the auction difficult for the opponents. They could easily misjudge whether West has a strong or a weak hand for this bid, and East–West might get away undoubled.

♠ J 3
♥ K 10 8 5
♦ A Q 7 3
♣ J 4 2

Cuebid 3♣. With interest in game, West starts with a further cuebid of North's suit. If East rebids 3♥ to show a minimum, West passes and stops in partscore. If East bids anything else, showing a good hand in the context of the Michaels cuebid, West can bid 4♥.

♠ Q 4
♥ J 5
♦ Q J 9 4 3
♣ A Q 10 3

Bid 2NT. This is an invitational bid, promising strength in the minor suits. The tendency is to avoid this bid, since finding enough tricks may be difficult if West can't establish any of the suits or get easily from one hand to the other.

♠ 8 4
♥ 5
♦ K Q 10 9 8 5
♣ A 7 5 2

Bid 2♦. This bid is non-forcing and sends the message that West would rather play in diamonds than pick hearts or spades.

♠ K 4
♥ 5
♦ J 8 7 4 3
♣ Q 8 6 5 2

Bid 2♠. This isn't the type of hand East was hoping West would hold. Nonetheless, West should do best by choosing one of East's suits. If East has only five spades, the partnership will be in a seven-card fit — that's the occasional price to pay when you use this convention. Besides, the auction isn't over yet. The opponents may bid and rescue East–West from a poor contract.

When partner uses the Michaels cuebid over a major suit, it shows at least five cards in the other major suit and an unidentified minor suit. The responses are similar to those after a minor-suit cuebid, with the exception that 2NT now asks for partner's minor suit.

Here are examples of responding to a Michaels cuebid after the auction shown. What does West call on the following hands?

WEST	NORTH	EAST	SOUTH
	1♠	2♠	Pass
?			

♠ Q 9 7 3
♥ 9 8 4
♦ 8 6 2
♣ K 7 5

Bid 3 ♥. East is showing hearts and a minor. West doesn't know which minor suit East holds, but doesn't care. West does know there is an eight-card fit in East's major suit. With no interest in game, West bids the suit at the cheapest available level.

Bidding a worthless three-card suit for the first time at the three level may appear unusual, but that's the way the convention works.

♠ Q 10 7 4 2
♥ 5
♦ K 7 5
♣ J 9 7 3

Bid 2NT. Without a fit for the known major suit, West bids 2NT to find out which minor suit East holds. West hopes it's clubs, but intends to pass whichever suit East bids.

♠ 8 7
♥ A Q 8
♦ A 9 7 4
♣ Q 10 6 3

Jump to 4 ♥. West has a fit with East's heart suit, and whether East's other suit is clubs or diamonds, West has a fit with that suit as well. It looks as though East–West have a good play for game. West jumps to game without giving the opponents any further information.

The Rest of the Auction

After a Michaels cuebid, the auction can take off in a number of ways. The opponents' subsequent bidding may take away some of the options. Here are some guidelines:

- The player making the Michaels cuebid can compete further holding extra length in one of the suits.

- A strong hand for the Michaels cuebid is usually shown by cuebidding again or by doubling if the opponents compete.

- A bid of 3NT by the advancer (responder to the Michaels cue-bidder) is always natural — to play.

- If 2NT is no longer available for the advancer to ask for partner's minor suit, the advancer can bid 4♣ or 4NT. Partner can pass 4♣ or correct to 4♦. 4NT forces partner to bid the minor at the five level.

Here are examples of the Michaels cuebid in action:

West	WEST	NORTH	EAST	SOUTH	East
♠ A 10 9 8 3			Pass	1 ♦	♠ K 6 4
♥ K J 10 8 5 3 2	2 ♦	Pass	2 ♠	3 ♦	♥ Q 6
♦ 8	3 ♥	4 ♦	4 ♥	Pass	♦ J 7 2
♣ —	Pass	Pass			♣ Q J 8 7 3

Initially, East doesn't have much interest in game opposite West's cuebid showing both majors and simply gives preference to spades. With a very distributional hand, however, West bids again, showing extra length in hearts. This bid convinces East, holding useful cards in both of West's suits, to bid game.

West	WEST	NORTH	EAST	SOUTH	East
♠ 10 6				1 ♠	♠ 8
♥ K J 8 7 3	2 ♠	4 ♠	4NT	Dbl	♥ A 4
♦ K Q 10 7 2	5 ♦	Dbl	Pass	Pass	♦ J 9 6 4 3
♣ 2	Pass				♣ J 9 8 6 3

West makes a Michaels cuebid, showing hearts and a minor suit. When North jumps to 4♠, East can no longer use 2NT to find out which minor suit West holds. Wanting to compete, East bids 4NT to ask for West's minor. This should not be misinterpreted by West as the Blackwood convention asking for aces, since the partnership has not yet agreed on a trump suit. West bids the minor suit. The contract is doubled by the opponents, but it will be defeated only one trick. That will be a successful sacrifice, since the opponents would have made their 4♠ contract.

West	WEST	NORTH	EAST	SOUTH	East
♠ K J 8 6 3		Pass	Pass	1 ♥	♠ Q 2
♥ 9 7	2 ♥	3 ♥	4 ♣	Pass	♥ 8 4 2
♦ 3	Pass	Pass			♦ A 10 7 5
♣ A J 10 7 3					♣ K 8 6 2

West's 2 ♥ cuebid shows spades and an unidentified minor suit. When North raises to 3 ♥, East wants to compete in a minor suit. East must be careful not to bid 3NT, since that would be to play and West would pass. Instead, East bids 4♣ to find out which minor West holds. With clubs,

West passes. With diamonds, West would have bid 4 ♦ . Sequences such as this show why both members of the partnership should discuss any conventions they want to use before sitting down to play.

West					East
♠ A K Q 7 6 3	WEST	NORTH	EAST	SOUTH	♠ 4
♥ A K J 9 7			Pass	1♣	♥ 10 8 2
♦ 5 2	2♣	3♣	Pass	Pass	♦ 10 8 7 6 4 3
♣ —	4♣	Pass	4♥	Pass	♣ 10 5 4
	Pass	Pass			

West uses the Michaels cuebid to show the major suits, even though West holds a very strong hand. After North's raise, East is pleased to pass, since West presumably has a weak hand with the major suits. West's subsequent cuebid of the opponents' suit changes all that. It shows a strong hand and forces East to choose one of the major suits. East shows preference for the heart suit and that's enough for West. East will be anxiously waiting to see what the dummy looks like, since East wasn't expecting to be declarer.

Other Uses of the Michaels Cuebid

Once the partnership is familiar with the basic form of the Michaels cuebid, its use can be extended to other situations.

Consider each of the following auctions:

WEST	NORTH	**EAST**	SOUTH
	1 ♦	Pass	Pass
2 ♦	Pass	?	

Most partnerships would treat West's 2 ♦ bid as a Michaels cuebid, showing both major suits. It won't be natural, since West could pass with a lot of diamonds. It could be used as a strong cuebid, but since West could start with a takeout double when holding a strong hand, a Michaels cuebid is a more practical application.

WEST	NORTH	EAST	SOUTH
	2 ♥	3 ♥	Pass
?			

When North opens with a weak two-bid, the partnership could use the immediate cuebid to show a very strong hand, but many partnerships prefer to use it to show a Michaels cuebid. If that's the partnership agreement, East is showing spades and a minor suit. Without a fit for spades, West bids 4♣ to play in East's minor suit, since 3NT would be to play. East would correct 4♣ to 4♦, if East's minor is diamonds.

WEST	NORTH	**EAST**	SOUTH
	1♣	Pass	1NT
2♣	Pass	?	

West's 2♣ bid can be used as a Michaels cuebid, showing both major suits. This type of sequence should be discussed beforehand, since some players might give it some other interpretation.

WEST	NORTH	EAST	SOUTH
	3♣	4♣	Pass
?			

Most partnerships would assume that East's bid shows both major suits, although some partnerships would use East's cuebid to show any two-suited hand. Again, the partnership should discuss whether or not the Michaels cuebid applies in this situation.

WEST	NORTH	**EAST**	SOUTH
Pass	1♥	Pass	2♥
3♥	Pass	?	

Since West passed originally, the 3♥ bid can be given little interpretation other than a Michaels cuebid, showing spades and a minor. Even if West weren't a passed hand, most players would assume this is a Michaels cuebid.

WEST	NORTH	**EAST**	SOUTH
	1♣	Pass	1♠
2♣	Pass	?	

West's 2♣ bid would be treated as natural by most players. Some would use 2♣ as a Michaels cuebid, but it definitely requires partnership agreement since it's not standard practice. West could make a takeout double to show hearts and diamonds, or perhaps use the unusual notrump.

THE UNUSUAL NOTRUMP

When an opponent opens the bidding, it's rare for the next hand to bid to hold a balanced hand of 20 or more points — the type of hand to open the bidding 2NT with. Even with such a strong hand, a player would start by making a takeout double and then jumping in notrump. This means that a jump to 2NT over an opponent's opening bid can be used to show something other than a very strong balanced hand. The most common use of a jump in notrump is to show a two-suited hand — two five-card or longer suits. Since its introduction in 1948 by Al Roth and Tobias Stone, a jump overcall of 2NT over a major suit has been conventionally used by the majority of players to show both minor suits. This is called the *unusual notrump* convention, and it asks partner to pick one of the minor suits.

For example, suppose North bids 1 ♥ and this is East's hand:

♠ 7
♥ 5
♦ A J 9 4 3
♣ A 10 8 7 6 5

It's difficult to know what to do. After a 2 ♣ overcall, South might jump to 4 ♥ and East–West could miss a potential fit in diamonds. If East overcalls in diamonds, the club suit could be overlooked.

If the partnership has agreed to play the unusual notrump convention, however, the problem is solved by jumping to 2NT, asking West to pick a minor suit. This is similar to the Michaels cuebid convention in that it shows both of the minor suits with one bid. Even if South immediately jumps to game, West has a good description of East's hand and will be in a position to judge what to do.

Forcing West to bid at the three level may seem risky, but the unusual notrump gives the choice of two suits. A safe landing spot will quite likely be found. Of course, if West has two little diamonds and a singleton club, it might get a little difficult. In the long run, provided there are lots of cards in the two suits, the bid is likely to succeed more often than not. 2NT describes East's hand and takes away a lot of bidding room from the opponents.

Most modern partnerships have extended the use of the unusual notrump to show the two lowest-ranking unbid suits, rather than specifically clubs and diamonds. If an opponent opens the bidding 1 ♥ or 1 ♠, a jump to 2NT would still show clubs and diamonds, the two lowest-ranking unbid suits. If the opening bid is 1♣, however, a jump to 2NT would show diamonds and hearts, the two lowest-ranking unbid suits; and if the opening bid is 1♦, a jump to 2NT would show clubs and hearts.

There is a down side to using the unusual notrump. As well as describing the hand to partner, it describes the hand to the opponents. This may help them during the play, either on defense or on offense (one of them would be declarer). So, like the Michaels cuebid, this convention is used only with a weak hand — less than an opening bid — when the partnership hopes to find a profitable sacrifice, or with a very strong hand, when ✗ the partnership hopes to buy the contract. With hands in between, bid naturally, overcalling the higher-ranking suit first and planning to show the other suit on the rebid.

What does East call with the following example hands after the auction shown?

WEST	NORTH	**EAST**	SOUTH
	1♠	?	

♠ 9
♥ 3
♦ Q J 9 8 7 3
♣ K J 10 8 4

Jump to 2NT. This shows a weak hand with both minor suits. East is suggesting that the partnership may be able to compete to prevent the opponents from buying the contract. Even if East–West can't win the contract, taking bidding room away from the opponents may push them to the wrong contract. Watch the vulnerability. Vulnerable and the opponents are not means East–West probably shouldn't get involved in the auction. The opponents may be able to collect more by doubling than the value of any contract they can make. At equal or favorable vulnerability, however, most players would take the risk.

♠ K 2
♥ —
♦ A K J 8 7
♣ A Q J 8 6 3

Jump to 2NT. The unusual notrump may be used with a very strong hand and both minor suits. East intends to compete further after West picks a minor suit. Given the opportunity, East can cuebid the opponent's suit on the next round of bidding to show the extra strength.

♠ Q 6
♥ 7 3
♦ A K J 10 7
♣ A J 9 3

Overcall 2 ♦. The unusual notrump tends to show at least five cards in each suit. Some players might use the convention with less distribution, but it's not common practice. Also, this hand is neither very weak nor very strong. It's best to bid naturally with this type of hand.

What does East call with the following example hands after the auction shown?

WEST	NORTH	EAST	SOUTH
	1 ♦	?	

♠ 7 5
♥ K J 10 8 6
♦ —
♣ A J 10 8 6 3

Jump to 2NT. This shows the two lowest-ranking unbid suits, hearts and clubs. It's the best way to compete before the opponents start bidding spades.

♠ Q 3
♥ J 10 7 6 4
♦ 7
♣ K J 8 6 3

Pass. Don't use the unusual notrump just because the shape is right. Some bidding judgment is required. A few players might bid 2NT if their side is non-vulnerable and the opponents are vulnerable, but it's not recommended. If the opponents declare the contract, the information about East's distribution may help declarer more than East–West.

♠ 8
♥ 4
♦ A J 9 8 6 4
♣ Q J 10 6 3

Pass. If the opening bid were 1 ♥ or 1 ♠, East would use the unusual notrump. Over 1 ♦, a bid of 2NT would show hearts and clubs, not diamonds and clubs. Some partnerships prefer to use the unusual notrump to always show the minor suits — which would be useful here — but that's not standard practice.

♠ A J 10 8 6
♥ Q J 8 7 4
♦ 8 2
♣ 9

Cuebid 2 ♦. This is the hand for a Michaels cuebid, not the unusual notrump. The two conventions work well together. Over 1 ♦, for example, a Michaels cuebid shows both majors and the unusual notrump shows hearts and clubs. With spades and clubs, East would have to bid naturally, or East–West would need to learn some even fancier two-suited convention.

Advancing After the Unusual Notrump

The responses after an unusual notrump follow a similar pattern to those following a Michaels cuebid:

- A simple preference to one of partner's suits shows no interest in game.

- A jump in one of the suits is weak and preemptive, if the bid is below the game level.

- A jump to the game level could be weak and preemptive or could be bid with the intention of making the contract.

- A cuebid of the opponent's suit is forcing for one round and shows at least game-invitational values. With a minimum for the unusual notrump — 5 to 8 high-card points — partner makes the cheapest available bid in one of the suits. Any other rebid shows a reasonable hand according to the vulnerability.

- 3NT is to play.

- A bid of the other suit — the suit not bid by the opponents or shown by partner — is to play.

What does West respond with the following example hands after the auction shown?

WEST	NORTH	EAST	SOUTH
	1♥	2NT	Pass
?			

♠ K Q 9 7 6
♥ J 8 6 4
♦ 10 2
♣ Q 3

Bid 3♣. This isn't the hand East was hoping for, but East has asked West to pick a minor suit and West should comply. West should not consider passing and playing in notrump; finding a source of tricks will be difficult.

♠ A 10 8 3
♥ J 8 5
♦ Q 9 7 4
♣ 7 3

Jump to 4♦. With a good fit with one of East's suits and not much defensive strength, West makes a preemptive jump to the four level. It's non-forcing, but East could bid again with a very distributional hand.

♠ J 8 4 2
♥ 4
♦ K 8 4
♣ Q 8 7 6 3

Jump to 5♣. There is a good fit with both of East's suits, but no strength elsewhere. Jumping to the five level makes the auction difficult for North–South who can probably make a game or a slam. If doubled, the penalty is unlikely to be more than the value of North–South's contract.

♠ A 8 4
♥ 8 7 4
♦ Q 10 4 2
♣ A 9 3

Cuebid 3♥. With high cards in East's suits, there is enough strength to invite East to the game level. If East bids 4♣, the cheapest available bid in the suits West has shown, West signs off in 4♦. East is showing a minimum hand such as: ♠9 ♥5 3 ♦K 9 7 5 3 ♣ K Q 10 5 2. If East bids anything else, West bids game. East should have something better than a minimum, such as: ♠10 2 ♥5 ♦A J 9 7 5 ♣K Q J 5 2.

♠ A K Q J 8 7 3
♥ 9 4
♦ K 4
♣ 6 5

Jump to 4♠. This is to play. West would rather play in spades than in one of East's suits. Game is possible with a little help from East in the minor suits.

The Rest of the Auction

After using the unusual notrump, the auction can proceed in many different ways, especially since the opponents will usually compete.

Here are sample auctions:

West						East
♠ 8 3		WEST	NORTH	EAST	SOUTH	♠ 10
♥ 5				Pass	1♠	♥ A 9 7 6
♦ K J 7 5 4		2NT	4♠	5♦	5♠	♦ Q 9 8 6 3
♣ A 10 9 6 3		Pass	Pass	Pass		♣ J 7 5

After West shows the minor suits, East competes to the five level after North jumps to game. Unwilling to defend 5 ♦, South pushes on to 5 ♠. This contract is likely to be defeated, if West gets a heart ruff and neither North nor South is void in clubs. East–West's bidding has pushed the opponents higher than they'd like to be. Even if North–South had judged perfectly to double 5 ♦, that contract would be defeated only one or two tricks — less than the value of North–South's spade game.

West	WEST	NORTH	EAST	SOUTH	East
♠ A			Pass	1 ♦	♠ 9 5 3
♥ A K J 8 7	2NT	3 ♠	Pass	4 ♠	♥ 10 6 4 2
♦ 2	Dbl	Pass	5 ♥	Pass	♦ 10 8 6
♣ K Q 10 8 7 3	Pass	Pass			♣ 9 4 2

With a strong hand, West makes an unusual notrump bid to show hearts and clubs. East is under the assumption that West has a weak hand and passes after North bids 3 ♠. When South raises to game, West doubles to show a very strong hand for the unusual notrump. With seven cards in West's suits and no defense elsewhere, East judges well to bid at the five level. If East can't make 5 ♥, the opponents were probably going to make 4 ♠.

West	WEST	NORTH	EAST	SOUTH	East
♠ 5				1 ♥	♠ K 8 7 4 3
♥ 8 6	2NT	Dbl	3 ♣	Dbl	♥ Q 9 7 3
♦ K Q 9 7 3	Pass	Pass	Pass		♦ J 5
♣ K 10 9 4 2					♣ Q 3

Even the best of conventions can lead to an occasional bad result. East will probably look quickly to see whether or not the partnership is vulnerable!

Other Uses of the Unusual Notrump

The most common use of the unusual notrump is a jump to 2NT, after an opponent's opening bid in one of a suit. Most partnerships, however, use the convention in a number of other situations.

Consider each of the following auctions:

West					East
♠ K J 7 2					♠ 3
♥ 6 3					♥ K Q 10 9 5
♦ 10 5 4					♦ Q J 8 7 6 3
♣ A Q 8 3					♣ 5

WEST	NORTH	EAST	SOUTH
			1♣
Pass	1♠	2NT	Pass
3♦	Pass	Pass	Pass

East's jump to 2NT is considered the unusual notrump by most players. With a very strong balanced hand, East could start with a double.

West					East
♠ —					♠ Q J 8 7 3
♥ 7 3					♥ A 9 6 5
♦ A Q 8 7 3					♦ 10 4
♣ K 10 9 7 6 2					♣ J 5

WEST	NORTH	EAST	SOUTH
	Pass	Pass	1NT
2NT	Pass	3♣	Pass
Pass	Pass		

Most partnerships treat West's 2NT as a takeout for the minor suits.

West					East
♠ 7 2					♠ K 10 8 6
♥ A 3					♥ 10 8 5
♦ K J 10 4					♦ A 8 6 3
♣ Q 10 8 3 2					♣ K 5

WEST	NORTH	EAST	SOUTH
			1♥
Pass	2♥	Pass	Pass
2NT	Pass	3♦	Pass
Pass	Pass		

West's 2NT in the balancing position is certainly unusual. The common agreement is that this shows the minor suits. With support for all of the unbid suits, West could make a takeout double. With a strong hand, West could have acted immediately.

West					East
♠ 10 5					♠ Q 9 6 3
♥ Q J 8 7 3					♥ A 5 2
♦ 4					♦ K 9 3
♣ A J 9 7 4					♣ Q 6 2

WEST	NORTH	EAST	SOUTH
Pass	1♦	Pass	1♠
1NT	2♦	2♥	3♦
Pass	Pass	Pass	

Since West passed originally, the 1NT bid can't be showing a strong hand. Most players would assume that this is unusual, showing a weak hand with clubs and hearts. With a stronger hand, West could make a takeout double to show the two suits or jump to 2NT with a very distributional hand.

West	WEST	NORTH	EAST	SOUTH	East
♠ 5				4♥	♠ Q J 8 4 2
♥ 4	4NT	Pass	5♦	Pass	♥ J 9
♦ A Q J 8 6	Pass	Pass			♦ K 10 7 3
♣ A K J 7 5 3					♣ 9 2

Most partnerships agree to use West's bid to show both minor suits. A double of 4 ♥ is used as a takeout double with support for all three unbid suits. This agreement isn't universal, however, so it should be discussed beforehand.

Some potential uses of the unusual notrump definitely require considerable discussion by the partnership beforehand.

Consider the following auctions:

West	WEST	NORTH	EAST	SOUTH	East
♠ 10 5		1♦	Pass	1♠	♠ 9 7
♥ Q J 8 7 3	1NT	2♠	5♣	Pass	♥ A 5
♦ 4	Pass	Pass			♦ A J 8 7 3
♣ A J 9 7 4					♣ K Q 8 3

Since West isn't a passed hand, West could have a balanced hand of 15 to 18 points and be making a natural overcall of 1NT. Without prior discussion, that's what East should assume. With clubs and hearts, West could either make a takeout double with a good hand or could jump to 2NT, the unusual notrump, with a weak distributional hand.

When both opponents have bid, entering the auction with 1NT with a balanced hand of 15 to 18 points is dangerous. East isn't likely to hold much, and the opponents know a lot about each other's hands. If West gets doubled for penalty and is defeated, it's unlikely that the opponents can make a game because of West's 15 to 18 points. West is caught in between the two opponents.

Because of the danger of overcalling with a natural 1NT in this position, many partnerships prefer to treat West's 1NT overcall (in the previous auction) as unusual, showing a weak distributional takeout for clubs and hearts. This doesn't commit the partnership to the three level, only the two level, so there's less danger of an opponent doubling for penalty. With clubs and hearts and a stronger, less-distributional hand, West can make a normal takeout double. With an extremely distributional hand, West can still jump to 2NT as the unusual notrump.

Each partnership needs to discuss its methods in this type of auction. It is equally important to discuss the meaning of a 2 ♦ or 2 ♠ bid by West in this sequence. Since there are many ways to compete in the other two suits, most partnerships treat a bid of either of the opponents' suits as natural when the opponents have bid two suits. North may have opened 1 ♦ on a three-card suit, and South may have responded 1 ♠ on a weak four-card suit. It's quite possible for West to have a good hand and a good diamond or a good spade suit.

West	WEST	NORTH	EAST	SOUTH	East
♠ 2				4 ♠	♠ J 4
♥ A K J 6 3	4NT	Pass	5 ♣	Pass	♥ Q 9 8 5
♦ A K 10 9 4 2	5 ♦	Pass	5 ♥	Pass	♦ 6
♣ 8	Pass	Pass			♣ Q J 10 7 5 2

When South's opening bid is 4 ♠, West can no longer overcall in a suit at the four level. East would have to bid at the five level to take out a double by West, in whatever suit East holds. If South had opened 4 ♥, West would have room to bid 4 ♠ with a good hand and long spades, or West could double with a strong hand and support for the unbid suits. Over 4 ♥, there would still be room left after a double for East to bid 4 ♠, if East doesn't want to defend for penalty.

Most partnerships play that a double of 4 ♠ by West is for penalty and a bid of 4NT by West is for takeout. Because there isn't much bidding room left over 4 ♠, West may bid 4NT with support for all of the unbid suits or only two of the unbid suits. When East bids a suit at the five level, West will pass with support and correct to one of the other two suits without support.

In the above auction, East responds 5 ♣, since West might have both minor suits. When West corrects to 5 ♦, East recognizes that West must hold diamonds and hearts. West would have overcalled 5 ♦ with only one suit. East corrects to hearts in the partnership's best trump fit.

West		East
♠ 5		♠ J 9 8 7 4
♥ 8		♥ 5 4 2
♦ A Q J 5 3		♦ K 10 7 6
♣ A K 10 9 7 5		♣ 3

WEST	NORTH	EAST	SOUTH
1♣	1♥	Pass	4♥
4NT	Pass	5♦	Pass
Pass	Pass		

West opens the bidding in the longer suit, 1♣, but the auction is up to the four level by the time West gets to make a rebid. Unwilling to defend 4♥, West makes an unusual bid of 4NT. This isn't the Blackwood convention asking for aces, since East has never bid and no suit has been agreed upon. With a strong hand and support for both of the unbid suits, West could double the 4♥ bid. So, East correctly interprets the 4NT bid as unusual, showing both minor suits, and picks diamonds as the trump suit. West couldn't afford to bid 5♦ over 4♥, since East might prefer clubs to diamonds and the partnership would be forced to the six level.

The last few auctions would only occur in an experienced partnership, where there had been considerable discussion beforehand. Both partners need to be clear on when a notrump bid is natural, when it's unusual and when it carries some other meaning — such as asking for aces. Otherwise, the unusual notrump may lead to an unusual contract!

SUMMARY

A direct cuebid of an opponent's suit can be used as a Michaels cuebid, showing a two-suited hand. By agreement, it also can be used in other situations.

Michaels Cuebid

- If the opening bid is 1♣ or 1♦, a direct cuebid of the opponent's suit shows at least five cards in each major suit.

- If the opening bid is 1♥ or 1♠, a direct cuebid of the opponent's suit shows at least five cards in the other major and five cards in an unspecified minor suit. Advancer (responder) can bid 2NT to ask for partner's minor.

The Michaels cuebid usually shows a weak, distributional hand, although it can be used with a strong hand.

Advancing After a Michaels Cuebid

- A simple preference to one of partner's suits shows no interest in game.

- A jump in one of partner's suits below the game level is weak and preemptive.

- A jump to game in one of partner's suits is to play. It could be weak and preemptive or be bid with the intention of making the contract.

- After a major-suit cuebid, 2NT asks for partner's minor suit. If 2NT isn't available, 4♣ or 4NT can be used to find out which minor partner holds.

- After a minor-suit cuebid, 2NT is invitational and a bid of the other minor is to play.

- A further cuebid of the opponent's suit is forcing for one round and shows at least game-invitational values. With a minimum for the Michaels cuebid — 5 to 8 high-card points — partner makes the cheapest available bid in one of the suits. Any other rebid shows a reasonable hand under the circumstances.

- 3NT is to play.

When an opponent opens, a direct overcall of 1NT shows a balanced hand of 15 to 18 points with some strength in the opponent's suit. Without partnership agreement, the only conventional bid used in response to a 1NT overcall is Stayman. The situation changes when the opponent's opening bid is followed by two passes. A balancing 1NT overcall shows 10 to 15 points. With a stronger hand, start with a takeout double.

A jump overcall to 2NT is commonly used to show a two-suited hand containing the two lowest-ranking, unbid suits. This is referred to as the unusual notrump.

The Unusual Notrump

- The player making the Michaels cuebid can compete further holding extra length in one of the suits.

- A jump overcall to 2NT shows a two-suited hand with at least five cards in each of the two lowest-ranking, unbid suits.

- The unusual 2NT usually promises a weak hand, although it can be used with a strong hand.

Like the Michaels cuebid, the partnership can agree to use the unusual notrump in situations other than a direct jump to 2NT over an opponent's opening bid.

Responses to the unusual notrump are as follows:

Advancing After the Unusual Notrump

- A simple preference to one of partner's suits shows no interest in game.

- A jump in one of the suits is weak and preemptive, if the bid is below the game level. A jump to the game level could be weak and preemptive or be bid with the intention of making the contract.

- A cuebid of the opponent's suit is forcing for one round and shows at least game-invitational values. With a minimum for the unusual notrump — 5 to 8 high-card points — partner makes the cheapest available bid in one of the suits. Any other rebid shows a reasonable hand under the circumstances.

- 3NT is to play.

- A bid of the other suit — the suit not bid by the opponents or shown by partner — is to play.

When an opponent makes a simple overcall over partner's opening bid, a cuebid of the opponent's suit shows a fit with opener's suit and at least the strength for a limit raise. Most partnerships use a jump raise of opener's suit in this situation as weak and preemptive, rather than invitational.

NOTE: See the Appendix (pages 353–355) for a discussion of these supplemental conventions and/or treatments.

Defense to Strong Club (Mathe)

Leaping Michaels

Unusual Over Unusual

Note: The following exercises illustrate the methods outlined in the summary.

Exercise One — Michaels Cuebid over a Minor

What call would East make with each of the following hands after North opens 1 ♦ ?

WEST	NORTH	**EAST**	SOUTH
	1 ♦	?	

1) ♠ Q J 9 6 5
   ♥ K J 10 8 3
   ♦ 8
   ♣ 7 2

2) ♠ A Q J 7 6
   ♥ A Q 10 8 6 3
   ♦ 4
   ♣ A

3) ♠ A Q 8 7 3
   ♥ A K J 3
   ♦ 7 3
   ♣ 6 4

Exercise Two — Michaels Cuebid over a Major

What call would East make with each of the following hands after North opens 1 ♥ ?

WEST	NORTH	**EAST**	SOUTH
	1 ♥	?	

1) ♠ K J 10 7 4
   ♥ 8 3
   ♦ 7
   ♣ K Q 10 7 5

2) ♠ Q 10 7 5 4 3
   ♥ —
   ♦ K 10 9 8 4 2
   ♣ 4

3) ♠ K Q 10 8 4
   ♥ K 4
   ♦ A Q 8 7 3
   ♣ 5

Exercise One *Answer* — Michaels Cuebid over a Minor

1) 2♦ (Michaels cuebid). The immediate cuebid of the opponent's minor suit shows both major suits and, typically, a weak hand. Competing to the two level doesn't carry too much risk if non-vulnerable, since West is likely to have a fit with at least one of the major suits. It would be riskier when vulnerable, but many players would still take a chance on competing.

2) 2♦ (Michaels cuebid). Although the cuebid usually shows a weak hand with both major suits, it can be used with a very strong hand. East plans to bid again after hearing which major suit West prefers.

3) 1♠. The distribution is not right for a Michaels cuebid, which promises at least five cards in each major. This hand is also too strong for a Michaels cuebid. Instead, overcall in the longer suit. East may get to show the hearts later in the auction.

Exercise Two *Answer* — Michaels Cuebid over a Major

1) 2♥ (Michaels cuebid). The cuebid shows spades and a minor suit. If West doesn't like spades, West can respond 2NT to find out which minor suit East has. East would then bid 3♣.

2) 2♥ (Michaels cuebid). East doesn't need much strength to get into the auction with a two-suited hand with such good distribution. With 6–6, East should be willing to compete in whichever suit West prefers.

3) 1♠. This is the right distribution for a Michaels cuebid, but the hand is too strong. West would expect a much weaker hand (see previous examples), and a game could be missed. East overcalls, intending to show the second suit, if given an opportunity later in the auction.

Exercise Three — Advancing After a Michaels Cuebid

What would West respond with each of the following hands after East uses a Michaels Cuebid?

WEST	NORTH	EAST	SOUTH
	1 ♥	2 ♥	Pass
?			

1) ♠ 10 7 2
   ♥ Q 8 7 6
   ♦ Q 8 3
   ♣ K 7 2

2) ♠ K 10 7 5
   ♥ 6
   ♦ J 9 6 2
   ♣ Q 6 5 4

3) ♠ 8
   ♥ 10 8 7 6 3
   ♦ K 4 2
   ♣ J 9 6 5

4) ♠ K Q 8 4
   ♥ A 8 3
   ♦ K 7 4
   ♣ K 8 2

5) ♠ K 10 5 4 2
   ♥ 6 5 3
   ♦ Q 7 6 5
   ♣ 10

6) ♠ 10 7
   ♥ 6
   ♦ A J 9 8 3
   ♣ A K 10 6 2

Exercise Three *Answer* — Advancing After a Michaels Cuebid

1) 2♠. East is showing at least five spades and five cards in a minor suit. West puts the partnership in its eight-card fit at the cheapest available level.

2) 3♠ (or 4♠). There is at least a nine-card fit in spades and also a nine-card fit in whichever minor suit East holds. 3♠ may not make, but if that's the case, the opponents can probably make, at least a game in hearts. West should not leave room for them to find their best spot. If West is aggressive, West might jump to 4♠.

3) 2NT. West doesn't like spades; 2NT asks which minor suit East holds. West intends to pass whether East bids 3♣ or 3♦.

4) 3♥. With an excellent fit in spades and a strong hand, West expects to make at least 4♠. Slam is still a possibility, since West also has a useful king in whichever minor suit East holds. Cuebidding the opponent's suit shows at least game-invitational values. If East makes a minimum bid, 3♠ for example, West bids game. By bidding game in this manner, West shows interest in slam. If East shows a good hand by jumping to 4♠, West can investigate bidding slam. East–West might make a slam, if East has as little as:

    ♠A 10 9 7 2   ♥7 2   ♦A Q 10 6 3   ♣6.

5) 4♠. The partnership has at least a ten-card fit in spades. If East's other suit is diamonds, there is a good fit in two suits. If East's other suit is clubs, there isn't more than one loser in that suit, and East won't have many hearts and diamonds. If 4♠ doesn't make, the opponents will have at least a game — and maybe a slam — in hearts.

6) 4NT. Whichever minor suit East holds, there is a tremendous fit. West asks East to show the minor suit at the game level.

Exercise Four — More about the Michaels Cuebid

What call does West make with each of the following hands after an opponent has interfered?

1) ♠ Q 8 6
♥ J 3
♦ Q 9 6 3
♣ K 10 7 4

WEST	NORTH	EAST	SOUTH
	1♣	2♣	3♣
?			

2) ♠ 7 3
♥ 4
♦ A J 7 4 2
♣ A Q 8 6 3

WEST	NORTH	EAST	SOUTH
	1♥	2♥	4♥
?			

3) ♠ 2
♥ Q J 8 6 4
♦ 9 3
♣ A Q 10 7 5

WEST	NORTH	EAST	SOUTH
			1♠
2♠	3♠	3NT	Pass
?			

4) ♠ Q 2
♥ 10 8 6 3
♦ 7 5 2
♣ 9 7 5 3

WEST	NORTH	EAST	SOUTH
	1♦	2♦	3♦
Pass	4♦	Double	Pass
?			

5) ♠ K J 10 8 6 3
♥ 6
♦ A Q 8 7 5 2
♣ —

WEST	NORTH	EAST	SOUTH
			2♥
?			

Exercise Four *Answer* — More about the Michaels Cuebid

1) Pass. The opponent's 3♣ bid has let West off the hook. It's no longer necessary for West to give preference to one of East's major suits.

2) 4NT. East is showing spades and a minor suit. West asks East to bid the minor suit at the five level. Even if East–West can't make 5♣ or 5♦, the opponents can probably make 4♥.

3) Pass. East's 3NT is to play. East would have bid 4♣, if interested in playing in a minor suit.

4) 4♥. East's initial Michaels cuebid showed a weak hand with both major suits. The subsequent cuebid, however, shows a strong hand. East wants to play in a major suit at the game level. West shows preference for hearts. Even though West has only 2 points, there is a good chance to make a game.

5) 3♥. This is an extended form of the Michaels cuebid, showing spades and a minor suit — if that is the partnership's agreement. When not certain of the agreement, it's safer to overcall 2♠ and hope to show the diamonds later.

Exercise Five — The Unusual Notrump

What call would East make with each of the following hands after North opens 1♥?

WEST	NORTH	**EAST**	SOUTH
	1♥	?	

1) ♠ 7
   ♥ 5
   ♦ K J 8 7 6 5
   ♣ A J 10 8 5

2) ♠ 8 4
   ♥ 7 3
   ♦ A K J 8 7
   ♣ A K 10 2

3) ♠ A J 9 8 7
   ♥ 8 6
   ♦ 3
   ♣ K Q 10 8 5

Exercise Six — Advancing After the Unusual Notrump

What call would West make with each of the following hands after North opens 1♥, and East overcalls 2NT?

WEST	NORTH	EAST	SOUTH
	1♦	2NT	Pass
?			

1) ♠ K 9 7 5 3
   ♥ Q 10 8
   ♦ K 5 2
   ♣ J 4

2) ♠ K Q 7 4
   ♥ 5
   ♦ Q 8 6 5
   ♣ J 9 6 3

3) ♠ J 8 3
   ♥ A 8 7 5 3
   ♦ 9 4
   ♣ K 10 2

4) ♠ A J 8 3
   ♥ K 8 3
   ♦ 10 7 4
   ♣ Q J 2

5) ♠ 6
   ♥ Q 2
   ♦ 10 9 7 6
   ♣ K 9 8 7 4 2

6) ♠ A K J 10 8 7 3 2
   ♥ 4
   ♦ 8 3
   ♣ A 2

Exercise Five *Answer* — The Unusual Notrump

1) 2NT (unusual 2NT). This shows the two lower-ranking unbid suits, clubs and diamonds. If West has a fit for one of the suits, East–West should be safe at the three level.

2) 2♦. The unusual 2NT shows at least five cards in both lower-ranking unbid suits. Also, it tends to show a weak hand. Bidding 2NT with this hand would send the wrong description to West. East settles for an overcall in the good five-card diamond suit.

3) 2♥ (Michaels cuebid) or 1♠. 2NT would show the two lower-ranking unbid suits, clubs and diamonds. The Michaels cuebid is available to show spades and a minor suit by bidding 2♥. Another option is a simple overcall of 1♠.

Exercise Six *Answer* — Advancing After the Unusual Notrump

1) 3♥. East's unusual 2NT shows the two lower-ranking unbid suits, clubs and hearts. Since West prefers hearts to clubs, the suit is bid at the cheapest available level.

2) 3♣. East is showing hearts and clubs. West has a distinct preference for clubs.

3) 4♥. East is showing hearts and clubs, so West has an excellent fit for both suits. If East holds as little as ♠7 ♥Q 10 9 6 4 2 ♦10 ♣A J 9 6 4, there could be game. In the meantime, the opponents will do well in spades or diamonds, if there is any room to explore.

4) 4♥. West has only three hearts, but East has at least five. There also are some fitting cards in clubs and the useful ♠A. Game is likely, if East holds something like ♠4 ♥A Q 10 5 2 ♦9 3 ♣K 10 7 6 4.

5) 5♣. West has a tremendous fit in clubs and some help in hearts. Although West doesn't have much in high cards, West also doesn't have much defense against a spade or diamond contract by the opponents. 5♣ may be a good sacrifice.

6) 4♠. West isn't interested in either of East's suits, but doesn't need much from East to make game, even if East is void in spades. West's jump to game in spades says, "This is where I'd like to play."

Exercise Seven — More About the Unusual Notrump

What call would West make with each of the following hands after the auction goes as indicated?

1) ♠ J 8 7 4
    ♥ 3
    ♦ A Q 8 7 3
    ♣ K 5 2

WEST	NORTH	EAST	SOUTH
	1♥	2NT	4♥
?			

2) ♠ Q 9 8 6 3
    ♥ K 8 4
    ♦ Q 2
    ♣ Q 10 5

WEST	NORTH	EAST	SOUTH
	1♥	Pass	2♥
Pass	Pass	2NT	Pass
?			

3) ♠ K J 7 2
    ♥ J 8 5 3
    ♦ 7 2
    ♣ Q 6 3

WEST	NORTH	EAST	SOUTH
		Pass	1♣
Pass	1♠	1NT	Double
?			

4) ♠ J 8 4
    ♥ Q 10 8 6 4
    ♦ J 10 2
    ♣ Q 8

WEST	NORTH	EAST	SOUTH
	1NT	2NT	Pass
?			

5) ♠ Q J 8 7 6 3
    ♥ J 8 4
    ♦ Q 9 4
    ♣ 10

WEST	NORTH	EAST	SOUTH
	4♥	4NT	Pass
?			

Exercise Seven Answer — More About the Unusual Notrump

1) 5♦. East's jump to 2NT shows diamonds and clubs. With an excellent fit for diamonds and some help in clubs, West bids game. Even if 5♦ doesn't make, the opponents quite likely can make their game.

2) 3♣. East passed over 1♥, so the 2NT bid is certainly unusual! East is unwilling to pass the hand out in 2♥ and is making a competitive call with diamonds and clubs. With support for all three unbid suits, East would have doubled. With a preference for clubs, West bids 3♣.

3) 2♥. East passed originally, so the 1NT bid can't be natural. It is a light takeout for the unbid suits, hearts and diamonds, and tends to show at least five cards in each suit. West has a preference for hearts.

4) 3♦. With a strong hand, East would have doubled the opponent's 1NT opening, so the 2NT bid is unusual. West assumes it is for the lower two unbid suits, diamonds and clubs, and shows the slight preference for diamonds.

5) 5♦. The standard agreement is that East's 4NT bid is unusual, showing the two lower-ranking unbid suits — diamonds and clubs in this case. West shows a preference for diamonds.

Bid and Play — Michael's Cuebid Over a Minor

(E–Z Deal Cards: #4, Deal 1 — Dealer, North)

Suggested Bidding

WEST	NORTH	EAST	SOUTH
	1 ♦	2 ♦	Pass
2 ♥	Pass	Pass	Pass

With a balanced hand and only 13 HCP, North opens in the longest suit. East could make a simple overcall of 1 ♠, the higher-ranking of the two five-card suits. Playing the Michaels cuebid convention, however, East can show both major suits by cuebidding 2 ♦.

```
Dealer: North    ♠ K 8 3
Vul: None        ♥ 9 8
                 ♦ A Q 10 8 6
                 ♣ A 9 8
   ♠ 6                      ♠ A J 9 4 2
   ♥ A 7 2         N        ♥ K J 6 5 4
   ♦ K 9 4 3 2   W   E      ♦ 7
   ♣ K Q 7 5       S        ♣ 10 4
                 ♠ Q 10 7 5
                 ♥ Q 10 3
                 ♦ J 5
                 ♣ J 6 3 2
```

South doesn't have enough strength to take any action at the two level. West has a hand of opening-bid strength, but doesn't have a good fit with East's announced suits. With three-card heart support for East's "known" five-card suit, West can put the partnership in its eight-card fit by bidding 2 ♥. Since the Michaels cuebid typically shows less than the strength for an opening bid, West has no reason to go any higher than partscore. With some strength in the minor suits, West might consider bidding 2NT, but distributional hands should usually be played in the partnership's best trump fit. Developing tricks and getting back and forth between the two hands may be difficult in a notrump contract.

West's 2 ♥ bid should end the auction. North has nothing extra. The cuebid described East's hand, and South is content to defend with some length and strength in the majors and no fit in North's suit.

Suggested Opening Lead

North doesn't have an obvious lead. South hasn't shown any strength, and leading an ace may help declarer establish tricks. A spade lead may not succeed, since that suit was bid by East. A trump lead may be best.

It won't give much away, and it may prevent declarer from ruffing some of dummy's spade losers.

Suggested Play

Declaring a contract from the short side, the side with fewer trumps, requires a shift in perspective. From the West point of view, declarer has a lot of losers — one possible heart loser, five diamond losers and three club losers. It is usually easier to make a plan from the side with the most trumps, East in this case. Dummy has four spade losers, one heart loser, one diamond loser and one club loser. Declarer wants to ruff one or two spades with the trumps in the West hand and then lead spades to establish a trick through length, if the missing spades are divided 4–3.

For example, if North leads a trump, declarer might try playing the ♥J from dummy, although it is unlikely North led a heart holding the ♥Q. Whichever heart is played from dummy, declarer has to win the first trick with the ♥A. West can then lead a spade to dummy's ♠A and ruff a spade. With no quick entry back to dummy, West can lead the ♣K to establish the ♣Q as a winner. North will win the ♣A and probably lead another heart to prevent declarer from ruffing another spade loser. Declarer can win this with dummy's ♥K, in order to lead a third round of spades, and give the trick to the opponents.

The defenders won't be able to prevent declarer from eventually getting back to dummy to lead another spade and establish dummy's fifth spade as a winner. So, declarer will lose two spade tricks, one trump trick, one diamond trick and one club trick — taking exactly eight tricks.

Suggested Defense

The defenders do best to lead trumps at every opportunity to try to prevent declarer from ruffing spades in the West hand. If they don't lead trumps, declarer may take nine tricks by ruffing two spade losers in the West hand and then establishing the fifth spade. If declarer tries to ruff diamond losers in the dummy, the defenders may be able to hold declarer to six or seven tricks. Declarer should get at least one spade trick, four heart tricks and one club trick.

Partscore hands like this are complex, because both declarer and the defenders have a number of options at each trick.

If West plays in a notrump contract, the defenders should be able to take at least four diamond tricks, one heart trick and the ♣A — limiting declarer to at most seven tricks.

Bid and Play — Advancing After a Michael's Cuebid

(E–Z Deal Cards: #4, Deal 2 — Dealer, East)

Suggested Bidding

WEST	NORTH	EAST	SOUTH
		Pass	1♣
2♣	3NT	4♠	Pass
Pass	Dbl	Pass	Pass
Pass			

After South opens the bidding 1♣, West uses a Michaels cuebid to show both major suits. North isn't interested in defending at a low level and simply jumps to game in notrump. Now it's up to East. East should appreciate the value of the fit with West's spade suit and the lack of defensive prospects against North–South's contract. Since East–West aren't vulnerable and the opponents are, East

```
Dealer: East    ♠ Q 10 6
Vul: N–S        ♥ K 9 2
                ♦ K Q J 8
                ♣ A J 4
♠ K 9 7 4 3              ♠ A 8 5 2
♥ A 10 8 7 6 3    N      ♥ 4
♦ 3             W   E    ♦ 10 9 7 5 2
♣ 5                S     ♣ 9 8 3
                ♠ J
                ♥ Q J 5
                ♦ A 6 4
                ♣ K Q 10 7 6 2
```

might bid 4♠ as a sacrifice bid. East isn't planning to make the contract, but the penalty may be less than the value of North–South's game.

South doesn't want to double East's contract, but North has a good hand with good defensive prospects. North's penalty double ends the auction. If West had passed or overcalled 1♥, the auction would have gone very differently. East–West would be unlikely to uncover their spade fit, and North–South would be left to play in 3NT.

Suggested Opening Lead

South is on lead and will probably start with the ♣K, top of a sequence. South might also consider leading a trump, hoping to prevent East–West from getting too many tricks through ruffs.

Suggested Play

East has a lot of losers: one or more potential spade losers, if the suit doesn't divide 2–2, five diamond losers and three club losers. East should look at establishing West's hand as winners, rather than trying to eliminate all of those losers in the East hand. This is referred to as a dummy reversal.

From the point of view of the West hand, there is one loser in diamonds, one in clubs and a lot of heart losers. Declarer may be able to establish the heart suit by ruffing some of those losers.

Suppose South leads a club and continues with another club, forcing dummy to ruff. Declarer should immediately play the ♥ A and ruff a heart, starting to establish the suit. East can then play the ♠ A and a spade to dummy's ♠ K. The missing trumps divide 3–1, leaving declarer with a spade loser, but another heart can be led from dummy and ruffed with declarer's last trump. With the defenders' hearts dividing 3–3, dummy's remaining hearts are now established as winners. Declarer can ruff a club to dummy and start leading the heart winners. North can ruff a heart and take a diamond trick, but the rest of dummy's hand is all winners. Declarer makes the contract, losing one spade, one diamond and one club.

Declarer is very lucky to actually make this contract. If the defenders' hearts weren't divided exactly 3–3, declarer would have to lose a heart trick. On the other hand, the defenders' spades might have divided 2–2, leaving declarer with no losers in that suit. The deal illustrates the power of a trump fit. North–South are unlucky to be unable to defeat 4♠ even when they hold 29 high-card points. Favorable distribution will often overcome a lack of high cards.

East must be careful to use the entries wisely. Suppose South leads a trump initially. East must win this trick with the ♠ A, leaving the ♠ K in dummy. East must immediately lead hearts before drawing any more trumps. After ruffing a heart, declarer uses West's ♠ K as an entry to dummy to ruff another heart. If declarer draws trumps right away or tries ruffing some of the club or diamond losers in dummy, establishing the heart suit may become impossible.

Suggested Defense

Due to the lucky lie of the cards for declarer, the defenders can't defeat the contract, if declarer plays as previously mentioned. South should probably lead a trump initially, hoping to prevent declarer from ruffing heart losers, but that won't work. The defenders also can try leading two rounds of clubs, forcing dummy to ruff and hoping to run dummy out of trumps before the hearts can be established. Again, declarer can still succeed with the lucky division of the hearts.

North–South's best result is to push on to 4NT if East sacrifices in 4♠. That's difficult to do. North has no reason to expect East–West to make their contract. South, however, might think that the penalty derived will not be enough compensation for a vulnerable game and that the sixth club will produce a tenth trick in notrump. South, therefore, might bid 4NT to play. If North–South bid 5♣, that contract can be defeated at least one trick if East gets a heart ruff.

East–West's use of the Michaels cuebid convention gives them an opportunity to compete for the contract. Without intervention, North–South would make 3NT easily with an overtrick.

Bid and Play — Michael's Cuebid Over a Major

(E–Z Deal Cards: #4, Deal 3 — Dealer, South)

Suggested Bidding

WEST	NORTH	EAST	SOUTH
			Pass
1♠	2♠	4♠	4NT
Pass	5♦	Pass	Pass
Pass			

After South's pass, West opens the bidding in the higher-ranking of two five-card suits. North uses the Michaels cuebid to show at least five hearts and a five-card or longer minor suit. East jumps to 4♠, a preemptive raise, to try to keep North–South out of the auction. South knows the partnership has a fit in one of the minor suits, but can't be sure which one. With 2NT no longer available to ask for

```
Dealer: South   ♠ 4
Vul: E–W        ♥ K Q 7 6 5
                ♦ A J 7 3 2
                ♣ 10 7
    ♠ K Q J 7 5          ♠ A 10 9 8 2
    ♥ J 9 4 3 2    N     ♥ 10
    ♦ K         W   E    ♦ 10 9 8
    ♣ A 8          S     ♣ Q 4 3 2
                ♠ 6 3
                ♥ A 8
                ♦ Q 6 5 4
                ♣ K J 9 6 5
```

North's minor suit, South uses 4NT instead. North shows the diamond suit, and that ends the auction. East–West are vulnerable, so it's better to defend and hope to defeat the contract, rather than to bid higher.

Suggested Opening Lead

East starts by leading the suit bid by East–West. East should lead the ♠A. Against a suit contract, leading low when holding an ace is dangerous.

Suggested Play

Declarer has one spade loser, two heart losers, one diamond loser and two club losers. There's nothing that can be done about the spade loser, but declarer should be able to avoid a heart loser. The hearts might divide 3–3, or declarer can ruff a heart loser in dummy, or declarer can discard one or more heart losers by establishing club winners in the dummy. Declarer might be able to avoid a diamond loser with the help of a successful finesse against the ♦ K. A club loser could be avoided by leading toward dummy and hoping to guess whether East holds the ♣A or ♣Q.

The first critical decision is in the trump suit. Suppose East wins the ♠A and shifts to the ♥ 10. North wins this with South's ♥A and has to decide how to play the trump suit. It might appear tempting to lead the ♦ Q, so that the finesse can be repeated if West has the ♦ K and doesn't cover. Without the ♦ 10, however, declarer can't afford to lead the ♦ Q. West would play the ♦ K on the ♦ Q, and after declarer wins tricks with the ♦ A and ♦ J, East gets a trick with the ♦ 10. Missing both the ♦ K and the ♦ 10, declarer should lead a low diamond from dummy. This works, since West's ♦ K appears, and declarer can draw trumps without losing a trick. It also would work if West started with the doubleton ♦ K. Declarer could finesse and then play the ♦ A. If West started with three diamonds including the ♦ K, there's no way for declarer to take all of the diamond tricks.

Having handled the diamond suit successfully, North needs to guess how to play the club suit. Since West opened the bidding and East has already turned up with the ♠A, it's more likely that West holds the ♣A than East. Declarer's best hope is that East started with the ♣Q. North should lead the ♣10, and if East doesn't cover, take the finesse by playing a low club from dummy. Once this is successful, declarer should be able to take the rest of the tricks, losing only one spade trick and one club trick.

Suggested Defense

After leading the ♠A, East should switch to the singleton ♥10. If West can win a trick before trumps are drawn, East may get a heart ruff. Declarer can draw trumps before letting West gain the lead but may make a mistake.

If declarer does successfully draw trumps and later leads the ♣10, East should play low. Looking at the clubs in dummy, there's nothing for the defense to promote by covering with the ♣Q. If East plays low, declarer may misguess and play dummy's ♣K, hoping East started with the ♣A. If declarer does that, East will eventually get a third trick for the defense with the ♣Q.

Note that North–South did well to get into the auction with their diamond fit by using the Michaels cuebid convention. If East–West were allowed to play in 4♠, they might make that contract. If North–South don't lead trumps often enough, West might get away with losing only one heart trick, one diamond trick and one club trick.

Bid and Play — The Unusual Notrump

(E–Z Deal Cards: #4, Deal 4 — Dealer, West)

Suggested Bidding

WEST	NORTH	EAST	SOUTH
1♠	2NT	4♠	5♦
Pass	Pass	Pass	

After West's opening bid, North enters the auction by using the unusual notrump. Over the 1♠ bid, North's 2NT shows at least five cards in each of the two lowest-ranking unbid suits, diamonds and clubs. East makes a preemptive jump raise to 4♠ to try to buy the contract and keep North–South out of the auction. This shouldn't deter South, who knows from the unusual notrump bid that the

```
Dealer: West   ♠ 4
Vul: Both      ♥ J
               ♦ Q J 8 6 5
               ♣ A Q J 7 6 3
♠ Q J 9 6 3              ♠ A 10 8 7 5
♥ A K 10          N      ♥ 9 7 6 3 2
♦ K            W   E     ♦ 9 7
♣ 10 9 4 2        S      ♣ 8
               ♠ K 2
               ♥ Q 8 5 4
               ♦ A 10 4 3 2
               ♣ K 5
```

partnership has at least a 10-card fit in diamonds. South also has a useful card in North's other suit, clubs. It looks best to compete to 5♦, rather than quietly defend 4♠.

Neither East nor West has enough to safely bid to the five level, and neither has enough to double 5♦. Their best hope is that the contract can be defeated.

Suggested Opening Lead

West will probably start with the ♥A, top of touching high cards. After seeing the singleton heart in dummy, West will probably switch to the ♠Q, top of touching cards in the partnership's agreed suit.

Suggested Play

Declarer has to lose one spade trick and one heart trick for sure. The rest of declarer's heart losers can be ruffed in dummy or discarded on the extra club winners. The success of the contract hinges around avoiding a loser in the trump suit.

Declarer is missing the ♦ K, and the normal play would be to take a diamond finesse, hoping that East holds the ♦ K. Declarer has some indications, however, that the finesse won't work. West opened the bidding, and there are very few high cards in the East–West hands. East has shown up with the ♠ A. That leaves only 10 high-card points for West to hold — the ♠ Q, the ♠ J, the ♥ A and the ♥ K — unless West also holds the ♦ K. It's unlikely West would open the bidding without the ♦ K. Further, East might not have made a preemptive raise to 4♠ with both the ♠ A and the ♦ K. Everything points to West holding the ♦ K.

If that's the case, declarer's best chance to make the contract is to play the ♦ A, hoping West's ♦ K is a singleton. Playing the ♦ A results in a spectacular success for declarer. Declarer avoids a diamond loser and makes the contract.

Even if declarer does lose a trick to West's ♦ K, North–South shouldn't be too disappointed. East–West can make the 4♠ contract by guessing how to handle the heart suit. So, down one should still be a good result.

Suggested Defense

There's little the defenders can do once North–South bid to 5♦ except to keep quiet and hope that declarer misguesses the diamond suit. If they bid on to 5♠, the defenders will get at least one spade trick, one diamond trick, and one club trick. West can restrict the heart losers to one by playing one high heart and finessing against South's ♥ Q when North's ♥ J appears.

CHAPTER 5
Blackwood and Gerber

BLACKWOOD AND GERBER

Slam bidding is one of the most exciting parts of the game. It's not surprising that there are a number of conventions related to it. Before venturing to the slam level, the partnership wants to make sure that it can meet three requirements: sufficient combined strength, a suitable strain in which to play the contract and enough controls. Most slam-related conventions are concerned with the last of these requirements, controls.

Slam Requirements

There are three main factors to consider when bidding a slam:

- Combined strength.
- Trump fit.
- Controls.

Combined Strength

It's generally accepted that the partnership requires:

- 33 or more combined points for a small slam.
- 37 or more combined points for a grand slam.

This idea allows some slams to be bid on sheer power. Here are some examples.

West	WEST	NORTH	EAST	SOUTH	East
♠ K Q 6 3	1NT	Pass	6NT	Pass	♠ A J 5
♥ Q 8 4	Pass	Pass			♥ A K 7
♦ K Q 6 2					♦ J 10 8
♣ A 9					♣ K Q 8 3

West's opening bid shows 15 to 17 HCP. Holding 18 HCP, East knows the partnership has a combined total of between 33 and 35 points. That's enough for a small slam, but not enough for a grand slam. West, having limited the hand with the 1NT opening bid, respects East's decision and passes.

West			East
♠ A K 10			♠ J 5
♥ K Q 6			♥ A J 3
♦ Q J 10 7 4			♦ A K 2
♣ A J			♣ K Q 10 6 5

WEST	NORTH	EAST	SOUTH
2NT	Pass	7NT	Pass
Pass	Pass		

West's 2NT opening bid shows 20 or 21 HCP. With 18 HCP plus 1 for the five-card suit, East is comfortable that the partnership holds more than 37 combined points.

West			East
♠ K J 7			♠ A Q 3
♥ Q 9 7 4			♥ A 10 6 5 3 2
♦ J 6			♦ A 7
♣ K Q J 3			♣ A 6

WEST	NORTH	EAST	SOUTH
1♣	Pass	1♥	Pass
2♥	Pass	6♥	Pass
Pass	Pass		

Slams bid on power aren't restricted to notrump contracts. West's raise to 2♥ shows a minimum-strength hand of 13 to 15 points and agrees on hearts as the trump suit. With 18 high-card points and 2 for the six-card suit, East can bid a small slam with the assurance that the partnership holds at least 33 points and at most 36.

Using the combined strength of the hands to determine the appropriate level is referred to as quantitative bidding and allows the partnership to have slam-invitational auctions such as the following:

West			East
♠ Q 10 4			♠ K J 7
♥ A Q 6 3			♥ K J 5
♦ K J 5 2			♦ Q 10 8
♣ K 7			♣ A Q J 2

WEST	NORTH	EAST	SOUTH
1NT	Pass	4NT	Pass
Pass	Pass		

West's 1NT opening bid shows 15 to 17 HCP, and East holds 17 high-card points. Adding up the combined strengths, East knows the partnership has 32 to 34 points. There should be enough for a slam contract if West has the top of the range for the opening bid — 16 or 17 HCP — but there may not be enough if West has a minimum of 15 HCP. East offers an invitation to slam by bidding one level beyond game — a quantitative raise to 4NT. With only 15 HCP, West declines the invitation by passing.

West	WEST	NORTH	EAST	SOUTH	East
♠ Q 10 3	1NT	Pass	5NT	Pass	♠ A K 7
♥ K Q	7NT	Pass	Pass	Pass	♥ A 9 3
♦ A J 9 8					♦ K Q 6 4
♣ K Q 9 3					♣ A J 8

This is another form of quantitative raise, used by more experienced partnerships. A raise of an opening notrump bid to the five level asks partner to choose between a small slam and a grand slam. With 21 high-card points opposite partner's 1NT opening bid, East knows the partnership has at least the values for a small slam, but could have enough to take all of the tricks. The 5NT bid invites partner to bid a grand slam. With a minimum opening bid, West would decline the invitation by bidding 6NT. West has 17 HCP and is happy to go for the big bonus.

Trump Fit

Suppose West opens the bidding 1♠. This is East's hand:

♠ Q 7	There are 19 high-card points and 1 length point for
♥ A K 9 6 2	the fifth heart, a total of 20 points. Combined with
♦ K Q 8 3	West's minimum of 12 or 13 points for the opening
♣ A J	bid, it looks as though the partnership may have
	enough combined strength for the slam level.

Players familiar with the Blackwood convention — a bid of 4NT to ask how many aces partner holds — might be tempted to use it right away. Although this approach could work out, it's more likely to lead to an auction like this:

WEST	NORTH	EAST	SOUTH
1♠	Pass	4NT	Pass
5♦	Pass	?	

West's response to Blackwood shows one ace, so there is no grand slam. But which small slam is best — 6♥, 6♠ or 6NT? 6NT would be unfortunate if the opening lead is the ♣K and the combined hands look something like this:

West	WEST	NORTH	EAST	SOUTH	East
♠ K J 10 9 8 6	1♠	Pass	4NT (?)	Pass	♠ Q 7
♥ Q J 7	5♦	Pass	6NT	Pass	♥ A K 9 6 2
♦ A J 5	Pass	Pass			♦ K Q 8 3
♣ 3					♣ A J

There are 10 tricks — the ♣A, five heart tricks, and four diamond tricks, but that's not enough to make the contract. If extra winners are promoted in spades, the defenders can take their club winners. Choosing a final contract of 6♥ or 6♠ would have been better. 6♦ might even make.

The difficulty arises from launching into the slam level before determining the best strain. The Blackwood convention is used when the partnership has agreed on the trump suit or on notrump. Even though the partnership belongs at the slam level, the first priority is to look for the best strain.

If East starts with a forcing response of 2♥, the partnership can search for a trump fit and then bid the appropriate slam.

For example:

West	WEST	NORTH	EAST	SOUTH	East
♠ A J 10 6 3	1♠	Pass	2♥	Pass	♠ Q 7
♥ Q 8 4 3	3♥	Pass	6♥	Pass	♥ A K 9 6 2
♦ A J 7	Pass	Pass			♦ K Q 8 3
♣ 9					♣ A J

Once a fit is found, the slam can be bid. The partnership might use some of the conventional bids discussed later in the chapter. The important point is that the first priority is to explore for the best trump fit. Only after it is found should the slam be bid.

On some deals, the partnership might even belong in a grand slam, but finding a fit is the first priority.

Controls

Once a fit has been found and the partnership is headed for the slam zone, there's one final consideration. Suppose West opens the bidding 1♠, and this is East's hand:

♠ K Q 7 4   There is an excellent trump fit and the hand is
♥ K Q J 9   worth 22 points — 19 high-card points plus 3
♦ 6   dummy points for the singleton diamond. The
♣ A K J 5   partnership is headed for the slam zone. There
                   should be a minimum of 33 combined points, and
East knows where to play the contract. It might sound like the perfect
time to jump right to 6♠.

Most of the time, that will work well. There will be 12 tricks, and the
partnership can score a slam bonus. On occasion, however, the slam will
be defeated. For example, suppose these are the combined hands:

WEST	EAST
♠ A J 10 8 6 3	♠ K Q 7 4
♥ 7	♥ K Q J 9
♦ K Q J	♦ 6
♣ Q 10 8	♣ A K J 5

West has a sound 1♠ opening bid worth 15 points — 13 high-card
points plus 2 length points. The combined partnership strength is more
than the 33 points needed to consider bidding a slam. There is also an
excellent fit in spades. There are six spade winners and four club winners. Two extra winners can be promoted in either hearts or diamonds.
Unfortunately, the opponents are likely to take two tricks right away, the
♥ A and the ♦ A. (If the opening lead was a club or a spade originally,
declarer could draw trumps and cash the clubs, pitching the losing heart
on the fourth club.)

The basic problem is that the partnership has wasted strength in hearts
and diamonds. The ♥ K, the ♥ Q and the ♥ J are practically worthless
opposite a singleton heart. Similarly, West's ♦ K, the ♦ Q and the ♦ J
are not useful. It would be better if either partner held fewer high cards
and the high cards held were more effectively located. For example, let's
remove West's 6 high-card points in diamonds and replace them with only
4 points, the ♦ A. Now the combined hands look like this:

WEST	EAST
♠ A J 10 8 6 3	♠ K Q 7 4
♥ 7	♥ K Q J 9
♦ A 5 3	♦ 6
♣ Q 10 8	♣ A K J 5

With two fewer points, West can make a slam contract. The only loser is the ♥A. The two losing diamonds can be ruffed in dummy or discarded on the heart winners. In fact, even with fewer high cards, there is an excellent chance of making the slam:

WEST	EAST
♠ A J 10 8 6 3	♠ K 9 7 4
♥ 7	♥ 9 5 4 3
♦ A 5 3	♦ 6
♣ Q 10 8	♣ A K 7 5

Provided the missing trumps divide 2–1, West should have little trouble coming to 12 tricks: one diamond winner, four club winners, at least one diamond ruff in dummy and six more spade winners. The only loser is the ♥A. Yet, the combined partnership strength is barely enough for a game contract on most deals.

The key factor that makes a difference in the above hands is controls. A control is a holding that prevents the opponents from taking too many tricks in a suit. The ace is a *first-round control*, since it stops the opponents from taking the first trick in the suit. In a trump contract, a void also can serve as a first-round control, since it prevents the opponents from taking the first trick in the suit. A king represents a *second-round control*. The opponents can take the first trick in the suit with their ace, but the king will stop them on the second round. In a trump contract, a singleton can serve the same function as a king — a second-round control. For example, West's singleton heart in the last deal on the previous page prevents the opponents from taking more than one trick in the suit, although they hold all of the high cards.

When bidding a small slam, it's important to hold first-round control of at least three suits and at least second-round control of the fourth suit. Otherwise, the opponents could take the first two tricks and defeat the contract, before there is a chance to establish extra winners or discard losers. To bid a grand slam, it's important to have first-round control of all four suits. How does the partnership discover whether or not it holds enough controls to make a slam contract? One of the popular methods is the *Blackwood* convention.

THE BLACKWOOD CONVENTION

In the 1940s, Easley Blackwood wrote about one of the methods used by some of the expert players to determine the number of aces and kings held by the partnership. Blackwood's name was quickly associated with the method, and the Blackwood convention rapidly became a household phrase among bridge players. Its popularity stems from the fact that it is relatively easy for both partners to learn and works well on many slam-going hands.

Blackwood

The Blackwood convention, often just called Blackwood, works as follows. After a trump suit has been agreed on by the partnership, a bid of 4NT asks partner how many aces partner holds.

Partner responds as follows:

5♣	No aces or all four aces.
5♦	One ace.
5♥	Two aces.
5♠	Three aces.

If the partnership holds all of the aces, a bid of 5NT now asks partner how many kings are held.

Partner responds:

6♣	No kings.
6♦	One king.
6♥	Two kings.
6♠	Three kings.
6NT	Four kings.

The progression of responses is fairly easy to remember. The only quirk is the response of 5♣ to show either four aces or no aces — all or nothing. This dual meaning of the 5♣ response leaves room for the bid of 5NT to ask for kings. Since there is a difference of 16 high-card points between four aces and no aces, the player who asks for the number of aces should be able to interpret a 5♣ response.

Here are examples of putting Blackwood to work:

West					East
♠ A J 10 8 6 3					♠ K Q 7 4
♥ 7					♥ K Q J 9
♦ K Q J					♦ 6
♣ Q 10 8					♣ A K J 5

WEST	NORTH	EAST	SOUTH
1♠	Pass	4NT	Pass
5♦	Pass	5♠	Pass
Pass	Pass		

There are several things to note in this auction. East's immediate jump to 4NT agrees on spades as the trump suit by inference. If there has been no prior agreement on a suit, then a jump to 4NT implies that the last bid suit is the agreed trump suit. West's response is dictated by the convention and has nothing to do with West's diamond holding. East has taken over as captain for the partnership. Once West shows one ace, East determines that the partnership is missing two aces by adding the number of aces in both hands. Since the opponents can take the first two tricks, East signs off at the lowest possible level in the agreed trump suit. West must respect East's decision, since East has assumed the captaincy on the hand. East knows how many aces the partnership holds. West does not.

West					East
♠ A J 10 8 6 3					♠ K Q 7 4
♥ 7					♥ K Q J 9
♦ A 5 3					♦ 6
♣ Q 10 8					♣ A K J 5

WEST	NORTH	EAST	SOUTH
1♠	Pass	4NT	Pass
5♥	Pass	6♠	Pass
Pass	Pass		

East finds out that the partnership is missing only one ace and can now bid the excellent slam contract with full confidence. There's no point in bidding 5NT, since East isn't interested in a grand slam. Some duplicate players might disagree — hoping to reach the top matchpoint contract of 6NT, instead of 6♠ — but this is a dangerous practice. West may continue on to a grand slam under the illusion that the partnership holds all of the aces!

Here's an example of reaching a grand slam by using Blackwood:

West	WEST	NORTH	EAST	SOUTH	East
♠ K 7	1♦	Pass	1♥	Pass	♠ A J 5
♥ K J 9 2	3♥	Pass	4NT	Pass	♥ A Q 10 8 6 3
♦ A 10 8 6 3	5♥	Pass	5NT	Pass	♦ K 4
♣ A 9	6♥	Pass	7♥	Pass	♣ K 5
	Pass	Pass			

Although East expects that the partnership is headed for a slam contract once West opens the bidding, East is in no hurry until a suitable trump fit has been found. Once West raises hearts — with a jump since the hand revalues to 17 points, counting 1 dummy point for each doubleton — East uses Blackwood to check for aces. Since the partnership holds all of the aces, East looks for bigger things. The response of 6♥ lets East know that the partnership holds all of the kings as well as all of the aces. That makes the grand slam a good bet. East can ruff the spade loser in dummy after drawing trumps.

Showing a Void

Although the basic mechanics of Blackwood are quite straightforward, one frequently asked question is, "What do I respond when I have a void in a suit — should I treat the void as an ace?" This is a good question, because in a trump contract a void will often serve the same purpose as an ace — controlling the first round of the suit. The best advice, however, is not to show a void as an ace, unless the situation has been specifically discussed with partner. To see why, consider these two hands:

West	WEST	NORTH	EAST	SOUTH	East
♠ Q 8 6 3	1♦	Pass	1♥	Pass	♠ 9
♥ Q J 5 2	3♥	Pass	4NT	Pass	♥ A K 8 7 3
♦ A Q J 8 4	5♥ (?)	Pass	7♥	Pass	♦ K 6
♣ —	Pass	Pass			♣ A K J 10 5

South leads a spade, and the contract is one down. What went wrong? West's hand is originally valued as 12 high-card points plus 1 for the five-card diamond suit. After East responds 1♥, West has good support for hearts and can revalue the hand using dummy points in place of length points. West counts 5 points for the club void and revalues the hand to 17 points, enough for a jump raise. With extra strength, East uses Blackwood to find out how many aces the partnership holds. West has the ♦A, but is also void in clubs. Reasoning that the club void is the same as an ace, West shows two aces. East bids a grand slam, confidently expecting to take all 13 tricks.

Both East and West held first round control of clubs, and neither held first round control of spades. East thought West's two aces were the ♦A, and the ♠A. West thought the club void would be useful — which it would have been if East held the ♠A instead of the ♣A. That's one of the troubles with mixing aces and voids. Is there a solution? Some partnerships have an agreement on how to show both aces and voids in response to Blackwood.

There are various methods, but this is a popular approach after partner starts Blackwood:

- With no aces, respond 5♣ (don't show the void).
- With one ace and a useful void, jump to the six level in the void suit if it ranks lower than the agreed trump suit; otherwise, jump to the six level in the agreed trump suit.
- With two aces and a useful void, bid 5NT (partner will have to determine which is the void suit).

A useful void is a void in a suit that has not already been bid by one of the partners. A void is not shown in a suit in which partner has already shown some length and strength. Show a void in an unbid suit or a suit that has been bid by the opponents.

For example, the auction on the hands from the previous example would now go:

West	WEST	NORTH	EAST	SOUTH	East
♠ Q 8 6 3	1♦	Pass	1♥	Pass	♠ 9
♥ Q J 5 2	3♥	Pass	4NT	Pass	♥ A K 8 7 3
♦ A Q J 8 4	6♣	Pass	6♥	Pass	♦ K 6
♣ —	Pass	Pass			♣ A K J 10 5

West's 6♣ response to Blackwood shows one ace and a void in clubs. East doesn't know whether West's ace is in diamonds or spades, but it doesn't matter. The partnership is missing one ace, so a small slam is all that's in the cards. East knows that West's club void is wasted opposite the ♣A and the ♣K.

Suppose we change the West hand so that the void is in spades, rather than clubs:

West	WEST	NORTH	EAST	SOUTH	East
♠ —	1♦	Pass	1♥	Pass	♠ 9
♥ Q J 5 2	3♥	Pass	4NT	Pass	♥ A K 8 7 3
♦ A Q J 8 4	6♥	Pass	7♥	Pass	♦ K 6
♣ Q 8 6 3	Pass	Pass			♣ A K J 10 5

West's jump to 6♥ shows one ace and a void in a higher-ranking suit than the agreed trump suit — which must be spades. Now East knows that West's ace is the ♦A and that there are no spade losers. East confidently bids a grand slam, and the partnership takes all of the tricks.

The reason to jump to the six level in the agreed trump suit with a void in a higher-ranking suit is to retain the ability of stopping at a small slam. If West had jumped to 6♠ on the above hand, that might have proved disastrous if East's spades and clubs were reversed. Now the partnership would be missing the ♣A and could no longer go back to 6♥.

Showing a void in response to Blackwood requires a firm partnership understanding. If the partnership has not discussed handling voids, ignore a void when responding to Blackwood. Better to miss the occasional slam than to watch the opponents take their aces against a slam contract.

Stopping in 5NT

Another commonly asked question is, "How do I stop in 5NT, if I find out that the partnership is missing two aces?" This is a problem that sometimes arises when the partnership has found a minor-suit fit and the response to Blackwood doesn't leave enough room to stop at the five level in the agreed trump suit. Bidding 5NT compounds the problem, since partner will think it asks for kings. A slam contract could be reached missing two aces!

The usual agreement is the following:

- After bidding 4NT and hearing partner's response, the bid of a suit at the five level, which can't be meant as a trump suit, asks partner to bid 5NT.

To see how this works, look at the following hands and auction:

West					East
♠ K 8					♠ Q J 6
♥ K Q 3					♥ 10 7
♦ K Q					♦ A 6 3
♣ A Q 10 8 7 2					♣ K 9 6 4 3

WEST	NORTH	EAST	SOUTH
1♣	Pass	3♣	Pass
4NT	Pass	5♦	Pass
5♥	Pass	5NT	Pass
Pass	Pass		

With 19 high-card points plus 2 points for the six-card suit, West becomes interested in a slam contract when East makes a limit raise of the opening 1♣ bid. West hopes East has two aces and that the partnership can make a slam contract. West tries the Blackwood convention and is disappointed to hear that East holds only one ace.

There's more of a challenge than that, however. East's response of 5♦ to show one ace has taken the partnership beyond the safe level of 5♣. West knows the partnership can't make 6♣, since two aces are missing. The only chance to play at the five level and not go down is to bid 5NT and hope to take 11 tricks. Unfortunately, if West bids 5NT at this point, East will assume it's more of the Blackwood convention and will respond 6♦ to show one king. That's going from bad to worse.

Instead, West bids 5♥, a suit that hasn't been bid so far. East recognizes that this can't be a suggestion to play with that suit as trump, since it has not been mentioned before. So, East bids 5NT. Now West passes, and the partnership rests in a makable spot. After losing two tricks to the ♥ A and the ♠ A, West has the rest of the tricks.

INTERFERENCE BY THE OPPONENTS

Suppose West has the following hand:

♠ A J 9 6
♥ Q 5
♦ A K J 3
♣ K J 6

The bidding proceeds:

WEST	NORTH	EAST	SOUTH
1♦	1♥	1♠	4♥
4♠	Pass	4NT	5♥
?			

Having agreed on a trump suit, East's 4NT bid is Blackwood, asking for aces. The response is 5 ♥, to show two aces, but South bids 5 ♥ first. Now what?

It's unusual, but not impossible, for the opponents to interfere in an auction when the other side is considering bidding a slam. North–South have a lot of hearts and are hoping to find a good sacrifice. The first instinct may be to double South's bid for penalty, but that may not result in a sufficient penalty if a small slam or even a grand slam can be made. It looks as though South's bid has complicated what was about to be a simple auction.

It's true that South's bid has taken away some bidding room, but there is some compensation. There are two new calls available to West: pass and double. Many partnerships take advantage of this by coming to the following agreement when the opponents interfere directly over the 4NT bid:

- Double shows no aces.
- Pass shows one ace.
- The cheapest bid shows two aces.
- The next cheapest bid shows three aces.

With this agreement, bid 5♠, the cheapest available bid, to show two aces. With no aces, double. With one ace, pass South's 5 ♥ bid. With three aces, bid 5NT. The opponent's intervention no longer prevents the partnership from knowing how many aces there are. This agreement is usually referred to by the acronym DOPI: Double is O (zero) aces, Pass is I (one) ace.

Here are two additional points. If an opponent doubles the 4NT bid, the responder can simply ignore the double and make the normal response. Finally, if an opponent interferes by bidding 5NT or higher, the agreement is usually switched to DEPO: Double is an Even number of aces (zero, two or four), Pass is an Odd number of aces (one or three).

For example:

West		East
♠ Q J 10 6 4		♠ A K 8 5 3
♥ A 9 8		♥ K Q J 7 4
♦ A J 6 4		♦ 3
♣ 3		♣ K 9

WEST	NORTH	EAST	SOUTH
1♠	3♣	4NT	6♣
Dbl	Pass	6♠	Pass
Pass	Pass		

West's double shows an even number of aces. East figures that it must be two aces, rather than zero or four, and bids the slam.

WHEN IS 4NT BLACKWOOD?

To use Blackwood successfully, both partners should have a clear understanding about when 4NT is asking for aces and when it isn't. The easiest guideline is the following:

• 4NT is Blackwood only if a trump suit has already been agreed upon by the partnership.

This clarifies most situations.

For example:

WEST	NORTH	**EAST**	SOUTH
1♠	Pass	3♠	Pass
4NT	Pass	?	

The partnership has agreed on spades as the trump suit, so West's 4NT bid is Blackwood.

WEST	NORTH	EAST	SOUTH
1NT	Pass	4NT	Pass
?			

There has been no agreement on a trump suit, so East's 4NT bid isn't asking for the number of aces. East's 4NT bid is a quantitative, or invitational, raise, inviting West to bid 6NT with a maximum-strength hand for the 1NT opening bid, but to pass otherwise.

WEST	NORTH	EAST	SOUTH
1♠	Pass	2♣	Pass
3♣	Pass	4NT	Pass
?			

Clubs have been raised, so East's 4NT bid is Blackwood.

WEST	NORTH	EAST	SOUTH
1NT	Pass	2♣	Pass
2♦	Pass	4NT	Pass
?			

East has used Stayman and found that West doesn't hold a major suit. East's 4NT bid isn't Blackwood, since no trump suit has been uncovered. It's a quantitative raise. East has enough strength to invite opener to bid a slam, but also has a four-card major suit. East used Stayman to investigate for an eight-card fit in a major suit. When West doesn't have a major suit, East continues by making an invitational raise.

Sometimes, a trump suit can be agreed upon through inference, even though the suit has not been bid by both partners. For example:

WEST	NORTH	EAST	SOUTH
1♠	Pass	4NT	Pass
?			

East hasn't raised West's spade suit, but most partnerships would agree that 4NT is Blackwood. It sounds as though East has a lot of spades and a lot of points. East already knows where the deal should be played — spades — and is only interested in checking for the number of aces before bidding a slam.

WEST	NORTH	EAST	SOUTH
1♣	Pass	1♦	Pass
1♥	Pass	4NT	Pass
?			

East started by searching for a fit. The leap to 4NT suggests that the partnership has found its fit — hearts. Now East uses Blackwood to check for the number of aces.

There are some situations, unfortunately, which are not so clear.

WEST	NORTH	EAST	SOUTH
	4♠	4NT	Pass
?			

There has been no partnership agreement on a trump suit, which lends support to the argument that East's 4NT is probably not Blackwood. On the other hand, North's bid has taken away all of the bidding room that East–West would usually use to find their fit. What if East has a very strong hand and only needs to find out how many aces are held by West in order to bid a slam?

As discussed in the previous chapter, the usual agreement in this situation is that 4NT is similar to a takeout double, asking West to pick one of the other three suits or, perhaps, a two-suited hand (the unusual notrump). That's because a double of 4♠ is customarily used as a penalty double. Unless the partners discussed this situation, there's a lot of room for a misunderstanding. There's the possibility that the partnership may go off the tracks as soon as it starts to use a convention, even one as straightforward as Blackwood.

WEST	NORTH	EAST	SOUTH
1NT	Pass	2♣	Pass
2♠	Pass	4NT	Pass
?			

Even experienced partnerships may disagree on the interpretation of East's 4NT bid. Is East agreeing upon spades as the trump suit by inference and asking for aces, or is East now simply making a quantitative raise after using Stayman to search for a heart fit?

The standard agreement would be that 4NT is an invitational raise, if the partnership has not agreed on a trump suit. Most partnerships use the *Gerber convention* in this situation to ask for aces (see discussion in the next section). Many players, however, would probably treat East's 4NT bid as Blackwood. After all, if East does have a fit with spades and enough strength to investigate slam, how does East agree on spades as trump without risking being passed? A raise to 3♠ would be invitational, and a raise to 4♠ would be a sign-off bid.

Fortunately, there's not much of a problem if West has a better-than-average hand. If West would accept an invitational raise by continuing to the slam level, then West can respond to 4NT as though it's Blackwood and show the number of aces. If West bids 5♥ in this situation, for example, East is likely to assume that West is showing two aces. If East intended 4NT as Blackwood, East now can make the appropriate decision about bidding a slam. If East intended 4NT as an invitational raise, East now can bid 6NT to clarify the situation.

What if West has a minimum hand for the 1NT opening? Not so easy. In an inexperienced partnership, assuming that East meant 4NT as Blackwood would probably be best. In that case, opener shows the number of aces, and if East now leaps to 6NT, hopes the contract makes. Once the play is over, the partners should discuss the auction to avoid misunderstandings in the future.

Situations in which the meaning of a 4NT bid is not clear can lead to some uneasiness among the players at the table. One of the partners could take a long time to make a call, and everyone else will know it's one of those "Is it or isn't it?" situations. To avoid this, make your decision in reasonable tempo. If in doubt, treat the 4NT bid as Blackwood and hope for the best. Some partnerships go further and have an agreement that 4NT is always Blackwood. That's technically incorrect, but it may put the partnership at ease.

THE GERBER CONVENTION

Suppose West opens 1NT, and East holds this hand:

♠ K 7
♥ K J
♦ K 9 4
♣ K Q J 10 8 2

The hand is worth 18 points — 16 high-card points plus 2 points for the six-card suit. The partnership should be able to take 12 tricks in a notrump contract, provided the opponents don't have two aces to take first. Blackwood can't be used to find out how many aces West holds. A direct raise to 4NT would be a quantitative raise, not the Blackwood convention, since no trump suit has been agreed upon.

To get around this, John Gerber of Houston, Texas, came up with the idea of using a response of 4♣ to ask for aces, when partner has opened the bidding 1NT or 2NT. This agreement is appropriately called the *Gerber convention.*

Gerber

The Gerber convention works as follows. After a bid of 1NT or 2NT, a jump to 4♣ asks partner how many aces partner holds.

Partner responds as follows:

4♦	No aces or all four aces.
4♥	One ace.
4♠	Two aces.
4NT	Three aces.

If the partnership holds all of the aces, a bid of 5♣ now asks partner how many kings are held.

Partner responds as follows:

5♦	No kings.
5♥	One king.
5♠	Two kings.
5NT	Three kings.
6♣	Four kings.

The nice thing about the Gerber convention is that the responses are similar to those for Blackwood. The cheapest available bid — 4♦ in this case — shows no aces. Keep moving one step up the ladder for each ace held. The only exception is the response of 4♦ to show either no aces or all four aces. This is done to leave room for the bid of 5♣ to ask for kings.

Let's see how Gerber would help out with the earlier hands:

West		WEST	NORTH	EAST	SOUTH		East
♠ A Q J 6		1NT	Pass	4♣	Pass		♠ K 7
♥ Q 8 5 3		4♠	Pass	4NT	Pass		♥ K J
♦ A Q J		Pass	Pass				♦ K 9 4
♣ 9 4							♣ K Q J 10 8 2

West's response to Gerber shows two aces. East now knows the partnership is missing two aces. The most important thing to note about this auction is that after East has used Gerber, any bid other than 5 ♣ — which asks for kings — is a sign-off bid, placing the contract. So, East's 4NT bid isn't Blackwood. It merely places the partnership in the best contract. East–West stop safely in 4NT, avoiding a slam missing two aces.

West	WEST	NORTH	EAST	SOUTH	East
♠ A J 6 4	1NT	Pass	4♣	Pass	♠ K 7
♥ A 8 5 3	4NT	Pass	6NT	Pass	♥ K J
♦ Q J 3	Pass	Pass			♦ K 9 4
♣ A 4					♣ K Q J 10 8 2

Once West shows three aces, East puts the partnership in a slam contract, knowing that the opponents hold only one ace. The partnership should have enough combined strength to take 12 tricks.

Here is another example of the use of the Gerber convention:

West	WEST	NORTH	EAST	SOUTH	East
♠ A K 8 3	1NT	Pass	4♣	Pass	♠ 6
♥ K 9 3	4♠	Pass	5♣	Pass	♥ A 8 4
♦ A 8	5NT	Pass	7NT	Pass	♦ K Q J 10 9 6 2
♣ K 9 6 2	Pass	Pass			♣ A 3

With a slam-going hand in response to the 1NT opening bid, East inquires about the number of aces by using Gerber. If West had shown no aces, East could sign off in 5 ♦. If West had shown one ace, East could sign off in 6 ♦. When West shows two aces, East looks for bigger things. East's 5♣ bid is a continuation of the Gerber convention, asking for the number of kings. If West had shown zero or one king, East would settle for 6 ♦. If West had shown two kings, East would likely settle for 6NT. When West's response shows three kings, East can count on taking all 13 tricks and bids the grand slam in notrump.

WHEN IS 4♣ GERBER?

Gerber isn't an alternative to Blackwood. It's used in conjunction with Blackwood. Some partnerships like to treat every 4♣ bid as Gerber, under the illusion that it allows the partnership to stop at a lower level than does Blackwood, if the partnership doesn't have enough aces. This can be true on occasion, but the partnership shouldn't be looking for a slam contract, if it won't be safe to stop at the five level. More importantly, 4♣ is useful as a natural bid in many situations.

The most common guideline is the following:

- If partner's last bid was a natural 1NT or 2NT, then a jump to 4♣ is the Gerber convention.

This clarifies most situations.

For example:

WEST	NORTH	EAST	SOUTH
2NT	Pass	4♣	Pass
?			

East's jump to 4♣ is in response to West's natural opening bid of 2NT, so it's the Gerber convention, asking for aces.

WEST	NORTH	EAST	SOUTH
1♦	Pass	1♥	Pass
1NT	Pass	4♣	Pass
?			

East's jump to 4♣ follows a natural rebid of 1NT by West, so most partnerships would treat this as Gerber.

WEST	NORTH	**EAST**	SOUTH
1♣	Pass	2NT	Pass
4♣	Pass	?	

Assuming that East's 2NT response is a natural bid in the partnership style, West's 4♣ jump rebid would be Gerber, even though clubs have previously been bid by the partnership. West could rebid 3♣ to show a long club suit.

WEST	NORTH	**EAST**	SOUTH
1♠	Pass	3♠	Pass
4♣	Pass	?	

In this situation, West's 4♣ rebid isn't Gerber, since it didn't follow a natural notrump bid. To ask for aces, West could use Blackwood. The 4♣ bid in this situation is usually used as a control-showing cuebid, which will be discussed in a later chapter.

WEST	NORTH	EAST	SOUTH
1♠	Pass	2♥	Pass
3NT	Pass	4♣	Pass
?			

Following the guideline, East's 4♣ bid would be natural — showing clubs — rather than Gerber. Some partnerships would treat East's 4♣ bid as Gerber, but it's not the standard practice.

One common exception to the guideline occurs after the Stayman convention has been used:

WEST	NORTH	EAST	SOUTH
1NT	Pass	2♣	Pass
2♠	Pass	4♣	Pass
?			

Most players would interpret East's 4♣ bid as Gerber in this sequence. This is because East has no other way to agree on spades as trump and then ask for aces. A raise to 3♠ would be invitational, and a raise to 4♠ would be a signoff. A bid of 4NT at this point would be treated as a quantitative raise — East might want to use Stayman to look for a fit in hearts, and having failed to find one, might now want to make a slam-invitational raise.

Handling Interference

If an opponent doubles the 4♣ Gerber bid, most partnerships ignore the double and make the standard response to the convention. If an opponent makes an overcall over the 4♣ bid, it's no longer possible to use the standard responses. Most partnerships fall back on the same methods used when an opponent interferes over the Blackwood convention. The partnership can use DOPI: Double is O (zero) aces, Pass is I (one) ace.

This is a short form for the following scheme:

- Double shows no aces.
- Pass shows one ace.
- The cheapest bid shows two aces.
- The next cheapest bid shows three aces, and so on.

For example:

West	WEST	NORTH	EAST	SOUTH	East
♠ A Q J 5	1NT	Pass	4♣	4♦	♠ K 3
♥ A J 9 3	4♥	Pass	6♣	Pass	♥ K Q 5
♦ J 6	Pass	Pass			♦ 9
♣ Q 9 3					♣ A K J 10 8 4 2

After South's interference, West makes the next cheapest bid, 4♥, to show two aces. That's all East needs to know to bid the slam.

SUMMARY

After a trump suit has been agreed upon by the partnership, a bid of 4NT is the Blackwood convention asking partner how many aces partner holds. If the partnership holds all of the aces, a subsequent bid of 5NT asks partner how many kings partner holds.

Responses to Blackwood

Responding to 4NT:

5♣	No aces or all four aces.
5♦	One ace.
5♥	Two aces.
5♠	Three aces.

Responding to 5NT:

6♣	No kings.
6♦	One king.
6♥	Two kings.
6♠	Three kings.
6NT	Four kings.

Responding to Blackwood with a Void

- With no aces, respond 5♣ (don't show the void).

- With one ace and a useful void, jump to the six level in the void suit, if it ranks lower than the agreed trump suit; otherwise, jump to the six level in the agreed trump suit.

- With two aces and a useful void, bid 5NT (partner will have to determine which is the void suit).

Stopping in 5NT after Using Blackwood

After bidding 4NT and hearing partner's response, the bid of a suit at the five level, which can't be meant as a trump suit, asks partner to bid 5NT.

Handling Interference after 4NT

If Blackwood is doubled, ignore the double when making responses.

If an opponent overcalls after a 4NT bid, use DOPI:

- Double shows no aces.
- Pass shows one ace.
- The cheapest bid shows two aces.
- The next cheapest bid shows three aces.

After an opening bid of 1NT or 2NT or a natural response of 1NT or 2NT, a jump to 4♣ is the Gerber convention, asking partner how many aces partner holds. If the partnership holds all of the aces, a subsequent bid of 5♣ asks partner how many kings partner holds.

Responses to Gerber

Responding to 4♣:

4♦	No aces or all four aces.
4♥	One ace.
4♠	Two aces.
4NT	Three aces.

Responding to 5♣:

5♦	No kings.
5♥	One king.
5♠	Two kings.
5NT	Three kings.
6♣	Four kings.

Interference by the opponents over Gerber is handled in the same manner as interference over Blackwood.

NOTE: See the Appendix (pages 356–357) for a discussion of these supplemental conventions and/or treatments.

Key Card Blackwood
Roman Key Card Blackwood

Note: The following exercises illustrate the methods outlined in the summary.

Exercise One — Responding to Blackwood

What call does East make with each of the following hands after the auction goes as shown?

1)

WEST	NORTH	**EAST**	SOUTH
1♥	Pass	3♥	Pass
4NT	Pass	?	

♠ K 8 3
♥ A J 10 5
♦ Q 10 7 4
♣ J 8

2)

WEST	NORTH	**EAST**	SOUTH
	Pass	1NT	Pass
4NT	Pass	?	

♠ A Q J 5
♥ K 10 7
♦ A 10 9
♣ K 6 3

3)

WEST	NORTH	**EAST**	SOUTH
		1♦	Pass
1♠	Pass	2♠	Pass
4NT	Pass	5♦	Pass
5NT	Pass	?	

♠ A 9 6 3
♥ K 7 5
♦ K Q 10 3
♣ J 2

4)

WEST	NORTH	**EAST**	SOUTH
1♦	Pass	1♠	Pass
3♠	Pass	4NT	Pass
5♦	Pass	?	

♠ K Q 9 8 4
♥ 3
♦ K 4
♣ A K J 8 2

5)

WEST	NORTH	**EAST**	SOUTH
1♠	Pass	2♦	Pass
3♦	Pass	4NT	Pass
5♦	Pass	?	

♠ 4
♥ A K 10
♦ K J 9 8 7 3
♣ A K 3

Exercise One *Answer* — Responding to Blackwood

1) 5♦. This response shows one ace.

2) 6NT. West's 4NT bid is quantitative (invitational). With a maximum for the 1NT opening bid, East accepts West's invitational raise.

3) 6♥. After East shows the number of aces in response to 4NT, West asks for the number of kings. The 6♥ response shows two kings.

4) 5♠. Two aces are missing, so East signs off at the five level in the agreed trump suit.

5) 6♦. Only one ace is missing, so East bids slam in the agreed trump suit.

Exercise Two — Blackwood and Voids

What call does East make with each of the following hands after the auction goes as shown?

1)

WEST	NORTH	**EAST**	SOUTH
	Pass	1♣	Pass
1♥	Pass	4♥	Pass
4NT	Pass	?	

♠ K 10 7 4
♥ K J 8 5
♦ —
♣ A K J 8 3

2)

WEST	NORTH	**EAST**	SOUTH
	1♦	Pass	Pass
1♥	Pass	4♥	Pass
4NT	Pass	?	

♠ —
♥ A J 9 6
♦ K Q 9 4 3
♣ K Q 8 6

3)

WEST	NORTH	**EAST**	SOUTH
1♣	Pass	1♥	Pass
1♠	Pass	3♠	Pass
4NT	Pass	?	

♠ A 7 6 3
♥ Q 10 8 7 2
♦ 10 9 7 3
♣ —

4)

WEST	NORTH	**EAST**	SOUTH
1♦	Pass	1♥	Pass
3♥	Pass	4NT	Pass
6♥	Pass	?	

♠ K 10 2
♥ A K J 8 7 5
♦ A
♣ K Q 6

5)

WEST	NORTH	**EAST**	SOUTH
		1♣	1♦
1♥	4♦	4♥	Pass
4NT	Pass	?	

♠ A 10 7 4
♥ Q J 8 3
♦ —
♣ A Q J 7 4

Exercise Two Answer — Blackwood and Voids

1) 6♦. The jump to 6♦ shows exactly one ace and a diamond void.

2) 6♥. The jump to the six level in the agreed trump suit shows one ace and a higher-ranking void. In this situation, West will know the void is in spades.

3) 5♦. Simply show one ace. The club void isn't likely to be useful, since clubs is one of West's suits.

4) 7♥. West's response has shown one ace and a higher-ranking void. West must hold the ♣A and a void in spades. There shouldn't be any losers in a 7♥ contract, since the spade losers can be ruffed in the dummy.

5) 5NT. This response shows two aces and a void. That may be enough for West to go for a grand slam.

Exercise Three — Using Blackwood

What call does East make with each of the following hands after the auction goes as shown?

1)

WEST	NORTH	EAST	SOUTH
		1♥	Pass
2♣	Pass	3♣	Pass
4NT	Pass	5♦	Pass
5♠	Pass	?	

♠ 3 2
♥ K Q 9 8 5
♦ A Q
♣ Q 10 7 6

2)

WEST	NORTH	EAST	SOUTH
1♥	Pass	3♥	4♦
4NT	5♦	?	

♠ J 8 3
♥ K J 8 3
♦ 9 4
♣ A Q 8 3

3)

WEST	NORTH	EAST	SOUTH
		2♣	Pass
2♦	Pass	2♥	Pass
3♥	Pass	4NT	Pass
5♦	Pass	?	

♠ A 9
♥ A K Q 9 6 3
♦ K Q J 3
♣ A

4)

WEST	NORTH	EAST	SOUTH
1♣	1♥	1♠	4♥
4♠	Pass	4NT	5♥
5♠	Pass	?	

♠ K Q 10 8 7 3
♥ 6
♦ A K J 4
♣ K 9

5)

WEST	NORTH	EAST	SOUTH
1♥	Pass	3♣	Pass
4♣	Pass	4NT	Pass
5♦	Pass	?	

♠ K 4
♥ K 3
♦ K 6
♣ A K J 10 9 7 4

Exercise Three *Answer* — Using Blackwood

1) 5NT. West's 5♠ bid can't be a suggestion to play with that suit as trump. It is a request for East to bid 5NT. West can then pass to allow the partnership to play in 5NT.

2) Pass. When the opponents interfere over Blackwood, pass shows one ace when playing DOPI.

3) 5NT. The partnership has all of the aces, so a grand slam is possible. East bids 5NT to ask about the number of kings West holds. If West holds one king, East should be able to take 13 tricks; if not, East will settle for a small slam.

4) 6♠. Playing DOPI, West's 5♠ bid shows two aces. Pass would show none; double would show one; the first available step would show two.

5) 5♠. The partnership is missing two aces, and it's too late to stop in 5♣. East bids 5♠, a suit that can't be a possible trump suit in light of the previous auction. This asks West to bid 5NT, which East will pass.

Exercise Four — The Gerber Convention

What call does East make with each of the following hands after the auction goes as shown?

1)

WEST	NORTH	**EAST**	SOUTH
1NT	Pass	?	

♠ A 5
♥ 3
♦ K Q J 8 7 6 3
♣ K Q 6

2)

WEST	NORTH	**EAST**	SOUTH
		2NT	Pass
4♣	Pass	?	

♠ K J 8
♥ A Q 8 7
♦ K Q 6 2
♣ A J

3)

WEST	NORTH	**EAST**	SOUTH
	Pass	1NT	Pass
2♣	Pass	2♠	Pass
4♣	Pass	?	

♠ Q J 8 4
♥ A 8
♦ A 10 7 5
♣ A J 3

4)

WEST	NORTH	**EAST**	SOUTH
		1♠	Pass
2♦	Pass	3NT	Pass
4♣	Pass	?	

♠ K J 9 6 2
♥ A Q
♦ Q J 3
♣ K Q 10

5)

WEST	NORTH	**EAST**	SOUTH
1NT	Pass	2♣	Pass
2♥	Pass	?	

♠ A K 7 4
♥ K Q 8 3
♦ K J 10 2
♣ 5

Exercise Four *Answer* — The Gerber Convention

1) 4♣ (Gerber). The partnership should have enough combined strength for a slam contract, if it holds enough first-round controls. East uses the Gerber convention to ask for the number of aces West holds.

2) 4♠. This response shows two aces. 4♦ would show none; 4♥ would show one.

3) 4NT. This response shows three aces.

4) 4♦. East gives preference to diamonds. West's 4♣ isn't Gerber because it wasn't a jump after a natural 1NT or 2NT bid.

5) 4♣ (Gerber). Use the Gerber convention to ask for aces. 4NT would be quantitative.

Bid and Play — Using Blackwood

(E–Z Deal Cards: #5, Deal 1 — Dealer, North)

Suggested Bidding

WEST	NORTH	EAST	SOUTH
	1♣	Pass	1♥/2♥
Pass	3♥	Pass	4NT
Pass	6♥	Pass	7♥
Pass	Pass	Pass	

North opens the bidding in the longest suit, and East passes. With 19 high-card points and a six-card suit, South knows the partnership is in the slam range. The first priority, however, is to find a trump fit. South could make a jump shift into 2♥, but a response of 1♥ is forcing and leaves more room to explore for the best strain.

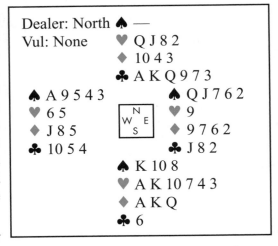

Dealer: North ♠ —
Vul: None ♥ Q J 8 2
♦ 10 4 3
♣ A K Q 9 7 3

♠ A 9 5 4 3   ♠ Q J 7 6 2
♥ 6 5   ♥ 9
♦ J 8 5   ♦ 9 7 6 2
♣ 10 5 4   ♣ J 8 2

♠ K 10 8
♥ A K 10 7 4 3
♦ A K Q
♣ 6

Assuming South bids only 1♥ and West passes, North's hand can be revalued in support of hearts. Counting 12 high-card points plus 5 dummy points for the spade void, the hand is worth 17 points, enough for a jump raise to 3♥.

Once the partnership has agreed upon the trump suit, South can use Blackwood to check for the number of aces. South doesn't want to be in a slam if two aces are missing. If the partnership is missing one ace, a small slam is the best spot. If North has two aces, South can investigate a grand slam.

North has one ace and a potentially useful void in spades. North shows this by jumping to 6♥ — showing one ace and a higher-ranking void. If South interprets this correctly, South will know that North holds the ♣A and a spade void. That should be enough for a grand slam. South will be able to ruff the spade losers with dummy's trumps. Trusting North, South bids 7 ♥.

Suggested Opening Lead

West is on lead against 7 ♥. If North–South have not already supplied an explanation of the auction, West can ask for one. West is probably aware that the ♠ A will be ruffed, but might lead it anyway. It's always possible that the opponents have had a misunderstanding. If the ♠ A is ruffed, it's unlikely to matter. East–West probably don't have much else, if the opponents have bid a grand slam.

Suggested Play

West should have little difficulty taking all of the tricks in a heart contract. Any spade losers can be ruffed in dummy or discarded on the extra club winners in dummy.

Suggested Defense

There's nothing East–West can do to prevent declarer from taking 13 tricks in a heart contract.

Hand Variation of Deal 1 — Blackwood and a Void

Instructions

To construct this variation of the previous deal, do the following:

- From the North hand, take the ♦ 10, ♦ 4 and ♦ 3 and give them to East.
- From the East hand, take the ♠ 7, ♠ 6 and ♠ 2 and give them to North.

Suggested Bidding

WEST	NORTH	EAST	SOUTH
	1 ♣	Pass	1 ♥ /2 ♥
Pass	3 ♥	Pass	4NT
Pass	6 ♦	Pass	6 ♥
Pass	Pass	Pass	

North has one ace and a potentially useful void in diamonds. North can show this by jumping to 6 ♦ — showing one ace and a void in diamonds. South now knows that the partnership is missing either the ♠ A or the ♣ A. South settles for a small slam in hearts by bidding 6 ♥. North accepts South's decision.

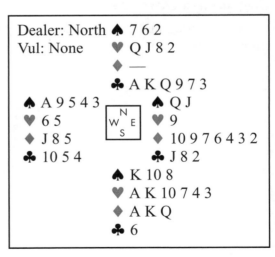

Dealer: North ♠ 7 6 2
Vul: None   ♥ Q J 8 2
               ♦ —
               ♣ A K Q 9 7 3
♠ A 9 5 4 3   ♠ Q J
♥ 6 5   ♥ 9
♦ J 8 5   ♦ 10 9 7 6 4 3 2
♣ 10 5 4   ♣ J 8 2
               ♠ K 10 8
               ♥ A K 10 7 4 3
               ♦ A K Q
               ♣ 6

Suggested Opening Lead

West is on lead against 6 ♥. West has to decide whether to lead the ♠ A or pick another suit. Some players always lead an ace against a slam contract. A better approach is to listen to the auction before deciding what to lead. On this auction, the opponents have bid very strongly, so it's quite likely they can take 12 or all 13 tricks. Leading the ♠ A is probably the best chance for the defense. It's possible, though unlikely, that the opponents have bid to slam missing both the ♠ A and ♠ K. A more likely possibility is that East started with a singleton spade. West may be able to give East a ruff by leading the ♠ A and a second round of spades.

Suggested Play

South should have little difficulty making the slam, whether or not West leads the ♠ A. If West doesn't lead the ♠ A, declarer can take all 13 tricks by discarding dummy's spades on the ♦ A K Q and then ruffing spade losers in dummy or discarding them on dummy's extra club winners.

Suggested Defense

There's nothing East–West can do to prevent declarer from taking 12 tricks in a heart contract. The ♠ A turns out to be the best lead. Otherwise, declarer can take all 13 tricks.

Bid and Play — Signing Off with Blackwood

(E–Z Deal Cards: #5, Deal 2 — Dealer, East)

Suggested Bidding

WEST	NORTH	EAST	SOUTH
		1♣	Pass
3♣	Pass	4NT	Pass
5♦	Pass	5♥	Pass
5NT	Pass	Pass	Pass

East isn't quite strong enough for a conventional (artificial) 2♣ opening and starts the auction with 1♣, planning to show the extra strength later. South passes, and West makes a limit raise of 3♣ with 11 high-card points and five-card support.

East can visualize a slam if West holds two aces, so East jumps to 4NT, the Blackwood convention.

```
Dealer: East    ♠ 10 5 2
Vul: N–S        ♥ Q J 8 4 2
                ♦ J 10 5 3 2
                ♣ —
     ♠ J 8 4              ♠ A K Q
     ♥ 7 3          N     ♥ K 9
     ♦ K Q 6      W   E   ♦ 8
     ♣ A J 10 6 2    S    ♣ K Q 9 8 5 4 3
                ♠ 9 7 6 3
                ♥ A 10 6 5
                ♦ A 9 7 4
                ♣ 7
```

West's 5♦ response shows one ace. East knows the partnership can't make a slam.

Unfortunately, West's 5♦ response puts the partnership beyond the safe resting spot of 5♣. East can't bid 5NT, since that would ask for the number of kings. Instead, East bids 5♥, a suit in which the partnership can't possibly want to play. This asks West to bid 5NT. When West bids 5NT, East passes. 5NT may not be a safe contract, but it may have a chance. East can expect West to hold some strength in diamonds, since there isn't room for much else if West has enough strength for a limit raise. Since two aces are missing, 6♣ would have no chance.

Suggested Opening Lead

South is on lead and has a difficult choice. The usual lead against a notrump contract would be the ♥5, fourth highest from the stronger of the four-card suits. From the auction, South has a clue that North doesn't have much, because East–West were trying to get to slam. South might prefer the safer lead of a spade, hoping to give nothing away and to make declarer do all of the work to take 11 tricks.

Suggested Play

The 5NT contract is a challenge. If South leads a heart, East will have an easy time. East can win the ♥K and then quickly take seven club tricks and three spade tricks to make the contract.

If South leads a spade, declarer has to find an 11th trick. The best choice is to lead a diamond, hoping South has the ♦A. If North has the ♦A, declarer will have to hope that North also holds the ♥A. Otherwise, the contract will be defeated by several tricks. North could return a heart, trapping East's ♥K. On the actual layout, East is safe. South holds both aces and can't prevent declarer from taking 11 tricks — three spades, one diamond and seven clubs. A lucky escape for East–West.

Suggested Defense

Due to the unfortunate location of the ♦A, the defenders can't do anything to prevent declarer from taking 11 tricks.

Bid and Play — Blackwood, DOPI AND DEPO

(E–Z Deal Cards: #5, Deal 3 — Dealer, South)

Suggested Bidding

WEST	NORTH	EAST	SOUTH
			Pass
1♠	3♥/4♥	4NT	5♥
5♠	Pass	7♠	Pass
Pass	Pass		

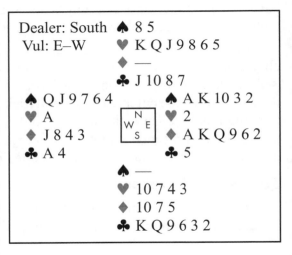

Dealer: South ♠ 8 5
Vul: E–W ♥ K Q J 9 8 6 5
♦ —
♣ J 10 8 7

♠ Q J 9 7 6 4   ♠ A K 10 3 2
♥ A   ♥ 2
♦ J 8 4 3   ♦ A K Q 9 6 2
♣ A 4   ♣ 5

♠ —
♥ 10 7 4 3
♦ 10 7 5
♣ K Q 9 6 3 2

South doesn't have the right type of hand to open the bidding. South can't open a weak two-bid when the six-card suit is clubs, and with a void and side four-card major, it would be a bit off-center to open 3♣. West's hand is too strong for a weak two-bid in spades, so West starts with 1♠. With a good seven-card suit, North can make a weak jump overcall to 3♥. North is unlikely to be defeated more than two tricks considering the nice side-suit holding in clubs. Some players might even venture 4♥ with the North hand.

With an excellent fit for spades and a good hand, East uses Blackwood to ask how many aces West holds. By inference, the jump to 4NT agrees on spades as the trump suit. East doesn't want to show the diamond suit or do something else, because the opportunity to use Blackwood may not be there when the bidding comes back around. There should be no losers in spades or diamonds, so a small or grand slam will hinge on the number of aces held by West.

With an excellent fit for North's hearts — North is showing seven of them — South should take some action over the 4NT bid to make the auction more difficult for the opponents. With such a good distributional hand, South might even envision the partnership making a 5 ♥ contract, if North is short in diamonds. South should bid at least 5 ♥. An adventuresome South might jump to 6 ♥ to put more pressure on East–West.

If South does bid 5 ♥, West can bid 5 ♠ to show two aces in response to Blackwood. Playing the DOPI convention, a double would show no aces, a pass would show one ace and the next available step, 5 ♠, would show two aces. If South jumps to 6 ♥, West could double to show an even number of aces, if the partnership is using DEPO — double even, pass odd. East now would have to guess whether West held no aces (highly unlikely) or two aces (most likely). If South chooses to bid 5 ♣ rather than 5 ♥, West would bid 5 ♦ to show two aces when playing the DOPI convention.

Over West's 5 ♠ bid, North should pass, having already described the hand with the preemptive jump overcall. Assuming East trusts West's 5 ♠ bid to be the DOPI conventional response, East can now jump to 7 ♠. The partnership should have no losers. Even if West doesn't hold the ♠Q, the partnership has at least a ten-card fit which should be good enough. A jump to 7NT would be possible, but could lead to disaster if West is short in diamonds and there are diamond losers. Getting to a grand slam in spades over the opponents' interference should be good enough.

Suggested Opening Lead

North is on lead and will probably start with the ♥ K, although this probably won't develop a trick for the defense. East–West are unlikely to bid a grand slam in spades without the ♥ A, so North might consider leading a club. It's always possible that the opponents have had a misunderstanding and are missing an ace. That's a little unlikely, since South might have made a Lightner double asking for an unusual lead holding a minor-suit ace or a void. North's opening lead won't make much difference.

Suggested Play

There's nothing to the play. Declarer can draw trumps and claim all of the tricks.

Suggested Defense

North–South can't prevent East–West from making a grand slam. The best North–South can do is to throw up interference and hope that East–West land in the wrong contract.

North–South will do very well if allowed to play in a heart contract, even if they are doubled. They are unlikely to lose more than two tricks — the ♣A and the ♥A — since East–West don't figure to find their club ruff.

Bid and Play — Gerber Over Notrump

(E–Z Deal Cards: #5, Deal 4 — Dealer, West)

Suggested Bidding

WEST	NORTH	EAST	SOUTH
Pass	1NT	Pass	4♣
Pass	4♠	Pass	5♣
Pass	5NT	Pass	7NT
Pass	Pass	Pass	

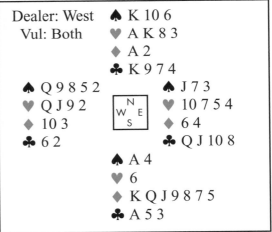

With a balanced hand and 17 high-card points, North opens 1NT. East passes. South can visualize a slam if the partnership isn't missing two aces. South uses Gerber, a jump to 4♣, to ask for the number of aces. A jump to 4NT would be a quantitative (invitational) jump and not the Blackwood convention.

Dealer: West ♠ K 10 6
Vul: Both ♥ A K 8 3
♦ A 2
♣ K 9 7 4

♠ Q 9 8 5 2   ♠ J 7 3
♥ Q J 9 2   ♥ 10 7 5 4
♦ 10 3   ♦ 6 4
♣ 6 2   ♣ Q J 10 8

♠ A 4
♥ 6
♦ K Q J 9 8 7 5
♣ A 5 3

After West's pass, North bids 4♠, the third step, to show two aces — 4♦, the first step, would show no aces or all four aces; 4♥ would show one ace.

South now knows the partnership holds all of the aces and can try for bigger things by bidding 5♣ to ask for the number of kings. North responds 5NT, the fourth step, to show three kings — 5♦ would show no kings; 5♥ would show one king; 5♠ would show two kings; and 6♣ would show all four kings.

South can now be certain that the partnership has all 13 of the tricks: the ♠A and ♠K, the ♥A and ♥K, seven diamond tricks and the ♣A and ♣K. South can bid a grand slam. Although South was originally planning to play the contract with diamonds as the trump suit, South might as well bid the slam in notrump. That contract is worth more than 7♦ and is slightly safer — no possibility of the opponents getting a ruff on the first trick.

Suggested Opening Lead

East is on lead and would start with the ♣Q, top of a sequence.

Suggested Play

There isn't much to the play. North has 13 sure tricks: two spades, two hearts, seven diamonds and two clubs.

Suggested Defense

If North–South reach 7NT, East–West will just have to wait for the next deal.

CHAPTER 6
Finding Key Cards

FINDING KEY CARDS

The most well-known conventions for slam bidding are the Blackwood and Gerber conventions discussed in the previous chapter. These conventions uncover the number of aces and kings held by the partnership. When it comes to looking for specific controls, including singletons and voids, a different approach is required.

When Blackwood Isn't Enough

Suppose West has the following hand:

♠ A K 9 7 5 4
♥ 8 2
♦ K Q
♣ A K 7

The bidding starts like this:

WEST	NORTH	EAST	SOUTH
1♠	Pass	3♠	Pass
?			

East's jump to 3♠ is a limit raise, showing 11 or 12* points and at least four-card support for spades. It appears timid to settle for game, when partner could easily hold the right cards to make a slam. On the other hand, you don't want to jump to 6♠ and watch the defenders take the first two tricks with the ♥A and the ♦A or the ♥A and the ♥K.

At first glance, it appears that Blackwood would solve the problem, since that will tell how many aces East holds. If East shows no aces, West stops safely at the five level. With two aces, a slam contract is reasonable. What if East shows only one ace? Now there's a dilemma. The success of a slam depends on which ace it is.

Suppose the auction continues like this:

WEST	NORTH	EAST	SOUTH
1♠	Pass	3♠	Pass
4NT	Pass	5♦	Pass
?			

*Assuming that the partnership has agreed that opener might have a 12 point hand.

The partnership might have either of these combined hands:

1) West	East
♠ A K 9 7 5 4	♠ Q 10 6 3
♥ 8 2	♥ A Q 5
♦ K Q	♦ 8 2
♣ A K 7	♣ Q J 6 2

2) West	East
♠ A K 9 7 5 4	♠ Q 10 6 3
♥ 8 2	♥ Q 5 3
♦ K Q	♦ A 8
♣ A K 7	♣ Q J 6 2

6♠ is an excellent contract with the first East hand, since the defenders can take only one trick, the ♦ A. 6♠ is not a successful contract with the second East hand, since the defenders can take the first two tricks with the ♥ A and the ♥ K.

Blackwood, therefore, won't always give the relevant information. The response tells how many aces the partnership holds, but it won't always tell which aces the partnership holds. The principal use of the Blackwood convention is to keep the partnership out of slam when too many aces are missing.

CUEBIDDING FIRST-ROUND CONTROLS

When information is needed about specific aces, cuebidding is the accepted method.

Cuebidding Aces

The way cuebidding works when looking for a slam is that, instead of asking how many aces partner holds, it shows partner an ace. Partner can then show another specific ace, and so on.

How does partner know when the bid is a cuebid and when it is simply a new suit being bid? It's not always easy to tell.

A general guideline is the following:

> When the partnership is already committed to a game contract, the bid of a suit in which the partnership can't want to play is a cuebid, showing interest in reaching a slam contract.

Look at this auction:

WEST	NORTH	**EAST**	SOUTH
1♠	Pass	3♠	Pass
4♣	Pass	?	

The partnership has already agreed on spades as the trump suit, so West's 4♣ bid can't be suggesting that the partnership play with clubs as trump. West's 4♣ bid also commits the partnership to at least the game level. If West wanted to stop in partscore, West would have passed the 3♠ response. West's 4♣ bid, therefore, is a cuebid. The 4♣ bid also shows interest in reaching a slam contract, since West could simply bid 4♠ with no interest in going beyond game.

What does East do after West starts cuebidding? With no interest in slam, East can simply retreat to the agreed trump suit by bidding 4♠. With enough for a slam, East could jump to 6♠ or use the Blackwood convention to find out exactly how many aces West holds. Most of the time, however, East will cuebid an ace in return, leaving the next decision to West.

Let's see how this might work with the earlier hands:

West	WEST	NORTH	EAST	SOUTH	East
♠ A K 9 7 5 4	1♠	Pass	3♠	Pass	♠ Q 10 6 3
♥ 8 2	4♣	Pass	4♥	Pass	♥ A Q 5
♦ K Q	6♠	Pass	Pass	Pass	♦ 8 2
♣ A K 7					♣ Q J 6 2

After East makes a limit raise, West cuebids the ♣A, showing interest in slam. Uncertain about whether or not there is a slam, East cuebids the ♥A. That's what West wanted to hear, so West has all of the information needed to bid the slam.

West	WEST	NORTH	EAST	SOUTH	East
♠ A K 9 7 5 4	1♠	Pass	3♠	Pass	♠ Q 10 6 3
♥ 8 2	4♣	Pass	4♦	Pass	♥ Q 5 3
♦ K Q	4♠	Pass	Pass	Pass	♦ A 8
♣ A K 7					♣ Q J 6 2

The auction starts the same way, but after West's 4♣ cuebid, East cuebids 4 ♦, showing the ♦ A. This isn't what West wanted to hear about, so West goes back to the agreed trump suit and the partnership stops safely at the game level.

It's important to note that West's 4♠ bid isn't a cuebid. The partnership must be able to stop in the agreed trump suit. More on this later.

What if East didn't hold any aces?

West	WEST	NORTH	EAST	SOUTH	East
♠ A K 9 7 5 4	1♠	Pass	3♠	Pass	♠ Q 10 6 3
♥ 8 2	4♣	Pass	4♠	Pass	♥ K Q 3
♦ K Q	Pass	Pass			♦ J 8
♣ A K 7					♣ Q J 6 2

After West cuebids 4♣, East doesn't have an ace to cuebid and simply goes back to the agreed trump suit. West now knows that the partnership is missing two aces and is happy to settle for a game contract. Again, West's 4♠ bid isn't a cuebid of the ♠ A but a sign-off in the agreed trump suit.

And what if East held both aces?

West	WEST	NORTH	EAST	SOUTH	East
♠ A K 9 7 5 4	1♠	Pass	3♠	Pass	♠ Q 10 6 3
♥ 8 2	4♣	Pass	4♦	Pass	♥ A J 3
♦ K Q	4♠	Pass	5♥	Pass	♦ A 8 3
♣ A K 7	6♠	Pass	Pass	Pass	♣ 10 6 2

The auction starts the same way, with East making a limit raise and West cuebidding 4♣ to show slam interest and the ♣ A. With two aces, East starts by showing the ♦ A. That's not the ace West wanted to hear about, so West retreats to 4 ♠. East now shows the second ace by bidding 5 ♥. That is what West wanted to know to confidently bid the slam.

This last set of hands brings up an important point:

> With a choice of cuebids, it is best to make the cheapest available cuebid first.

Holding both the ♦ A and ♥ A, East made the cheaper available cuebid, 4 ♦. That didn't deny holding the ♥ A, it simply showed the ♦ A. If East had bid 4♥, however, it would have shown the ♥ A, but would have denied the ♦ A.

Cuebidding a Void

In a trump contract, a void can be as effective as an ace, since it controls the first round of a suit. The opponents can't take the first trick in a suit in which declarer has either the ace or a void. Cuebid a void as though it were an ace.

Consider the following auctions:

West	WEST	NORTH	EAST	SOUTH	East
♠ A K 9 7 5 4	1♠	Pass	3♠	Pass	♠ Q 10 6 3
♥ K 8 2	4♣	Pass	4♥	Pass	♥ A Q 5
♦ K Q J 5	6♠	Pass	Pass	Pass	♦ 8 2
♣ —					♣ Q J 6 2

After East makes a limit raise, West cuebids 4♣ to show first-round control of clubs. East doesn't know that West has a void and not the ♣A, but that doesn't make much difference. East cooperates by cuebidding the ♥A, and that's enough for West to bid the slam contract. West knows there can't be a grand slam, since East bypassed 4♦, denying a first-round control in diamonds.

The Blackwood convention wouldn't have been effective in this auction. If West bid 4NT instead of cuebidding 4♣, East would have shown one ace. West wouldn't know whether to bid a slam, since East might hold the ♣A instead of the ♥A, and the defenders could take the first two tricks.

What if East held the ♣A?

West	WEST	NORTH	EAST	SOUTH	East
♠ A K 9 7 5 4	1♠	Pass	3♠	Pass	♠ Q 10 6 3
♥ K 8 2	4♣	Pass	4♠	Pass	♥ Q 6 5
♦ K Q J 5	Pass	Pass			♦ 8 2
♣ —					♣ A Q J 2

Holding the ♣A, East will be a little surprised to hear West cuebid 4♣, showing first-round control in clubs. East infers that West holds a void, so the ♣A is essentially a wasted high card. East doesn't have the ♦A or ♥A to cuebid, so East signs off in the agreed trump suit, and the partnership stops safely at the game level. East doesn't bother bidding 5♣ to show the ♣A, since East knows that card is a redundant feature.

Either player may cuebid a void.

West	WEST	NORTH	EAST	SOUTH	East
♠ A K 9 7 5 4	1♠	Pass	3♠	Pass	♠ Q 10 6 3
♥ K 7 2	4♣	Pass	4♥	Pass	♥ —
♦ K Q 5	6♠	Pass	Pass	Pass	♦ J 8 6 2
♣ A					♣ K 10 7 5 2

East holds only 6 high-card points, but counts the heart void as 5 dummy points, making the hand strong enough for a limit raise. With slam aspirations, West cuebids 4♣, and East cooperates by cuebidding 4♥, showing first-round control of hearts. West assumes that East holds the ♥A, but not the ♦A, and determines that slam should be a reasonable gamble. West won't be disappointed to discover that East has a heart void instead of the ace. That may even be better, since West can now ruff any heart losers in dummy. The partnership reaches an excellent slam contract with only 25 combined high-card points.

Finding the Ace of Trump

The partnership bids only controls outside of the trump suit. A bid of the trump suit isn't a cuebid; it simply shows nothing further to add at that point in the auction. How does the partnership find the trump ace? Most of the time, the Blackwood convention would be used once the needed information is uncovered through cuebidding.

West	WEST	NORTH	EAST	SOUTH	East
♠ K Q 9 7 5 4	1♠	Pass	3♠	Pass	♠ A 10 6 3
♥ 7 2	4♣	Pass	4♥	Pass	♥ A 8 5
♦ K Q J 4	4NT	Pass	5♥	Pass	♦ 10 2
♣ A	6♠	Pass	Pass	Pass	♣ K 8 6 2

West doesn't want to use the Blackwood convention right away. Even if East holds two aces, the defenders might be able to take the first two heart tricks if East holds the ♠A and the ♦A. West starts by cuebidding the ♣A. East cooperates by showing the ♥A. West knows that East doesn't have the ♦A, since East skipped over diamonds, but slam should have a reasonable chance if East holds the ♠A as well as the ♥A. To discover whether East holds the ♠A, West now bids Blackwood. East shows two aces, so West knows they must be the ♠A and ♥A. West bids the slam, confident that the defenders can't take the first two heart tricks.

West	WEST	NORTH	EAST	SOUTH	East
♠ K Q 9 7 5 4	1♠	Pass	3♠	Pass	♠ J 10 6 3
♥ 7 2	4♣	Pass	4♥	Pass	♥ A 8 5
♦ K Q J 4	4NT	Pass	5♦	Pass	♦ 10 2
♣ A	5♠	Pass	Pass	Pass	♣ K Q 9 2

The auction begins as in the previous example with West showing the ♣A and East showing the ♥A. West checks for the number of aces using Blackwood and signs off at the five level, after discovering that East doesn't hold a second ace.

CUEBIDDING SECOND-ROUND CONTROLS

Cuebidding is initially used to show first-round controls — aces and voids — but can be used to show other controls as well. A king is a second-round control, since it offers protection against the defenders taking the second trick in the suit. A singleton has the same effect as a king; the opponents may be able to take the ace in that suit, but they can't take a second trick.

Cuebidding Kings and Singletons

Generally aces or voids are shown first in cuebidding sequences. If there's still some question as to the best contract, the partnership continues by showing kings or singletons. Let's look at some sample auctions to see how this might work.

West	WEST	NORTH	EAST	SOUTH	East
♠ A K Q 10 6 3	2♣	Pass	2♦	Pass	♠ J 8 5 2
♥ Q J 9	2♠	Pass	3♠	Pass	♥ K 7 6 3
♦ —	4♣	Pass	4♠	Pass	♦ Q 10 5
♣ A K Q 6	5♦	Pass	5♥	Pass	♣ 8 4
	6♠	Pass	Pass	Pass	

West, playing weak two-bids, starts with a strong artificial 2♣ opening and then shows the spade suit after East's waiting bid of 2♦. East raises to 3♠ to show support. West can't use the Blackwood convention at this point, since West won't know what to do if partner shows either one ace or no aces. Instead, West cuebids the ♣A. East doesn't have a first-round control to show and goes back to the agreed trump suit. West hasn't had enough and shows the diamond void by cuebidding 5♦. Having denied the ♥A by failing to cuebid 4♥ on the previous round, East can afford to bid 5♥, showing a second-round control in the suit, the ♥K. That's what West wanted to hear, and the partnership reaches an excellent slam.

West	WEST	NORTH	EAST	SOUTH	East
♠ A K Q 10 6 3	2♣	Pass	2♦	Pass	♠ J 8 5 2
♥ Q J 9	2♠	Pass	3♠	Pass	♥ 3
♦ —	4♣	Pass	4♠	Pass	♦ Q 10 7 5 3
♣ A K Q 6	5♦	Pass	5♥	Pass	♣ J 8 4
	6♠	Pass	Pass	Pass	

A singleton works as well as a king. On these two hands, the auction begins the same way. After agreeing on spades as the trump suit, West cuebids the ♣A. Without a first-round control to show, East returns to 4♠, the agreed upon trump suit. When West persists by showing the first-round diamond control, East can show the second-round control in hearts. That gets the partnership to an excellent slam.

West	WEST	NORTH	EAST	SOUTH	East
♠ A K Q 10 6 3	2♣	Pass	2♦	Pass	♠ 9 8 5 2
♥ Q J 9	2♠	Pass	3♠	Pass	♥ 8 6
♦ —	4♣	Pass	4♦	Pass	♦ A K 8 7
♣ A K Q 6	5♣	Pass	5♦	Pass	♣ 8 4 2
	5♠	Pass	Pass	Pass	

Cuebidding will often reveal an overabundance of values in one suit and a lack of control in another. On these two hands, the auction starts the same way as before, with West beginning a cuebidding sequence with 4♣ to show the ♣A. East shows the ♦A. This isn't useful to West, since West also has first-round control of diamonds, but West tries again by bidding 5♣, showing the ♣K. East now bids 5♦ to show the ♦K. Finally, West has to stop at 5♠, since neither partner has first- or second-round control of the heart suit. The partnership keeps out of slam, since East's ♦A K are wasted (redundant) values.

A void can serve as a first-round control and a second-round control in a suit.

Look at the next example:

West				East
♠ A K Q 10 6 3				♠ J 9 8 2
♥ Q J 9				♥ —
♦ —				♦ Q 8 6 4 3
♣ A K Q 6				♣ J 8 4 2

WEST	NORTH	EAST	SOUTH
2♣	Pass	2♦	Pass
2♠	Pass	3♠	Pass
4♣	Pass	4♥	Pass
5♦	Pass	5♥	Pass
7♠	Pass	Pass	Pass

After West cuebids the ♣A, East shows first-round control of hearts by cuebidding 4♥. West shows first-round control of diamonds by cuebidding 5♦. Having shown first-round control of hearts, East can now show second-round control of hearts by cuebidding 5♥. This is all that West needs to know to bid the grand slam.

Finding the King of Trump

The partnership can't cuebid the trump king. A bid of the agreed upon trump suit is used as the way to stop a cuebidding sequence with nothing further to say. To discover whether partner holds the trump king, the partnership usually has to fall back on the Blackwood convention — although there are other techniques which will be discussed shortly.

Here's an example:

West				East
♠ 8 4				♠ A K 6
♥ A K				♥ 7 3
♦ A 10 9 5 4 3				♦ K 8 7 6 2
♣ A K Q				♣ 7 3 2

WEST	NORTH	EAST	SOUTH
1♦	Pass	3♦	Pass
3♥	Pass	3♠	Pass
4NT	Pass	5♦	Pass
5NT	Pass	6♥	Pass
7NT	Pass	Pass	Pass

After East's jump raise, West is interested in reaching a slam. West doesn't want to use Blackwood right away because of the two low spades. If East were to show no aces, West couldn't be sure whether or not there is a slam. The partnership might be missing the ♠A and the ♠K. West starts by cuebidding. When East shows a first-round control in spades, West knows there is no danger of losing the first two spade tricks and can visualize the possibility of a grand slam. Further cuebidding might uncover the ♠K, but it wouldn't tell West whether East held the ♦K. So West simply reverts to the Blackwood convention. East's first response confirms possession of the ♠A, and East's second response shows two kings, which must be the ♠K and the ♦K. West confidently bids the grand slam in notrump instead of diamonds, because the same 13 tricks are available and the score is higher. If East had shown one king, West wouldn't know whether it was the ♠K or the ♦K, but it wouldn't matter. Whichever king is missing, the partnership should stop in 6NT. If the partnership is missing the ♠K, there would be 12 running tricks after a spade lead. If the partnership is missing the ♦K, there would be double stoppers in the other suits, so declarer would probably have time to set up the diamond suit by giving up a trick to the ♦K.

CUEBIDDING OTHER CONTROLS

Cuebidding controls requires partnership cooperation. Cuebidding takes practice, but can be more effective than using the Blackwood or Gerber conventions when the partnership is interested in specific controls, not just the number of aces and kings.

An experienced partnership at times goes further than aces and kings, finding out about a key queen or a doubleton — a third-round control. Knowledge of third-round controls is usually unnecessary. If the partnership has enough aces and kings and enough combined strength for a slam, there is usually a reasonable play for the contract.

The location of the trump queen, however, can be critical. There are some useful methods for discovering whether or not the partnership holds this card.

Trump Quality

In addition to making sure the partnership has enough controls for a slam contract, one critical area of concern is the trump suit itself. The partnership may be able to escape a loser missing the king or queen in a suit other than trumps, but avoiding losers in the trump suit itself is much more difficult.

Trump Asking Bids

The partnership could consider a slam contract in a major suit and be concerned about the quality of the trump suit. A jump or raise to five of the major suit asks partner to bid the slam with good trump support but to pass otherwise. This agreement requires good judgment from both partners. The question being asked of partner is, "In light of the auction so far, do you have better trump support than I might expect?"

Here are examples:

West	WEST	NORTH	EAST	SOUTH	East
♠ —	1♥	Pass	3♥	Pass	♠ A J 7
♥ Q 10 7 5 2	3♠	Pass	4♦	Pass	♥ J 8 4 3
♦ K Q 3	5♥	Pass	Pass	Pass	♦ A J 8 4
♣ A K Q 6 3					♣ 7 2

After East's limit raise, West has some interest in reaching a slam contract. The Blackwood convention won't be of much use; whether East shows one or two aces, West won't have any idea whether slam is a good prospect or not. Instead, West looks for specific controls by starting with a cuebid of 3♠, showing first-round control of spades. East's response of 4♦, showing first-round control of diamonds, is encouraging because it appears there are no losers outside of the trump suit. West's only concern is the trump suit itself. Blackwood will not give West the answer, so West jumps to 5♥, saying, "How good is your trump support in light of your earlier limit raise?" With poor trump support for the jump raise, East declines the invitation by passing. The partnership avoids getting to a slam missing the ace and king of the trump suit.

West	WEST	NORTH	EAST	SOUTH	East
♠ —	1♥	Pass	3♥	Pass	♠ J 7 3
♥ Q 10 7 5 2	3♠	Pass	4♦	Pass	♥ K J 8 4
♦ K Q 3	5♥	Pass	6♥	Pass	♦ A J 8 4
♣ A K Q 6 3	Pass	Pass			♣ 7 2

The auction starts the same way, but when West asks about the quality of the heart support, East accepts the invitation and bids the slam.

West		East
♠ 10 8 6 5 2		♠ J 9 7 4 3
♥ A K J		♥ 8 5
♦ —		♦ K 9 7 5 2
♣ A K Q J 5		♣ 3

WEST	NORTH	EAST	SOUTH
1♠	Pass	4♠	Pass
5♠	Pass	Pass	Pass

East makes a weak and preemptive raise to game of West's opening bid. West still feels there might be a slam, if East has good quality spades for the raise. With poor spades, East declines the invitation. With better spades, perhaps ♠ A 9 7 4 3 or ♠ K Q 7 4 3, East would accept the slam try. Notice that West isn't asking about anything except the quality of the trump suit; otherwise, West would have used Blackwood or started a cuebidding sequence.

Auctions such as these are very delicate and rely on excellent partnership cooperation and judgment. They can't be used when the agreed trump suit is a minor. For another way to find information about partner's holding in the trump suit, see *Key Card Blackwood* in the Appendix.

Grand Slam Force

Trump quality is especially important if the partnership is contemplating a grand slam. The partnership wants to make sure there are no potential losers in the trump suit. One commonly used convention to find out about honors in the trump suit was devised by Ely Culbertson in 1936, and popularized by his wife, Josephine.

The *grand slam force* works this way. When the partnership has agreed on a trump suit and is interested in reaching a grand slam:

> A bid of 5NT asks partner to bid a grand slam if holding two of the top three trump honors. Otherwise, partner signs off at the six level in the agreed trump suit.

The grand slam force can be used only if 5NT wouldn't be a natural notrump raise or part of another convention, such as Blackwood. To illustrate this, consider the following auctions:

West		East
♠ J 8 3		♠ A K Q
♥ A Q 8 5		♥ K 9 7 6 3
♦ K Q 10 7 3		♦ —
♣ 3		♣ A K Q 10 5

WEST	NORTH	EAST	SOUTH
1♦	Pass	1♥	Pass
2♥	Pass	5NT	Pass
7♥	Pass	Pass	Pass

After West raises hearts, East jumps to 5NT as the grand slam force, asking West to bid a grand slam with two of the top three honors. With the ♥A and the ♥Q, West accepts the invitation by bidding the grand slam.

West		East
♠ J 8 3		♠ A K Q
♥ Q J 8 5		♥ K 9 7 6 3
♦ A K Q 7 3		♦ —
♣ 3		♣ A K Q 10 5

WEST	NORTH	EAST	SOUTH
1♦	Pass	1♥	Pass
2♥	Pass	5NT	Pass
6♥	Pass	Pass	Pass

The auction starts the same way, but with only one of the top three honors, the ♥Q, West declines the grand slam invitation and signs off in a small slam.

West		East
♠ J 8 3		♠ A K Q
♥ A 8 4 2		♥ K 9 7 6 3
♦ A K 10 7 3		♦ —
♣ 3		♣ A K Q 10 5

WEST	NORTH	EAST	SOUTH
1♦	Pass	1♥	Pass
2♥	Pass	5NT	Pass
6♥	Pass	Pass	Pass

This is similar to the previous example, except that West holds the ♥A, instead of the ♥Q. Without two of the top three honors, West signs off in 6♥. The partnership may make a grand slam, if the missing hearts divide exactly 2–2, but that's against the odds. The partnership generally wants to avoid bidding a grand slam when there's the possibility of a trump loser. Getting the small slam bonus should be enough.

West		East
♠ K 8		♠ A 7 3
♥ A K 9 5		♥ Q J 7 6
♦ A J 7 5 3		♦ K 6
♣ 3 2		♣ A Q J 6

WEST	NORTH	EAST	SOUTH
1♦	Pass	1♥	Pass
3♥	Pass	4NT	Pass
5♥	Pass	5NT	Pass
6♥	Pass	Pass	Pass

After West's jump raise, East uses Blackwood to check for the number of aces. When West shows two aces, East's 5NT bid asks for the number of kings as a continuation of Blackwood. 5NT isn't the grand slam force. When West shows two kings, East settles for a small slam. Had West shown three kings, East would have bid the grand slam.

West		East
♠ 9		♠ A K 10 8 3
♥ 7 4 2		♥ —
♦ A K 10 8 5 3		♦ Q J 6
♣ 10 3 2		♣ A K Q 5 4

WEST	NORTH	EAST	SOUTH
2♦	Pass	5NT	Pass
7♦	Pass	Pass	Pass

After West opens with a weak two-bid in diamonds, East uses the grand slam force to find out whether or not West has the ♦ A and ♦ K. The 5NT bid suggests that the last suit mentioned is trump. With two of the top three honors, West bids the grand slam. If West held only the ♦ A or the ♦ K, the partnership would stop in a small slam. The auction is quick and efficient.

Experienced partnerships can use more complex methods for inquiring about trump honors. See Key Card Blackwood in the Appendix and Other Responses to a Grand Slam Force in the Appendix. For most partnerships, the occasional use of the basic grand slam force should be enough.

SUMMARY

To find out about the specific aces and kings held by the partnership, rather than the number of aces and kings, use cuebidding controls:

Guidelines for Cuebidding Controls

- When the partnership is already committed to a game contract, the bid of a suit, in which the partnership can't want to play, is a cuebid, showing interest in reaching a slam contract.

- Use cuebidding when the Blackwood convention won't necessarily give the information needed to decide whether the partnership belongs in a slam contract.

- First-round controls — aces and voids — are usually shown before second-round controls — kings and singletons.

- With a choice of controls to show, bid the cheapest control — the next one up the line — to leave the maximum amount of room.

- Controls are not shown in the trump suit itself. A bid of the agreed upon trump suit says there is nothing further to say at that point.

- After the partnership discovers what it needs to know through cuebidding, the Blackwood convention can be used if there is still room available.

Since controls in the trump suit cannot be shown through cuebidding, the quality of the trump fit must be determined using other methods. One common agreement is the following:

Trump Asking Bids

- A jump or raise to five of an agreed-upon major suit asks partner to bid the slam with good trump support but to pass otherwise.

Grand Slam Force

When the partnership has agreed on a trump suit and is interested in reaching a grand slam, it can use the grand slam force provided 5NT wouldn't be a natural notrump raise or part of another convention:

- A bid of 5NT asks partner to bid a grand slam holding two of the top three trump honors. Otherwise, partner signs off at the six level in the suit agreed upon as trump.

NOTE: See the Appendix (pages 357–359) for a discussion of these supplemental conventions and/or treatments.

Other Responses to a Grand Slam Force
Using the Grand Slam Force after Blackwood

Note: The following exercises illustrate the methods outlined in the summary.

Exercise One — Cuebidding First-Round Controls

What call does West make on each of the following hands after the auction has started?

1) ♠ A K 9 7 4 2
♥ 7 5
♦ K J 2
♣ A 3

WEST	NORTH	EAST	SOUTH
		1 ♦	Pass
1 ♠	Pass	3 ♠	Pass
?			

2) ♠ Q 5
♥ K 10 9 3
♦ A Q 6 2
♣ 9 7 4

WEST	NORTH	EAST	SOUTH
		1 ♥	Pass
3 ♥	Pass	3 ♠	Pass
?			

3) ♠ A K Q 7 3
♥ Q J 9 8 2
♦ —
♣ A Q 8

WEST	NORTH	EAST	SOUTH
1 ♠	Pass	3 ♠	Pass
?			

4) ♠ A K Q J
♥ A K Q 10 7 5
♦ Q 3
♣ 6

WEST	NORTH	EAST	SOUTH
2 ♣	Pass	2 ♦	Pass
2 ♥	Pass	3 ♥	Pass
3 ♠	Pass	4 ♥	Pass
?			

5) ♠ A 9 3
♥ Q J 6 5
♦ A 8 6 2
♣ 7 5

WEST	NORTH	EAST	SOUTH
	Pass	1 ♥	Pass
3 ♥	Pass	4 ♣	Pass
4 ♦	Pass	4 ♥	Pass
?			

Exercise One *Answer* — Cuebidding First-Round Controls

1) 4♣. Cuebid the ♣A. Don't use Blackwood with two low hearts.

2) 4♦. East has cuebid the ♠A. Cooperate by showing the ♦A.

3) 4♣. Cuebid the ♣A. Don't use Blackwood with a void.

4) Pass. East doesn't appear to have either the ♣A or the ♦A.

5) 4♠. East has shown interest in slam by starting a cuebidding sequence. The 4♦ cuebid didn't inspire East to go beyond the game level, but West has more to show. East may hold two or three low spades and be afraid to move beyond the game level if the partnership doesn't have a control in spades.

Exercise Two — Cuebidding Second-Round Controls

What call does West make on each of the following hands after the auction has started?

1) ♠ A J 5
    ♥ K 7 2
    ♦ K 10 8 5 3
    ♣ 8 3

WEST	NORTH	EAST	SOUTH
		1 ♦	Pass
3 ♦	Pass	3 ♥	Pass
3 ♠	Pass	4 ♣	Pass
?			

2) ♠ 9 6
    ♥ Q 8 6 3
    ♦ A K 9 4
    ♣ Q 10 5

WEST	NORTH	EAST	SOUTH
		1 ♥	Pass
3 ♥	Pass	3 ♠	Pass
4 ♦	Pass	5 ♣	Pass
?			

3) ♠ 6
    ♥ J 10 7 3
    ♦ 9 6 4 3
    ♣ A 9 5 4

WEST	NORTH	EAST	SOUTH
		2 ♣	Pass
2 ♦	Pass	2 ♥	Pass
3 ♥	Pass	3 ♠	Pass
4 ♣	Pass	4 ♦	Pass
?			

4) ♠ A K J 10 8 7 4
    ♥ Q 6
    ♦ A
    ♣ A K Q

WEST	NORTH	EAST	SOUTH
2 ♣	Pass	2 ♦	Pass
2 ♠	Pass	3 ♠	Pass
4 ♣	Pass	4 ♠	Pass
5 ♦	Pass	5 ♥	Pass
?			

5) ♠ Q 9 6 3
    ♥ 10 8 6 5
    ♦ —
    ♣ Q J 7 4 2

WEST	NORTH	EAST	SOUTH
		2 ♣	Pass
2 ♦	Pass	2 ♠	Pass
3 ♠	Pass	4 ♣	Pass
4 ♦	Pass	4 ♥	Pass
?			

Exercise Two *Answer* — Cuebidding Second-Round Controls

1) 4♥. After East's 3♥ cuebid, West showed first-round control in spades. When East continues cuebidding, West now can show a second-round control in hearts — the king. East has already shown first-round control of hearts, so there is no ambiguity when West cuebids 4♥.

2) 5♦. West has already shown first-round control of diamonds and now has an opportunity to show second-round control as well.

3) 4♠. A singleton is as good as a king when it comes to second-round controls. East has already shown first-round control of the suit; West can show second-round control.

4) 6♠. East doesn't have first-round control of hearts, since East didn't cuebid 4♥ over West's 4♣ cuebid. East is now showing second-round control of hearts — the ♥K or a singleton — so a small slam in spades should be a good contract.

5) 5♦. A void acts as both a first-round control and a second-round control of a suit. Having shown first-round control of diamonds, West now has an opportunity to show second-round control.

Exercise Three — Trump Asking Bids

What call does West make on each of the following hands after the auction has started?

1) ♠ J 10 8 7 5

WEST	NORTH	EAST	SOUTH
1♠	Pass	3♠	Pass
4♣	Pass	4♦	Pass
?			

♥ —
♦ K Q 6
♣ A K Q 10 5

2) ♠ J 8 4

WEST	NORTH	EAST	SOUTH
		1♥	Pass
3♥	Pass	3♠	Pass
4♣	Pass	5♥	Pass
?			

♥ 10 9 7 5
♦ Q 5
♣ A K J 6

3) ♠ A K J 8

WEST	NORTH	EAST	SOUTH
1♦	Pass	1♠	Pass
4♠	Pass	5♠	Pass
?			

♥ K Q
♦ K Q J 7 3
♣ 9 4

Exercise Three *Answer* — Trump Asking Bids

1) 5♠. The cuebidding sequence has revealed that East holds first-round control of diamonds. The only losers are likely to be in the spade suit. It's not necessary to show first-round control in hearts. 4♠ would be a sign-off, so jump to 5♠ to ask about trump quality. Slam will be a good proposition if partner holds something like ♠A Q x x, ♠K Q x x, or ♠A 9 x x. It won't be good if East holds ♠Q x x x or ♠K x x x. Hopefully, East will make a reasonable decision.

2) Pass. East is asking about the quality of the trump support. Since West already promised four-card support with the limit raise, the holding couldn't be much weaker. West rejects the invitation by passing.

3) 6♠. East could have used Blackwood to ask about the number of aces or started a cuebidding sequence if interested in controls outside the trump suit. East's raise to the five level asks about the quality of West's trump support. It couldn't be much better, so West accepts the invitation and bids the slam.

Exercise Four — Grand Slam Force

What call does West make on each of the following hands after the auction has started?

1) ♠ J 5
    ♥ 9 3
    ♦ A K Q 8 2
    ♣ K 8 7 3

WEST	NORTH	EAST	SOUTH
1 ♦	Pass	2 ♣	Pass
3 ♣	Pass	5NT	Pass
?			

2) ♠ A Q 9 3
    ♥ K Q 8 4 2
    ♦ J 7 3
    ♣ 8

WEST	NORTH	EAST	SOUTH
1 ♥	Pass	1 ♠	Pass
2 ♠	Pass	5NT	Pass
?			

3) ♠ —
    ♥ A 6 4
    ♦ Q 9 6 3
    ♣ A K Q 10 8 2

WEST	NORTH	EAST	SOUTH
		3 ♦	Pass
?			

4) ♠ A
    ♥ A K Q J 3
    ♦ Q 9 3
    ♣ A K 8 2

WEST	NORTH	EAST	SOUTH
2 ♣	Pass	3 ♦	Pass
?			

5) ♠ K Q 8
    ♥ A 10 5
    ♦ Q J 7 3
    ♣ K 8 2

WEST	NORTH	EAST	SOUTH
1NT	Pass	5NT	Pass
?			

Exercise Four *Answer* — Grand Slam Force

1) 6♣. West has only one of the top three honors in clubs.

2) 7♠. West has two of the top three honors in the spade suit.

3) 5NT. West uses the grand slam force to ask if East has both the ♦A and the ♦K.

4) 5NT. West uses the grand slam force to ask if East has both the ♦A and the ♦K.

5) 6NT. East's 5NT is forcing to 6NT and invites partner to bid 7NT. It isn't the grand slam force convention, although it is similar in effect. West has a minimum and signs off in a small slam.

Bid and Play — Finding Key Cards

(E–Z Deal Cards: #6, Deal 1 — Dealer, North)

Suggested Bidding

WEST	NORTH	EAST	SOUTH
	1♠	Pass	3♠
Pass	4♣	Pass	4♥
Pass	5♣	Pass	5♥
Pass	5♠	Pass	Pass
Pass			

After North's opening bid of 1♠, South makes a limit raise to 3♠. North can see a potential slam contract, if South has either first-or second-round control of diamonds. Blackwood is unlikely to do any good. If South shows no aces or one ace, North still won't know what to do.

Instead, North cuebids the ♣A, showing interest in reaching slam and first-round control of clubs. South cue-

Dealer: North   ♠ A K 10 8 5 3
Vul: None   ♥ —
                 ♦ Q J 9 6 2
                 ♣ A K

♠ J 4   ♠ 2
♥ J 10 9 7   ♥ Q 6 5 4 2
♦ K 4   N   ♦ A 10 7 5
♣ 10 8 6 5 2 W   E   ♣ J 9 4
                 S
                 ♠ Q 9 7 6
                 ♥ A K 8 3
                 ♦ 8 3
                 ♣ Q 7 3

bids the ♥A in return. This isn't what North was hoping to hear, but North makes one more try by repeating the club cuebid to show second-round control of clubs. South cooperates by bidding 5♥ to show second-round control of hearts. Neither partner, however, has shown either first-or second-round control of diamonds, so North stops in 5♠. South, having shown both controls and having nothing further to add, accepts North's decision to stop short of slam.

If North were to use the Blackwood convention, South would show one ace, and North wouldn't know whether to bid the slam. Cuebidding is the only way for the partnership to make an accurate determination of whether it belongs in a slam contract.

Suggested Opening Lead

East is on lead. With all of the cuebidding in hearts and clubs, East should probably lead the unbid suit, diamonds. East should lead the ♦ A. It would be risky to lead away from an ace against a suit contract.

Suggested Play

There's not much to the play in 5 ♠. Declarer has to lose two diamond tricks and that's all.

Suggested Defense

The defenders should get two diamond tricks, whether or not East leads diamonds initially. That will be good if North–South reach a slam contract. If North–South stop below the slam level, there's nothing the defenders can do.

Hand Variation of Deal 1 — Finding Key Cards, part 2

Instructions

To construct a variation of the previous hand, make the following changes:

From the South hand, take the ♥ A and give it to East.

From the South hand, take the ♥ K and give it to West.

From the West hand, take the ♦ K and give it to South.

From the East hand, take the ♦ A and give it to South.

Suggested Bidding

WEST	NORTH	EAST	SOUTH
	1♠	Pass	3♠
Pass	4♣	Pass	4♦
Pass	4♥	Pass	5♦
Pass	7♠	Pass	Pass
Pass			

Once again after North's opening bid of 1♠, South makes a limit raise to 3♠. North can see a potential slam contract, if South has either first-or second-round control of diamonds. Blackwood is unlikely to do any good. If South shows no aces or one ace, North still won't know what to do.

Instead, North cuebids the ♣A, showing interest in reaching slam and first-round control of clubs. This time South cuebids the ♦ A in return. North shows first-round control of hearts, the void, by cuebidding 4♥. South shows second-round control of diamonds, the ♦ K, by cuebidding 5♦.

```
Dealer: North  ♠ A K 10 8 5 3
Vul: None      ♥ —
               ♦ Q J 9 6 2
               ♣ A K
♠ J 4                      ♠ 2
♥ K J 10 9 7    N          ♥ A Q 6 5 4 2
♦ 4           W   E        ♦ 10 7 5
♣ 10 8 6 5 2    S          ♣ J 9 4
               ♠ Q 9 7 6
               ♥ 8 3
               ♦ A K 8 3
               ♣ Q 7 3
```

That's all North needs to hear to bid the grand slam. The partnership doesn't appear to have any losers in any of the suits.

The North–South hands are identical to those in the original hand, except that South's hearts and diamonds have been exchanged. Now North–South can make a grand slam. They couldn't make even a small slam on the previous deal. Only through cuebidding can the partnership successfully reach the best contract both times.

Suggested Opening Lead

East is on lead. Despite all of the cuebids, East will probably lead the ♥ A. In case North–South have had a misunderstanding, East can hope to take the first trick.

Suggested Play

There's not much to the play in 7♠. Declarer should draw trumps right away to make sure that the defenders don't get a ruff.

Suggested Defense

The defenders can't defeat the grand slam in spades. East–West's only hope is that North–South don't reach that level, or if they do, they accidentally get to 7NT!

Bid and Play — When Blackwood Won't Help

(E–Z Deal Cards: #6, Deal 2 — Dealer, East)

Suggested Bidding

WEST	NORTH	EAST	SOUTH
		2♣	Pass
2♦	Pass	2♥	Pass
3♥	Pass	3♠	Pass
4♥	Pass	5♣	Pass
5♥	Pass	Pass	Pass

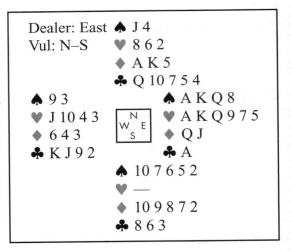

Dealer: East ♠ J 4
Vul: N–S　♥ 8 6 2
　　　　　♦ A K 5
　　　　　♣ Q 10 7 5 4

♠ 9 3　　　　　♠ A K Q 8
♥ J 10 4 3　　♥ A K Q 9 7 5
♦ 6 4 3　　　　♦ Q J
♣ K J 9 2　　　♣ A

♠ 10 7 6 5 2
♥ —
♦ 10 9 8 7 2
♣ 8 6 3

With 25 high-card points plus 2 length points for the six-card heart suit, East starts with a strong, conventional (artificial) 2♣ bid. West makes a waiting bid of 2♦, and East rebids 2♥ to show a strong two-bid. With good support and the ♣K, West raises to 3♥, leaving room for East to explore for slam.

With two potential diamond losers, East should not use Blackwood. Unless West shows an ace, East still won't know whether the partnership belongs in slam. West might have the ♦ K, and slam would be a good venture. East starts by cuebidding 3♠. Without an ace to cuebid, West signs off in 4♥. East makes one more try by cuebidding 5♣, still hoping West has something in diamonds. With three low diamonds, West signs off again in 5♥. Now East has nothing further to say.

Suggested Opening Lead

South is on lead and would start with the ♦ 10, top of a sequence in the unbid suit.

Suggested Play

If South leads a diamond, there's nothing much to the play. The defenders will take the first two diamond tricks, and declarer will take the rest. East's spade loser can be ruffed in dummy or discarded on dummy's ♣K.

If South doesn't lead a diamond, East can take 12 tricks by discarding one of the diamond losers on dummy's ♣K.

Suggested Defense

A diamond lead prevents declarer from taking 12 tricks. Other than that, there's nothing the defenders can do. If East–West reach a slam, however, finding the diamond lead will be critical.

Hand Variation of Deal 2 — Looking for Controls

Instructions

To construct a variation of the previous hand, make the following changes:

From the West hand, take the ♣K and give it to North.

From the North hand, take the ♦K and give it to West.

Suggested Bidding

WEST	NORTH	EAST	SOUTH
		2♣	Pass
2♦	Pass	2♥	Pass
3♥	Pass	3♠	Pass
4♥	Pass	5♣	Pass
5♦	Pass	6♥	Pass
Pass	Pass		

The bidding starts the same way. With 25 high-card points plus 2 length points for the six-card heart suit, East starts with a strong, conventional (artificial) 2♣ bid. West makes a waiting bid of 2♦, and East rebids 2♥ to show the strong two-bid. With good support and the ♦K, West raises to 3♥, leaving room for East to explore for slam.

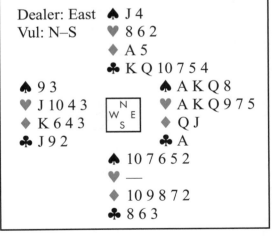

Dealer: East   ♠ J 4
Vul: N–S   ♥ 8 6 2
               ♦ A 5
               ♣ K Q 10 7 5 4

♠ 9 3   ♠ A K Q 8
♥ J 10 4 3   ♥ A K Q 9 7 5
♦ K 6 4 3   ♦ Q J
♣ J 9 2   ♣ A

               ♠ 10 7 6 5 2
               ♥ —
               ♦ 10 9 8 7 2
               ♣ 8 6 3

Once again, with two potential diamond losers, East doesn't use Blackwood. East starts by cuebidding 3♠. Without an ace to cuebid, West signs off in 4♥. East makes one more try by cuebidding 5♣, still hoping West has something in diamonds. Having denied first-round control of diamonds with the earlier 4♥ bid, West can afford to show second-round control of diamonds by bidding 5 ♦. This is all East needs to hear to bid the slam. East knows there isn't a grand slam, since the partnership must be missing the ♦ A.

Suggested Opening Lead

South is on lead and would start with the ♦ 10, top of a sequence in the unbid suit.

Suggested Play

After South leads a diamond and North takes the ♦ A, there's nothing to the rest of the play. East's spade loser can be ruffed in dummy or discarded on dummy's ♦ K.

Suggested Defense

There's nothing the defenders can do to defeat 6 ♥. If East–West get to 6NT instead of 6 ♥, the slam can be defeated by leading a club.

Bid and Play — Cuebid Controls on the Way to Blackwood

(E–Z Deal Cards: #6, Deal 3 — Dealer, South)

Suggested Bidding

WEST	NORTH	EAST	SOUTH
			1♠
Pass	3♠	Pass	4♣
Pass	4♦	Pass	4NT
Pass	5♥	Pass	6♠
Pass	Pass	Pass	

Dealer: South ♠ A 10 8 3
Vul: E–W   ♥ 7 2
               ♦ A K 8 5
               ♣ 9 7 3

♠ 5   ♠ 9
♥ K Q 10 9   N   ♥ 8 6 5 4 3
♦ 10 7 3   W   E   ♦ Q J 9 4
♣ K 8 6 4 2   S   ♣ J 10 5

               ♠ K Q J 7 6 4 2
               ♥ A J
               ♦ 6 2
               ♣ A Q

South doesn't have quite enough for a strong two-bid, so South settles for an opening bid of 1♠. After West's pass, North makes a limit raise to 3♠, and East passes. South is interested in slam, but can't use Blackwood with two low diamonds. If North were to show one ace, South couldn't be sure that the partnership isn't losing the first two diamond tricks. Instead, South shows some interest in slam by cuebidding 4♣ to show first-round control of clubs.

With an excellent hand for the limit raise, North cooperates by cuebidding 4♦ to show first-round control of diamonds. South could continue by cuebidding 4♥, but that won't accomplish much. Cuebidding won't tell South whether the partnership has the ♠A, since spades, the suit agreed upon as trump, is the suit used to sign off with. Instead, South can revert to the Blackwood convention, now that North is known to hold the ♦A. The partnership can't be losing the first two tricks in diamonds. When North shows two aces in response to Blackwood, South simply bids the small slam.

There isn't much point in looking for a grand slam. North, having made only a limit raise, can't hold enough in high cards. Even if South bid 5NT and North showed one king, South would settle for a small slam. In fact, South might have jumped to 6♠ directly over the 4♦ cuebid. If the partnership is missing the ♠A, North is likely to have enough high cards elsewhere to give slam at least a reasonable chance of success.

Suggested Opening Lead

West is on lead against 6♠ and will start with the ♥K, top of touching cards from a broken sequence.

Suggested Play

Declarer has two potential losers — one in hearts and one in clubs. One possibility is to take the club finesse. That has a 50% chance of success. There's a much better option, however, once West leads the ♥K. West's lead of the ♥K indicates possession of the ♥Q. Since declarer has the ♥J, West can be put back on lead later in the play with that card. If declarer can arrange things so that West is forced to lead a club at that point, there will be no need to rely on the club finesse.

Declarer starts by winning the ♥A and drawing the opponents' trumps, which takes only one round with the ♠K. Declarer now goes about eliminating the diamond suit from the North and South hands. Dummy's ♦A and ♦K are played, and a third round of diamonds is ruffed. Declarer crosses to dummy's ♠A and ruffs dummy's last diamond, leaving the following cards in the North–South hands:

North
♠ 10 8
♥ 7
♦ —
♣ 9 7 3

South
♠ Q J 7
♥ J
♦ —
♣ A Q

Now is the right time to lead the ♥J, putting West back on lead. That will eliminate the remaining hearts from the North–South hands. West will be left with nothing but losing choices. If West leads a club, the lead will be into declarer's ♣A and ♣Q. If West leads another heart, declarer can ruff in dummy and discard the ♣Q from the South hand. Whatever West does, declarer makes the contract without relying on the club finesse.

This line of play is a strip and end play. Declarer first strips West out of any useful options by drawing trumps and eliminating the diamonds. Then declarer throws West on lead toward the end, forcing West to lead a club — or to give declarer a ruff and a sluff. Declarer has to visualize the possibility and then bring it about.

Suggested Defense

The defenders can't do anything to prevent declarer from making the slam, if declarer finds the winning line of play. Even if West initially leads a spade or a diamond, declarer can still play the same way — eliminate the spades and diamonds and then play the ♥A and ♥J to endplay West. This is declarer's best line of play, since even if East were to hold the ♥K or ♥Q, declarer could still fall back on the club finesse as a second chance.

Bid and Play — The Grand Slam Force

(E–Z Deal Cards: #6, Deal 4 — Dealer, West)

Suggested Bidding

WEST	NORTH	EAST	SOUTH
2♥	Pass	5NT	Pass
7♥	Pass	Pass	Pass

West starts with a weak 2♥ bid. East can visualize a grand slam, if West holds a six-card suit headed by the ♥K and the ♥Q. West should be able to take 13 tricks by establishing the spade suit or by ruffing diamond losers in the dummy. East uses the grand slam force to find out whether partner holds two of the top three honors in hearts. With the king and the queen, West accepts by bidding 7♥. East–West reach the grand slam in three bids.

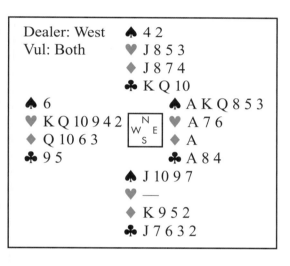

Dealer: West
Vul: Both

♠ 4 2
♥ J 8 5 3
♦ J 8 7 4
♣ K Q 10

♠ 6
♥ K Q 10 9 4 2
♦ Q 10 6 3
♣ 9 5

♠ A K Q 8 5 3
♥ A 7 6
♦ A
♣ A 8 4

♠ J 10 9 7
♥ —
♦ K 9 5 2
♣ J 7 6 3 2

West shouldn't try to bid the grand slam in notrump. If the spades don't break — as on the actual deal — there may not be 13 tricks in notrump.

Suggested Opening Lead

North is on lead and will probably start with the ♣K, top of the broken sequence in clubs.

Suggested Play

Outside of the heart suit, declarer has three diamond losers and one club loser. Provided the missing spades divide no worse than 4–2, declarer should be able to establish the spade suit and use it to discard all four losers.

The first challenge is the trump suit. There will be no difficulty drawing the missing trumps if they are divided 2–2 or 3–1. Declarer should, however, guard against the possibility that the missing hearts are divided 4–0. Declarer does this by winning the ♣A and then leading up to the ♥K. If both opponents follow suit, declarer can simply finish drawing trumps. If North were to show out on the first round, declarer could then play a heart to dummy's ♥A and take a finesse against South's ♥J.

On the actual deal, South shows out on the first round of hearts. Declarer now leads the ♥10 to trap North's ♥J. If North plays low on the ♥10, it wins the trick, and declarer can win the third round of hearts with dummy's ♥A. The remaining challenge is to return to the West hand to draw the last trump. Declarer accomplishes this by playing one high spade from dummy and then leading a low spade and ruffing it. This has a two-fold purpose. It is the safest way to return to the West hand, since North will only be able to overruff when holding a singleton spade. At the same time, it helps to establish dummy's remaining spades as winners when the missing spades are divided 4–2 and not 3–3.

Once in the West hand, declarer plays the ♥Q to draw North's remaining trump. Declarer can now cross to dummy with the ♦A and take the remaining spade winners, discarding the club and diamond losers from the West hand.

The unfortunate trump break makes the play even more challenging than the bidding!

Suggested Defense

There's nothing the defenders can do if East–West reach the grand slam in hearts and declarer safely negotiates the pitfalls. If East–West bid 7NT, the defenders can defeat that contract. Declarer can't untangle the heart suit in a notrump contract. With the 4–2 spade division, East–West will probably be defeated five tricks in notrump.

CHAPTER 7
Leads and Signals

LEADS AND SIGNALS

The last area of conventions that the partnership must address is defensive carding. Most partnerships use standard methods, which require little discussion, with one or two exceptions.

OPENING LEADS AGAINST SUIT CONTRACTS

Here are the usual agreements for leads against suit contracts.

- The top card is led from two or more touching cards headed by an honor (**K**–Q–5, **Q**–J–7–4–2, K–**J**–10–5).
- The top card is led from a doubleton (**7**–2, **Q**–5).
- Otherwise, a low card is led — low from three cards or fourth highest from a suit of four or more cards (K–8–**6**, Q–8–7–**5**, 10–8–7–**3**–2).

There are exceptions.

Leading from a Suit Headed by the Ace

From a holding such as A–8–6 or A–J–10–3, leading away from the ace against a suit contract isn't usually a good idea. The ace may never win a trick, if declarer started with a singleton or can discard losers in the suit before the defenders regain the lead. It's better to avoid leading the suit, if possible, unless the suit was bid and raised by the partnership. If the suit is to be led, however, leading the ace is usually best to try to make certain of at least one trick.

Dealer: South ♠ Q 10 8 7
♥ K J 7 3
♦ 5
♣ K 9 7 5

♠ 9 6 2   ♠ A 5 4 3
♥ 6 4   ♥ 9 2
♦ A 10 8 3   ♦ J 7 6 4
♣ 10 8 6 2   ♣ A Q 4

♠ K J
♥ A Q 10 8 5
♦ K Q 9 2
♣ J 3

WEST	NORTH	EAST	SOUTH
			1 ♥
Pass	3 ♥	Pass	4 ♥
Pass	Pass	Pass	

If West leads a low diamond, declarer will make the contract with an overtrick. Declarer can win the first diamond trick, draw trumps and drive out the ♠A. All the defenders get is the ♠A and ♣A. Declarer can ruff two diamond losers in dummy and discard two losers on the established spade winners.

The defenders can defeat the contract, if West leads the ♦A and then switches to a club. Whether East–West will actually defeat the contract depends on West eventually leading a club after winning a trick with the ♦A. That may or may not happen, but leading a low diamond at trick one doesn't give the defenders a chance.

It's interesting to note that leading a low diamond wouldn't do any harm if North–South were in a notrump contract. West would still get the ♦A later in the play — and likely one or two more diamond tricks in the process. It is only against a suit contract that leading a low card from a suit headed by the ace is usually unwise.

Leading from a Suit Headed by the Ace–King

For many years, the bridge world led the king from an ace-king combination. During the time when this was standard practice, you did not know if partner was leading the king from the ace-king or the king-queen. (This made it difficult for you to give partner the correct attitude on the lead – more about attitude signals later in this chapter.) Modern bridge theory is to lead the ace from a suit headed by the ace and king. This play is consistent with leading the top card from two or more touching honors. Although this is the way most partnerships agree to lead from a suit headed by the ace-king, it does require partnership agreement.

If your agreement is to lead the ace from a suit such as A–K–7–5, then lead the king from a doubleton A–K. When the ace is played next, partner will be alerted by this unusual sequence of plays and picture a doubleton. This might be essential information to get a ruff in the suit when partner gains the lead.

Here is an example:

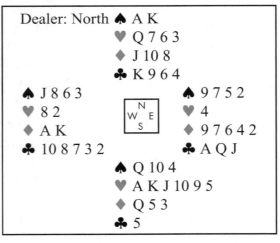

WEST	NORTH	EAST	SOUTH
	1 ♣	Pass	1 ♥
Pass	2 ♥	Pass	4 ♥
Pass	Pass	Pass	

Suppose West takes the two diamond winners and shifts to a club. East wins the first trick and might be faced with the dilemma of whether to play another club or to lead a diamond. East's decision may be even more challenging if South makes the crafty play of dropping the ♦ Q on the second round of diamonds.

If East–West usually lead the ace from a suit headed by the ace–king, West should reverse this practice by leading the ♦ K followed by the ♦ A. This unusual play should alert East that West started with a doubleton diamond. On winning a club trick, East should return a diamond rather than try to cash a second club winner.

If East–West usually lead the king from a suit headed by ace–king, West should lead the ♦ A followed by the ♦ K to make East aware of the situation. Again, East should return a diamond.

This type of partnership agreement is important in helping the defenders decide what to do.

Suppose we modify the hands slightly:

Dealer: North ♠ A K
♥ Q 7 6 3
♦ J 10 8
♣ K 9 6 4

♠ J 8 6 3   ♠ 9 7 5 2
♥ 8 2   ♥ 4
♦ A K 3   ♦ 9 7 6 4 2
♣ 10 8 7 3   ♣ A Q J

(N W E S)

♠ Q 10 4
♥ A K J 10 9 5
♦ Q 5
♣ 5 2

WEST	NORTH	EAST	SOUTH
	1♣	Pass	1♥
Pass	2♥	Pass	4♥
Pass	Pass	Pass	

The defense starts the same way, with West taking two diamond tricks and shifting to a club. This time, East needs to take a second club winner. If East returns a diamond, South can discard a club loser and make the contract. So, West should lead the high diamonds in the usual partnership agreement — ♦ A followed by the ♦ K, if the partnership usually plays the ace from ace–king.

Leading from Three Low Cards

The partnership also should agree on the lead from a suit with three low cards, such as 7–5–2. Some partnerships prefer that the lead of a low card, such as the 2, guarantees at least one honor in the suit. Some partnerships prefer to lead the top card from three low cards (**7**–5–2). This is referred to as top of nothing. Others prefer to lead the middle card (7–**5**–2), then follow with the highest card — so partner won't think it's a doubleton — and finally play the lowest card. This is referred to as MUD — **m**iddle, **u**p, **d**own.

Here is an example of the lead from three low cards:

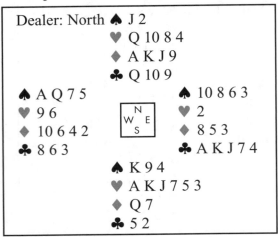

WEST	NORTH	EAST	SOUTH
	1 ♦	Pass	1 ♥
Pass	2 ♥	Pass	4 ♥
Pass	Pass	Pass	

Not wanting to lead from the spade holding, West elects to lead a club and strikes gold. East wins the first trick with the ♣J and takes a second winner with the ♣K. East needs to know if there is a third winner coming from the club suit. If East leads the ♣A, South ruffs, draws trumps and discards two spade losers on dummy's extra diamond winners. To defeat the contract, East must shift to a spade instead of playing a third round of clubs.

If West leads the top of three low cards, East will have a difficult decision. East won't be able to tell for certain whether West started with two or three clubs. If East–West use MUD leads from three low cards, West will start by leading the middle card, the ♣6. On the second round of the suit, West will play up, the ♣8. Now East knows that West holds a third club and leading another round of clubs won't do any good.

The defenders also should defeat the contract if they lead low from three low cards. West will lead the ♣3 and follow with a higher club on the second round. East will know West doesn't have a singleton or doubleton and may find the shift to spades.

OPENING LEADS AGAINST NOTRUMP CONTRACTS

When leading partner's suit against a notrump contract, the same guidelines can be used as leading against a suit contract. When leading your own suit, use the following:

- The top card of touching cards is led from a three–card sequence, a broken sequence or an interior sequence headed by an honor (**K**–Q–J–6–5, **Q**–J–9–4, A–**J**–10–5–2).

- Otherwise, a low card is led — fourth highest from a suit of four or more cards (K–8–**6**, Q–8–7–**5**, 10–8–7–**3**–2).

Leading from a Sequence

Leading the top card from a solid sequence, three or more touching cards, avoids giving declarer an extra trick in the suit in many situations.

For example:

NORTH (Dummy)
♥ 8 5

WEST   EAST
♥ K Q J 7 2   ♥ 9 6 3

SOUTH (Declarer)
♥ A 10 4

If West were to lead a low heart, declarer would win the first trick with the ♥ 10 and have the ♥ A left as a second trick. By leading the ♥ K, West avoids giving declarer a cheap trick.

Similarly, leading top of a broken sequence may avoid giving declarer an undeserved trick:

NORTH (Dummy)
♥ K 8 5

WEST   EAST
♥ Q J 9 7   ♥ 6 3 2

SOUTH (Declarer)
♥ A 10 4

If West leads a low heart, declarer will get three tricks in the suit. If West leads the ♥ Q, declarer can be restricted to two tricks in the suit provided East next leads the suit for the defenders.

With only two touching honors — without the ♥ 9 in the above example — West is usually better off leading fourth best.

For example, consider this layout:

NORTH (Dummy)
♥ K 10 8

WEST   EAST
♥ Q J 7 2   ♥ 9 6 3

SOUTH (Declarer)
♥ A 5 4

If West leads the ♥ Q, declarer can win the first trick with the ♥ A. Later South can lead toward dummy's ♥ K 10 and take the finesse to take three tricks in the suit. If West leads the ♥ 2, declarer may insert dummy's ♥ 10 on the first round of the suit and take three tricks, but declarer is more likely to play dummy's ♥ 8 (the best technical play), hoping West started with ♥ Q 9 7 2 or ♥ J 9 7 2, rather than ♥ Q J 7 2. East's ♥ 9 will force the ♥ A and restrict declarer to two tricks in the suit.

Leading top of an interior sequence is designed to trap high cards in declarer's and dummy's hands.

For example:

NORTH (Dummy)
♥ Q 9 7
WEST .... EAST
♥ A J 10 6 3 .... ♥ K 5 2
SOUTH (Declarer)
♥ 8 4

The lead of the ♥ J traps North's ♥ Q, and the defenders take the first five tricks against a notrump contract. The lead of a low heart wouldn't be successful if declarer played a low heart from dummy.

NORTH (Dummy)
♥ 8 4
WEST .... EAST
♥ A J 10 6 3 .... ♥ K 5 2
SOUTH (Declarer)
♥ Q 9 7

The lead of the ♥ J is equally successful if South holds the ♥ Q, as in this example. East should play the ♥ K on the first round of the suit — third hand high — and lead back the suit, so that the defenders take all five heart tricks.

NORTH (Dummy)
♥ 8 4
WEST .... EAST
♥ A J 10 6 3 .... ♥ 7 5 2
SOUTH (Declarer)
♥ K Q 9

If West leads the ♥ J in this situation, declarer can win the first trick with the ♥ Q. Provided East next leads the suit for the defenders, however, East–West will take the next four tricks in the suit. The lead of a low heart would not be as successful.

There are many possible layouts when leading from sequences, and the guidelines don't always work. With nothing better to go on, however, they will usually get the defenders off to the best start.

Leading Fourth Highest — The Rule of Eleven

Without a sequence to lead from, the guideline is to lead a low card, specifically the fourth highest card in the suit. The advantage of leading the fourth highest card is that partner knows the opening leader holds exactly three higher cards in the suit. Partner can sometimes put this knowledge to use by using the rule of eleven:

> Subtract the number on the card led from 11.
> The result is the number of cards higher
> than the one led in the other three hands.

Here is an example:

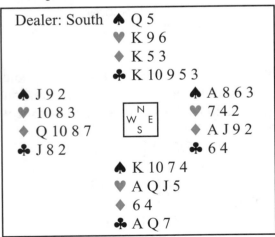

```
Dealer: South    ♠ Q 5
                 ♥ K 9 6
                 ♦ K 5 3
                 ♣ K 10 9 5 3
♠ J 9 2                        ♠ A 8 6 3
♥ 10 8 3          N            ♥ 7 4 2
♦ Q 10 8 7      W   E          ♦ A J 9 2
♣ J 8 2           S            ♣ 6 4
                 ♠ K 10 7 4
                 ♥ A Q J 5
                 ♦ 6 4
                 ♣ A Q 7
```

WEST	NORTH	EAST	SOUTH
			1NT
Pass	3NT	Pass	Pass
Pass			

West leads the ♦ 7 , and declarer plays a low diamond from dummy. East may be tempted to play the ♦ A, ♦ J or ♦ 9, but the only winning play is the ♦ 2! That leaves West on lead to play another diamond, trapping dummy's ♦ K. The defenders get four diamond tricks and the ♠ A. If East plays a higher diamond on the first trick, the ♦ J for example, East will be on lead at trick two. Now there is no way to defeat the contract. Declarer may even make an overtrick.

How does East know to play low on the first trick? The rule of eleven tells East to subtract the number on the card led by West — seven — from 11. The result is four, the number of cards higher than the ♦ 7 in the remaining three hands. East has three of the higher cards and can see the fourth in dummy, the ♦ K. That leaves no card higher than the ♦ 7 in declarer's hand. East confidently plays the ♦ 2 and the contract is defeated.

The Lead of an Ace against a Notrump Contract

Many partnerships have the agreement that the lead of an ace against a notrump contract asks partner to play an honor card, if one is held, otherwise to give a count signal (see later). For example, suppose the ace is led from a holding such as A–K–J–10–9. Holding the queen, partner would play it, and the rest of the tricks in the suit would be winners. If partner didn't hold the queen, partner would give a count signal. If the queen didn't appear in dummy, it could be predicted whether it was in declarer's hand and whether it was going to fall under the ace.

Here is an example:

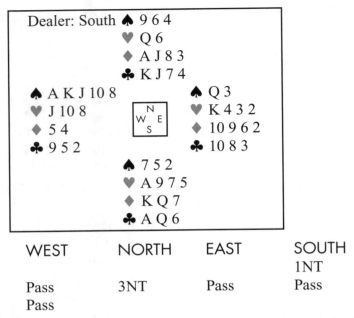

WEST	NORTH	EAST	SOUTH
			1NT
Pass	3NT	Pass	Pass
Pass			

West leads the ♠A. If East plays the ♠3, West won't know whether to continue leading spades or shift to another suit. If West doesn't continue with the ♠K, declarer will make the contract. If East plays the ♠Q on West's ♠A, the defenders won't have any trouble taking the first five tricks.

Could it be correct for West not to continue with spades at trick two?

Consider this layout:

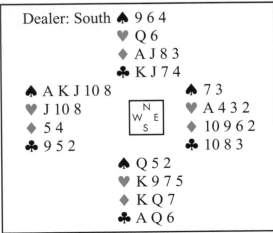

WEST	NORTH	EAST	SOUTH
			1NT
Pass	3NT	Pass	Pass
Pass			

Now declarer will make the contract if West leads a spade at trick two. West must shift to another suit. At some point, East will have an opportunity to win the ♥A and lead a spade to defeat the contract.

If the partnership has the agreement that the lead of an ace against a notrump contract asks partner to play an honor, lead the king from a suit headed by the ace and king if it wouldn't be a good idea for partner to play an honor. For example, lead the king from A–K–J–2, and partner would give an encouraging attitude signal (see later) holding the queen.

Leading from a Suit Headed by King–Queen–Ten

Most partnerships have an agreement similar to the previous one when leading from a suit headed by the K–Q–10–9. The queen is led, asking partner to play the jack when holding it, otherwise to give a count signal.

When it wouldn't be good for partner to play the jack, lead the king. For example, lead the king from K–Q–10–2, and partner would give an encouraging attitude signal holding the jack.

Leading from a Weak Suit

The partnership should agree on which card is led from a long suit that doesn't have an honor card. Many players prefer to lead the second highest card from such suits (9–**7**–5–2, 8–**5**–4–3–2). Without such an agreement, the fourth highest card is usually led (9–7–6–**3**–2).

Other Leads

Against both suit and notrump contracts, the defenders have choices other than the traditional lead of top of a sequence or fourth highest.

Third- and Fifth-Best Leads

The standard lead from a long suit is the fourth highest card (K–10–8–**6**–3), a convention dating back to the days of Hoyle, more than 250 years ago. Some partnerships prefer to use third- and fifth-best leads:

- The third highest card is led from a three-card or four-card suit (K–8–**3**, Q–10–**7**–5).
- The fifth highest card is led from a five-card or longer suit (Q–9–7–4–**2**, J–8–6–4–**3**–2).

The theoretical advantage of this approach is that the partnership can often tell more quickly, than when using fourth highest leads, exactly how many cards the leader started with in the suit. It does, however, require agreement between the players, and it has an affect on guidelines associated with fourth highest leads, such as the rule of eleven.

Zero or Two Higher Leads

Some partnerships have the agreement that the lead of the 10 or the 9 shows either zero higher cards or two higher cards in the suit, while the lead of the jack denies any higher honors. Leads of the ace, king and queen retain their standard meanings.

Under this agreement, lead the 10 from a holding such as **10**–9–8–5, but also lead the 10 from holdings such as K–J–**10**–5 or A–J–**10**–5 (against a notrump contract), since there are two higher honors in the suit. Lead the queen from **Q**–J–10–5, however. Lead the 9 from holdings such as K–10–**9**–5, Q–10–**9**–5 or A–10–**9**–5 (against a notrump contract), since there are two higher cards in the suit.

Here is an example of how this agreement might prove advantageous on defense.

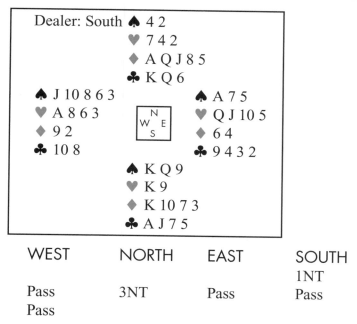

Dealer: South ♠ 4 2
♥ 7 4 2
♦ A Q J 8 5
♣ K Q 6

♠ J 10 8 6 3   ♠ A 7 5
♥ A 8 6 3   ♥ Q J 10 5
♦ 9 2   ♦ 6 4
♣ 10 8   ♣ 9 4 3 2

♠ K Q 9
♥ K 9
♦ K 10 7 3
♣ A J 7 5

WEST	NORTH	EAST	SOUTH
			1NT
Pass	3NT	Pass	Pass
Pass			

West leads the ♠ J, and East wins the first trick with the ♠ A. Without any agreement, East will be tempted to lead back a spade, since West might have started with something like ♠ K J 10 6 3 and be leading the top of an interior sequence. If East switches to another suit, the defenders may lose their opportunity to take the first five tricks.

With the agreement that the lead of a jack denies a higher honor in the suit, East knows that declarer holds the ♠ K and the ♠ Q. The best chance for the defense appears to be to switch to the ♥ Q. When East does that, the contract is defeated. Holding ♠ K J 10 6 3, West would have led the ♠ 10, showing zero or two higher honors.

The advocates of this type of agreement claim that it leads to improved accuracy on defense, since the opening leader will usually have no difficulty deducing the full layout. Opponents of this idea feel that it gives away too much information to declarer and prefer the more ambiguous standard honor leads.

Leading during the Middle Game

After the opening lead has been made, the defenders will often have an opportunity to lead a suit later in the hand. The usual agreement is that the same principles apply as on opening lead. For example, lead the top of touching honors and the fourth highest card from a suit not headed by touching honors.

Returning Partner's Suit

If partner leads a suit and there is a chance to return partner's lead, use the following guidelines:

- Lead the top card from a remaining doubleton (**7**–2, **Q**–5).
- Lead the top card from two or more touching cards headed by an honor (**Q**–J–7, **10**–9–5).
- Lead a low card otherwise — the original fourth-highest from three or more remaining cards (Q–8–**6**, 9–7–**5**, J–8–**3**–2).

This last guideline is best illustrated through an example.

Suppose West leads the ♥4 and this is the complete layout:

```
             NORTH (Dummy)
                ♥ J 8
 WEST                        EAST
 ♥ Q 9 7 4       ■          ♥ A 6 3 2
             SOUTH (Declarer)
                ♥ K 10 5
```

After winning a trick with the ♥A, East would return the ♥2, the original fourth-highest card. If East had started with ♥A 6 2, East would return the ♥6, top of the remaining doubleton. If East had started with ♥A 6 5 3 2, East would return the ♥3, the original fourth-highest. The card East returns may help West determine the complete layout of the suit, which may be useful in both notrump and suit contracts.

DEFENSIVE SIGNALS

In addition to the information conveyed through the cards led during the play, the defenders can exchange information in other ways.

The Attitude Signal

An attitude signal can be used with a choice of cards to play in a suit that partner has led, or when discarding in a suit. The conventional agreement is:

- A high card is an encouraging signal.
- A low card is a discouraging signal.

The terms "high" and "low" are relative. To encourage from a holding of K–3–2, the highest affordable card is the 3. Holding 10–8–7, the most discouraging card is the lowest card, the 7.

Here is an example of using the attitude signal on defense:

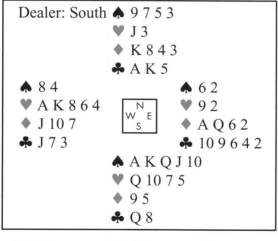

```
Dealer: South    ♠ 9 7 5 3
                 ♥ J 3
                 ♦ K 8 4 3
                 ♣ A K 5
        ♠ 8 4                    ♠ 6 2
        ♥ A K 8 6 4     N        ♥ 9 2
        ♦ J 10 7      W   E      ♦ A Q 6 2
        ♣ J 7 3          S       ♣ 10 9 6 4 2
                 ♠ A K Q J 10
                 ♥ Q 10 7 5
                 ♦ 9 5
                 ♣ Q 8
```

WEST	NORTH	EAST	SOUTH
			1 ♠
Pass	3 ♠	Pass	4 ♠
Pass	Pass	Pass	

West leads the ♥ A. East should play the ♥ 2, a discouraging signal, even with a doubleton. Hopefully, West now will find the shift to diamonds, which allows the defenders to defeat the contract with two heart tricks and two diamond tricks.

If East were to play the ♥9, an encouraging signal, on the first heart, West might continue by leading the ♥K and a third round of hearts. This would be the winning defense if East held a spade higher than dummy's ♠9 and didn't hold the ♦Q. Declarer can make the contract if West leads a third round of hearts. Declarer ruffs with a high trump in dummy, draws trumps and discards a diamond loser on dummy's extra club winner.

See also upside-down signals in the Appendix.

The Count Signal (Length Signal)

A count signal tells partner how many cards there are in a suit. The standard conventional agreement to show length in a suit is:

- High-low shows an even number of cards.
- Low-high shows an odd number of cards.

Count signals are commonly used when declarer is playing a long strong suit and it's important to tell partner exactly how many cards are held. They also may be used to convey information when following suit or discarding. It's often important for partner to know how many cards are held in a particular suit, so that partner can determine which cards to hold on to.

Here is an example of using a count signal on defense:

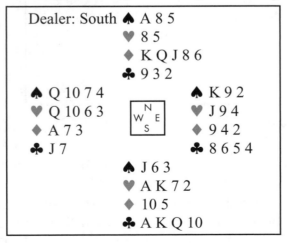

WEST	NORTH	EAST	SOUTH
			1NT
Pass	3NT	Pass	Pass
Pass			

West leads the ♠4. A low spade is played from dummy, and East wins the trick with the ♠K. East returns the ♠9 — top of the remaining doubleton — and the defenders win the second trick as declarer holds up with dummy's ♠A. A third round of spades is led, and declarer wins with dummy's ♠A. Declarer now leads a low diamond from dummy to the ♦10, which West ducks. The ♦5 is led toward dummy and West . . .

If East–West are using count signals, East will have played the ♦2 on the first round of diamonds, showing an odd number. East can't hold five diamonds, since declarer holds at least two. If East has a singleton diamond, it won't matter whether West holds up again with the ♦A, since declarer will always have a diamond left to reach dummy. West, therefore, can assume East holds exactly three diamonds, leaving declarer with a doubleton. West can safely win the second round of diamonds, and declarer will not have an entry to dummy's established tricks. If the defenders are careful from that point on, declarer will be held to eight tricks.

If West were to hold up the ♦A a second time, declarer could make the contract. Declarer would get one spade trick, two heart tricks, two diamond tricks and four club tricks. East's count signal is essential to the successful defense.

If East held a doubleton diamond, East would start with a high diamond, showing an even number. West would then have to hold up until the third round of diamonds and hope that declarer didn't have enough tricks without the diamonds.

Although some players like to give count signals frequently, this isn't a recommended tactic against a good declarer. While giving partner information, declarer also gets information. Declarer may be able to take advantage of this. Count signals should be given only when the information will be of more value to partner than to declarer, as in the above deal.

Trump Echo

The normal method of giving count in the trump suit is often reversed. A high-low in the trump suit is commonly used to show three trumps, and this practice is referred to as a trump echo. It's generally used as a signal when you are trying to get a ruff. It may be important for partner to know that you still have one trump left after two rounds have been played. With a doubleton trump, you would play low-high, telling partner you don't have a third trump left. As with other count signals, this should not always be used, since it may be of more value to declarer than to partner.

The Suit Preference Signal

A suit preference signal tells partner which of two suits to lead or return. It's used most often when defending against a trump contract. It doesn't apply to the suit led or to the trump suit. Instead, it indicates a preference for one of the two remaining suits:

- A high card shows preference for the higher-ranking suit.
- A low card shows preference for the lower-ranking suit.

Typically, a suit preference signal is used when partner leads a singleton against a trump contract and the first trick is won with the ace from a suit such as A–10–6–2. With a choice of cards to lead for partner to ruff, a high card, the 10, asks partner to return on the next lead the higher-ranking of the two remaining suits — excluding the trump suit — and a low card, the 2, asks partner to return the lower-ranking of the two remaining suits. With no preference for either suit, the 6, a middle card, is led.

Here is an example of a suit preference signal in action:

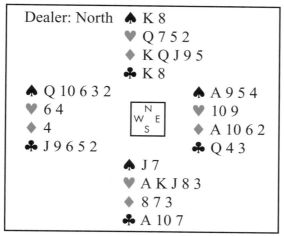

Dealer: North	♠ K 8
	♥ Q 7 5 2
	♦ K Q J 9 5
	♣ K 8

♠ Q 10 6 3 2   ♠ A 9 5 4
♥ 6 4   ♥ 10 9
♦ 4   ♦ A 10 6 2
♣ J 9 6 5 2   ♣ Q 4 3

                 ♠ J 7
                 ♥ A K J 8 3
                 ♦ 8 7 3
                 ♣ A 10 7

WEST	NORTH	EAST	SOUTH
	1 ♦	Pass	1 ♥
Pass	2 ♥	Pass	4 ♥
Pass	Pass	Pass	

West leads the ♦ 4. The ♦ K is played from dummy, and East wins the ♦ A. East is aware that the unusual lead of the opponent's suit is because West holds a singleton and is hoping for a ruff. East leads back the ♦ 10, a suit preference signal, for West to ruff. The ♦ 10 shows preference for the higher-ranking of the two "obvious" suits — spades and clubs. After ruffing the diamond, West leads a spade. East wins the ♠ A and gives West a second diamond ruff to defeat the contract.

If East held the ♣ A instead of the ♠ A, East would return the ♦ 2 at trick two, as a suit preference signal for clubs. With neither ace, East would return a middle diamond, the ♦ 6, showing no preference for either suit.

Attitude and count signals generally take priority over suit preference signals. Only when the situation clearly doesn't call for an attitude or a count signal does a suit preference signal come into play.

See also *Lavinthal signals* in the Appendix.

SUMMARY

Opening Leads against Suit Contracts

The standard leads against a suit contract are the following:

- The top card is led from a doubleton (**7**–2, **Q**–5).
- The top card is led from two or more touching cards headed by an honor (**K**–Q–5, **Q**–J–7–4–2, K–**J**–10–5).
- Otherwise, a low card is led — low from a suit of three cards and fourth highest from a suit of four or more cards (K–8–**6**, Q–8–7–**5**, 10–8–7–**3**–2).
- Leading a low card from a suit headed by the ace is usually unwise against a suit contract.

The partnership needs to agree which card is led from:

- A suit headed by the ace and king.
- Three low cards.

Opening Leads against Notrump Contracts

When leading partner's suit, use the same guidelines as leading against a suit contract. Otherwise, use the following:

- The top of touching cards is led from a three–card sequence, a broken sequence or an interior sequence headed by an honor (**K**–Q–J–6–5, **Q**–J–9–4, A–**J**–10–5–2).
- Otherwise, a low card is led — fourth highest from a suit of four or more cards (K–8–**6**, Q–8–7–**5**, 10–8–7–**3**–2).

The partnership also can agree:

- The lead of an ace against a notrump contract asks partner to play an honor card, if one is held, otherwise to give a count signal.

- To lead the queen from a suit headed by the K–Q–10–9 asking partner to play the jack when holding it, otherwise to give a count signal.

The partnership generally uses the same guidelines when leading later in the hand. The defenders also can use three types of defensive signals during the play:

Defensive Signals

Attitude signal:

- A high card is an encouraging signal.

- A low card is a discouraging signal.

Count signal:

- High-low shows an even number of cards.

- Low-high shows an odd number of cards.

Suit preference signal:

- A high card shows preference for the higher-ranking suit.

- A low card shows preference for the lower-ranking suit.

NOTES: See the Appendix (pages 359–360) for a discussion of these supplemental conventions and/or treatments.

Lavinthal Discards

Upside-down Carding

Note: The following exercises illustrate the methods outlined in the summary.

Exercise One — Opening Leads against Suit Contracts

West chooses to lead a diamond against the following auction. Which card would West select from each of the following hands?

WEST	NORTH	EAST	SOUTH
			1 ♠
Pass	3 ♠	Pass	4 ♠
Pass	Pass	Pass	

1) ♠ 8 3
   ♥ Q 8 5
   ♦ K Q J 6
   ♣ J 7 4 2

2) ♠ J 5
   ♥ J 9 7 5
   ♦ Q J 9 2
   ♣ J 8 4

3) ♠ 7 6 3
   ♥ 8 4 2
   ♦ A K 9 5
   ♣ J 8 3

4) ♠ J 7
   ♥ K 8
   ♦ Q 10 6 4 2
   ♣ J 6 5 3

5) ♠ Q 8 5
   ♥ Q 9 3
   ♦ 9 6 2
   ♣ J 7 5 3

6) ♠ J 8 5 3
   ♥ J 6
   ♦ A J 8 7 5
   ♣ Q 5

Exercise Two — Opening Leads against Notrump Contracts

What is West's opening lead from each of the following hands after the auction shown?

WEST	NORTH	EAST	SOUTH
			1NT
Pass	3NT	Pass	Pass
Pass			

1) ♠ Q J 10 8 5
   ♥ A 7 4
   ♦ 6 2
   ♣ 9 5 4

2) ♠ Q 7 3
   ♥ J 10 8 6 5
   ♦ K 8 4
   ♣ 8 4

3) ♠ K J 10 7 3
   ♥ 7 4 3
   ♦ K 9 5
   ♣ J 8

4) ♠ Q 8
   ♥ 9 5 4
   ♦ A K 7 4 3
   ♣ J 7 3

5) ♠ J 5 4
   ♥ K 6
   ♦ 8 4 2
   ♣ A K J 10 4

6) ♠ J 9 7 3
   ♥ K 10 6 2
   ♦ A 5
   ♣ J 4 3

Exercise One *Answer* — Opening Leads against Suit Contracts

1) ♦ K. Lead the top of touching high cards.

2) ♦ Q. The top of touching high cards is led from a broken sequence.

3) ♦ A. The partnership must agree on which card to lead from this holding. Without discussion, the standard lead from this combination is the ♦ A, but some partnerships prefer to lead the ♦ K.

4) ♦ 4. Without touching high cards, lead the fourth highest — unless the partnership has agreed to play third and fifth leads, in which case the ♦ 2 would be led.

5) ♦ 6 or ♦ 2 or ♦ 9. The partnership must agree on which card to lead from this holding. If the partnership uses MUD, the middle card would be led, the ♦ 6. If the partnership leads low from three or more cards, whether or not they include an honor, the ♦ 2 would be led. If the partnership leads top of nothing, the ♦ 9 would be led.

6) ♦ A. Avoid leading a low card from a suit headed by the ace against a suit contract — the ace may never win a trick.

Exercise Two *Answer* — Opening Leads against Notrump Contracts

1) ♠ Q. West leads the top of a solid (three-card or longer) sequence.

2) ♥ J. The top of touching high cards is led from a broken sequence.

3) ♠ J. The top of touching high cards is led from an interior sequence. If the partnership has agreed to play zero or two higher, the ♠ 10 would be led from this holding since there are two higher honors (the ♠ J would then deny a higher honor).

4) ♦ 4. With no solid, broken or interior sequence, lead fourth highest.

5) ♣ A. This is the card that would be led from a broken sequence. The partnership may have an agreement that East will play the ♣ Q at trick one when holding that card. If not, give a count signal. Otherwise East shows attitude.

6) ♥ 2. With a choice of four-card or longer suits, generally choose the stronger suit and lead fourth highest without a sequence in the suit.

Exercise Three — Rule of Eleven

After the following auction, West leads the ♥ 7, and a low heart is played from dummy. Which card does East play?

WEST	NORTH	EAST	SOUTH
			1NT
Pass	3NT	Pass	Pass
Pass			

NORTH
♠ J 7 6
♥ K 6 2
♦ A Q 10 6 3
♣ K 9

WEST
♥ 7

EAST
♠ 9 5 4
♥ A 10 9 3
♦ K 8 2
♣ 7 4 2

SOUTH

Exercise Three *Answer* — Rule of Eleven

♥ 3. Assuming West's lead is fourth highest, East can subtract from 11 to get the number of higher cards in the other three hands (11–7 = 4). One higher card is in dummy, and three higher cards are in East's hand. That means that declarer has no card higher than the ♥ 7. By playing low, East lets West win the first trick. West can lead the suit again to trap dummy's ♥ K. West has led fourth highest from ♥ Q J 8 7.

Exercise Four — Attitude Signals

After the following auction, West leads the ♦ K, and a low diamond is played from dummy. Which card would East play?

WEST	NORTH	EAST	SOUTH
	1 ♣	Pass	1 ♠
Pass	2 ♠	Pass	4 ♠
Pass	Pass	Pass	

```
                NORTH
                ♠ Q 8 6 2
                ♥ A Q
                ♦ J 7 4
                ♣ A 9 6 4
        WEST                EAST
        ♦ K                 ♠ 6 4
                ▮           ♥ J 7 5 2
                            ♦ Q 9 2
                            ♣ Q 8 5 3
                SOUTH
```

Exercise Four *Answer* — Attitude Signals

♦ 9. This is an encouraging attitude signal asking West to keep leading the suit. If the partnership leads the king from ace–king, East–West will take the first three tricks in the suit, if declarer has more than a doubleton. Besides, East doesn't particularly want West to switch to another suit.

Exercise Five — Count Signals

After the following auction, West leads the ♠2, and the ♠K is played from dummy, winning the trick. Which spade does East play? The ♣3 is led from dummy to the second trick. Which club does East play?

WEST	NORTH	EAST	SOUTH
			1NT
Pass	2NT	Pass	3NT
Pass	Pass	Pass	

```
                NORTH
                ♠ K 5
                ♥ J 9 3
                ♦ 8 4 2
                ♣ K J 8 6 3
    WEST                        EAST
    ♠ 2                         ♠ Q 9 4 3
              ███████           ♥ Q 10 5 2
              ███████           ♦ 9 7 5
              ███████           ♣ 7 4
                SOUTH
```

Exercise Five *Answer* — Count Signals

♠9 and ♣7. The ♠9 is an encouraging attitude signal. When West gains the lead, East would like West to continue leading spades. Since East holds the ♠Q, that should be successful if West holds either the ♠A or the ♠J. The ♣7 is a count signal, the start of a high-low to show an even number of cards in the suit. West may hold the ♣A and need to know how many times to hold up in order to limit declarer to as few club tricks as possible.

Exercise Six — Suit Preference Signals

After the auction has gone as follows, West leads a singleton heart. East wins the first trick with the ♥A and returns the ♥4. West ruffs the heart return. Which card does West play to trick three?

WEST	NORTH	EAST	SOUTH
			1♠
Pass	3♠	Pass	4♠
Pass	Pass	Pass	

NORTH
♠ K 10 8 3
♥ Q J 7 2
♦ Q 5
♣ Q J 6

WEST
♠ 7 4 2
♥ 3
♦ J 10 6 2
♣ K 10 5 4 2

EAST
♥ A

SOUTH

Exercise Six *Answer* — Suit Preference Signals

♣4. East has returned the lowest outstanding heart. This should be a suit preference signal for clubs, the lower of the two "obvious" choices — diamonds or clubs. Although a club lead is unattractive and a diamond lead appears safer, West respects East's signal. With an entry in diamonds, East would have returned a high heart. With no entry in either suit, East would have returned a middle heart. Partnership trust is what it is all about!

Bid and Play — Unusual Lead Signals a Doubleton

(E–Z Deal Cards: #7, Deal 1 — Dealer, North)

Suggested Bidding

WEST	NORTH	EAST	SOUTH
	1♠	Pass	3♠
Pass	4♠	Pass	Pass
Pass			

North, with an unbalanced hand and a five-card major, opens 1♠. After East passes, South makes a limit raise to 3♠. North accepts the invitation and bids game.

```
Dealer: North   ♠ A Q J 10 6
Vul: None       ♥ Q 2
                ♦ 9 8 6 3
                ♣ A Q
♠ 7 4                        ♠ 8 2
♥ A J 10 7        N          ♥ 9 8 6 5 3
♦ J 5 2        W   E         ♦ A K
♣ J 6 4 3         S          ♣ 10 9 8 5
                ♠ K 9 5 3
                ♥ K 4
                ♦ Q 10 7 4
                ♣ K 7 2
```

Suggested Opening Lead

East is on lead and should make a plan before choosing the opening lead. With a doubleton ♦ A K, East can visualize the possibility of getting a diamond ruff to defeat the contract, if there is an entry to West's hand. East should start by leading a high diamond. After seeing the dummy, there still may be time to change plans — if there is a singleton or doubleton diamond in dummy, for example.

To alert West that the ♦ A K is doubleton, East should reverse the standard partnership agreement of leading from a suit headed by the ace and king. If the partnership agreement is to lead the ace from a suit headed by the ace and king, East should lead the ♦ K. If the partnership agreement is to lead the king from a suit headed by the ace and king, East should start by leading the ♦ A. This "unusual" sequence of plays is intended to alert West to the possibility of a diamond ruff.

Suggested Play

North's 4♠ contract is precarious. There is a sure heart loser, and there are three potential diamond losers. If East leads something other than a diamond, North will have the opportunity to draw trumps and then play diamonds. If the diamonds lie favorably, as they do on the actual deal, declarer will lose one heart and only two diamond tricks and make the contract.

If the defenders lead diamonds initially and get their diamond ruff, they will defeat the contract by taking two diamonds, one ruff and the ♥A.

Suggested Defense

When East leads a high diamond, West will play the ♦2, a discouraging card. West can't see much future in the diamond suit. After looking at the dummy, however, East should continue with the other high diamond. East can see that there is still the possibility of getting a diamond ruff, if East can find a quick entry to the West hand.

After leading the second diamond, East's dilemma will be whether to lead a heart or a club to get to the West hand. With no help from West, this would be a pure guess. If East leads a club, declarer can win and draw trumps, making the contract. By leading a heart, the contract can be defeated.

On the second round of diamonds, West has an opportunity to help East find the winning defense. From East's unusual play in diamonds and the fact that East continued leading diamonds despite West's discouraging signal, West should realize that East has a doubleton diamond. With an entry in the heart suit but not the club suit, West should play the ♦J on the second round of diamonds! This is a suit preference signal for the higher-ranking of the two "obvious" suits, hearts and clubs. East should now lead a heart rather than a club, preferably the ♥9, top of nothing, to show no interest in having the suit returned. West can win the ♥A and, trusting East, lead back a diamond for East to ruff and defeat the contract.

If East–West do find this defense, all North–South can do is congratulate their opponents and move on to the next deal.

Bid and Play — Lead High to See the Dummy

(E–Z Deal Cards: #7, Deal 2 — Dealer, East)

Suggested Bidding

WEST	NORTH	EAST	SOUTH
		1♦	Pass
1♠	Pass	1NT	Pass
4♠	Pass	Pass	Pass

East has a balanced hand but it isn't strong enough to open 1NT. Instead, East opens 1♦ and rebids 1NT, after West's 1♠ response. West has enough to take the partnership to game and now knows there is an eight-card spade fit, since East has shown a balanced hand with at least two spades. West can then bid 4♠.

Dealer: East
Vul: N–S

```
              ♠ 4
              ♥ J 7 5 2
              ♦ A K 9 4
              ♣ 7 6 5 2
♠ A K Q 7 6 2        N        ♠ 5 3
♥ 6 4             W     E     ♥ A K 9 8
♦ J 6 5              S        ♦ Q 10 7 3
♣ Q J                         ♣ A 9 4
              ♠ J 10 9 8
              ♥ Q 10 3
              ♦ 8 2
              ♣ K 10 8 3
```

Suggested Opening Lead

North is on lead. Despite East's opening bid of 1♦, North should lead a high diamond. It may be possible to give South a ruff in diamonds, or North can choose to shift to another suit after seeing the dummy. North would make the agreed partnership lead from a suit headed by the ace and king.

Suggested Play

If the missing spades are divided 3–2, declarer would have no spade losers. There are only two diamond losers and a potential club loser. If the defenders don't lead clubs in time, declarer may be able to establish an extra winner in diamonds on which to discard the club loser.

The spades are divided 4–1, giving West an unexpected loser in that suit. The club finesse also loses to South's ♣K. Declarer has four losers and can be defeated. The defense, however, is a challenge.

Suggested Defense

If North leads a high diamond, South's play to the first trick will be important. North will interpret South's choice of cards as an attitude signal. If South plays the ♦8, that would be an encouraging signal, and North would continue with another high diamond and give South a ruff by leading a third round of diamonds.

From North's perspective, giving South a diamond ruff might be the only way to defeat the contract. South might have a singleton diamond and the ♠A, for example. It is up to South to give the appropriate attitude signal on the first trick.

From South's perspective, getting a diamond ruff will not help the defense. South has a natural spade trick without being given a ruff. After the ♠A K Q are played, South's ♠J always will be a winner for the defense. Since North's opening lead shows both the ♦A and ♦K, South knows the defenders already have three tricks, unless West holds a singleton diamond. The best source of a fourth defensive trick is in the club suit. If North can be persuaded to lead a club, South's ♣K should be a trick for the defense.

On the first trick, therefore, South should play the ♦2, a discouraging signal! South hopes that North will then shift to a club. Now declarer can't prevent the defenders from getting two diamond tricks, one club trick and one spade trick to defeat the contract.

If South plays the ♦8 on the first trick and North continues leading diamonds, South can ruff the third round, but now the defenders lose the race. Whatever South leads next, declarer can win, draw the remaining trumps and discard the club loser on dummy's established diamond winner.

If South makes a discouraging signal on the first trick, how does North know to switch to a club rather than a heart? It isn't clear-cut, but with both the ♥A and ♥K in the dummy, a club switch looks more promising than a heart switch. The defenders would have to lead hearts twice to drive out the ♥A and ♥K. By then, declarer would probably have been able to establish dummy's ♦Q on which to discard a heart loser. From North's perspective, if South doesn't want diamonds continued, a club lead is likely to be the best chance for the defenders. South might have the ♣K Q J, for example.

Bid and Play — Declarer Determines the Dangerous Opponent

(E–Z Deal Cards: #7, Deal 3 — Dealer, South)

Suggested Bidding

WEST	NORTH	EAST	SOUTH
			Pass
Pass	Pass	2♣	Pass
2♦	Pass	2NT	Pass
3NT	Pass	Pass	Pass

After three passes, East, with 24 high-card points, opens with a strong artificial 2♣ bid. West makes a waiting response of 2♦, and East rebids 2NT, showing a balanced hand of 22 to 24 points. West has enough to raise to game, ending the auction.

If the partnership doesn't use weak two-bids and the strong artificial 2♣ opening, East can simply open 2NT showing a balanced 22 to 24 points, and West will raise to 3NT.

```
Dealer: South   ♠ K 6 3
Vul: E–W        ♥ J 10 8 4
                ♦ 10 5 3
                ♣ A 5 4
♠ 5 4 2                      ♠ A J 8
♥ 9 7 2          N           ♥ A K Q 3
♦ 7 2          W   E         ♦ A K Q 4
♣ K Q 10 6 3     S           ♣ J 2
                ♠ Q 10 9 7
                ♥ 6 5
                ♦ J 9 8 6
                ♣ 9 8 7
```

Suggested Opening Lead

South is on lead against 3NT. With the spades being slightly stronger than the diamonds, South should start with the ♠10, top of the touching cards from an interior sequence.

Suggested Play

Declarer starts with seven sure tricks: one spade, three hearts and three diamonds. An eighth trick can be established in clubs, and a ninth trick might appear if the missing hearts divide 3–3.

Dummy's clubs would actually provide four tricks with an entry to the winners, once the ♣A is driven out. Unfortunately, there is no entry. It's possible, however, that the clubs will provide two tricks if the opponents hold up the ♣A until the third round. While that assumes a defensive error, it may be a better chance than relying on hearts to divide 3–3.

Declarer first has to decide what to do, if South leads a spade and North plays the ♠K at trick one. There are two possibilities. If declarer feels that South has the ♣A, it may be best to win the ♠A and lead clubs immediately. South may not hold up with the ♣A exactly one round and may play the ♠Q, setting up East's ♠J. Also, the hearts might divide 3–3. If declarer feels that North holds the ♣A, it may be best to hold up the ♠A in case South has a five-card spade suit.

There's no "right" decision for declarer. Winning the first spade is probably the better choice. If South holds the ♣A, declarer will have a couple of chances. If North holds the ♣A, declarer still will have some chances if the spades divide 4–3.

If East wins the ♠A at trick one, the best play is to lead two rounds of clubs, hoping the defenders duck twice. Then declarer can take nine tricks. If East holds up the ♠A until the third round, the best play is still to lead two rounds of clubs. East now knows for certain that the missing spades are divided 4–3. If the defenders correctly take the ♣A on the second round, there is still the chance that hearts will divide 3–3. Even when hearts don't divide 3–3, declarer can still make the contract by cashing the top diamonds, bringing the total to eight. Now, knowing that North holds a good heart and no spades, declarer can lead a heart to North's high heart and hope that North's last card is a club and not a diamond.

Suggested Defense

If South does lead the ♠10 against 3NT, North must be careful to play the ♠K on the first trick. North can't tell whether South is simply leading the top of a sequence or is leading from an interior sequence. If South doesn't hold a higher honor, playing the ♠K is unlikely to make much of a difference, since declarer can always get three tricks from the ♠A Q J when North has the ♠K. If South is leading from an interior sequence, it is important for North to play the ♠K to prevent East from taking a trick with the ♠J.

Playing the ♠K on the first trick is unlikely to lose and may gain. Playing the ♠K on the actual layout is essential. It also would be necessary if South had led the ♠10 from something like ♠A Q 10 9 or ♠A 10 9 8 7.

Declarer may win the ♠A at trick one or may hold up until the third round. In either case, the critical decision for North is when to play the ♣A. If North takes the ♣A on the first round, declarer has an easy route to nine tricks. If North waits until the third round, declarer again will make nine tricks.

How does North know to win the ♣A on the second round of the suit? South should give a count signal in clubs by playing low-high to show an odd number of clubs, three in this instance. If South holds three clubs, declarer can hold only two clubs, so it is safe for North to win the ace on exactly the second round of clubs. Provided the defenders are careful from that point onward, with North holding on to all four hearts and South holding on to all four diamonds, declarer will be held to eight tricks.

North will have to watch South's play in the club suit carefully. The ♣7 may look like a high club at first, but when South follows with the ♣8 or ♣9 on the second trick, North should know what is going on.

Bid and Play — The Rule of Eleven

(E–Z Deal Cards: #7, Deal 4 — Dealer, West)

Suggested Bidding

WEST	NORTH	EAST	SOUTH
Pass	1♠	Pass	1NT
Pass	2NT	Pass	3NT
Pass	Pass	Pass	

West passes. With 18 high-card points plus 1 for the five-card suit, North is too strong to open 1NT. North starts the auction with 1♠. East doesn't have quite enough for a take-out double and passes.

South, without the strength to bid a new suit at the two level, responds 1NT. With a hand worth 19 points, North can invite game by raising to 2NT, showing 18 or 19 points.

Dealer: West
Vul: Both

```
              ♠ A K 8 6 4
              ♥ K 5 4
              ♦ A Q 5
              ♣ Q 5
♠ Q J 7 5              ♠ 10 9
♥ Q 10 8 7      N       ♥ A J 9 2
♦ J 3        W   E      ♦ 9 7 4
♣ 8 7 2         S       ♣ A 9 6 3
              ♠ 3 2
              ♥ 6 3
              ♦ K 10 8 6 2
              ♣ K J 10 4
```

With 7 high-card points plus 1 point for the five-card suit, South accepts the invitation and bids 3NT. Aggressive North players might raise directly to 3NT.

Suggested Opening Lead

West is on lead. Although the spades are better than the hearts, West should lead the unbid suit, hearts. With no sequence, West leads the ♥7, fourth highest.

Suggested Play

If the diamonds divide 3–2, declarer has five tricks in that suit to go with two sure tricks in spades. The remaining tricks needed for the contract can be promoted in the club suit.

The only danger is the heart suit. If the missing hearts divide 4–4, there will be no problem if West holds the ♥ A, since dummy's ♥ K will be a winner. Declarer should be in no hurry to play dummy's ♥ K at trick one. East might hold ♥ A Q 10 or ♥ A J 9, for example. Playing the ♥ K at trick one would not be successful. Declarer should play a low heart from dummy on the first trick, hoping that East will win. Now East can't continue leading the suit without giving a trick to dummy's ♥ K.

Suppose East plays the ♥ 2 on the first trick. West wins and leads a second heart. Now declarer can play dummy's ♥ K, hoping that West has the ♥ A. On the actual lie of the cards, however, declarer cannot avoid losing four heart tricks and the ♣ A, if the defenders handle the heart suit correctly.

Suggested Defense

If West leads the ♥ 7 and declarer plays a low heart from dummy on the first trick, East must be careful to play the ♥ 2. This is not a discouraging signal. East expects West's ♥ 7 to win the first trick!

East determines this by applying the rule of eleven. Assuming West has led fourth highest, East can subtract 7 from 11, leaving four cards higher than the ♥ 7 in the remaining three hands. East holds three cards higher than the ♥ 7 and can see one higher card in the dummy. That leaves declarer with no cards higher than West's ♥ 7.

Playing the ♥ 2 on the first trick is the only way to defeat the contract. Once West's ♥ 7 wins the first trick, West can lead a second heart, trapping North's ♥ K. The defenders take the first four heart tricks to go with the ♣ A. If East plays the ♥ J or ♥ 9 on the first trick, the contract can no longer be defeated. East can't continue hearts without giving a trick to dummy's ♥ K, and declarer will be able to establish enough winners in clubs to make the contract.

CHAPTER 8
Two-Over-One

TWO-OVER-ONE

The two-over-one approach is popular enough throughout North America to warrant some discussion. Whether or not a partnership adopts this approach, there will be opponents who use it. One key to reaching good contracts is for both partners to recognize whether a particular bid is forcing, invitational or sign-off. Using the two-over-one approach reduces the number of potential misunderstandings, leaving both partners feeling more confident during the auction. Using this approach requires that the partnership adopt the *forcing 1NT convention*.

Two-Over-One

Suppose East holds the following hand:

> ♠ K 6
> ♥ Q 9 4
> ♦ A Q 10 6 5
> ♣ A 7 5

West opens the bidding 1 ♥, and the auction proceeds:

WEST	NORTH	**EAST**	SOUTH
1 ♥	Pass	2 ♦	Pass
3 ♦	Pass	?	

Now what? West might hold any of the following hands:

a) ♠ Q 7
♥ K 8 7 6 3
♦ K J 7 3
♣ K 4

b) ♠ Q 7
♥ A K J 6 3
♦ K 9 7 3
♣ 6 4

c) ♠ A 7
♥ A K 10 6 3
♦ K 9 7 3
♣ 6 4

Opposite hand a), 4 ♥ is a better contract than 5 ♦, but even that contract is in some jeopardy. Opposite hand b), a small slam in hearts or diamonds can be made. Opposite hand c), a grand slam is a possibility. Playing standard methods, exploring the options is difficult at this point in the auction. A bid of 3 ♥ — an old suit at the three level — would be invitational, not forcing. A jump to 4 ♥ would be a sign-off. If East makes any other bid, the heart fit is likely to be lost.

To avoid such situations, many partnerships prefer to use a conventional agreement. When responder's first bid is a new suit at the two level, all bids below the game level are forcing. Using this approach, East could bid 3♥ in the above auction to show the heart fit, with the assurance that West won't pass. That would make it easier for the partnership to explore for the best game or slam contract. This style is referred to as *two-over-one game forcing*.

TWO-OVER-ONE GAME FORCING

Two-over-one refers to responder's initial bid of a new suit at the two level when opener started with a one-level bid in a suit. A 2♦ response to opener's 1♥ bid is a two-over-one response. It doesn't apply to a jump to the two level — such as 2♠ in response to an opening bid of 1♥ — which would be a jump shift. "Game forcing" implies that neither partner can pass until at least the game level has been reached.

In standard methods, a new suit at the two level by responder shows 10 or more points. With less strength, responder may only bid a new suit at the one level or bid 1NT. If the partnership agrees to use two-over-one game forcing, responder will need 13 or more points to respond in a new suit at the two level. With fewer than 13 points, responder can't afford to commit the partnership to the game level, since opener may have as few as 12 points. As a consequence, responder will have many more hands that fall into the category of a 1NT response.

Here are examples of responding to an opening bid of 1♥ when using two-over-one game forcing:

♠ 7 3	Respond 2♣. With a hand worth 15 points — 13
♥ J 5	HCPs plus 2 points for the six-card suit — this is
♦ A 9 2	the same response that would be made using stan-
♣ A K J 7 6 4	dard methods. The only difference is that opener
	now knows that the partnership is committed to
	at least the game level.

♠ K Q 10 8 5
♥ 7 3
♦ K 3
♣ A J 6 2

Respond 1♠. Although there is enough strength to commit the partnership to game, start by showing the spade suit at the one level. A jump to 2♠ would be a jump shift, showing a much stronger hand. The 1♠ response is still forcing, although it could be made on as few as 6 points. Show strength in the subsequent auction. This same response would be made using standard methods.

♠ K 10 6 3
♥ 4
♦ A Q 10 8 5 2
♣ K 4

Respond 2♦. With 14 points — 12 HCPs plus 2 points for the six-card suit — there is enough strength to bid a new suit at the two level. With two suits to show, start with the longer suit. Show the spade suit later in the auction. The auction would start the same way using standard methods.

♠ K J 5
♥ 4 2
♦ K Q 10 8 3
♣ J 7 3

Respond 1NT. With 11 points — 10 HCPs plus 1 for the five-card suit — there isn't enough strength to commit the partnership to the game level by responding 2♦. Without a suit that could be bid at the one level, the remaining choice is to respond 1NT. Playing standard methods, respond 2♦ with this hand, since the partnership could still stop below the game level after a two-over-one response.

♠ J 10 7 4
♥ 3
♦ K 9
♣ A Q 9 8 7 3

Respond 1♠. Using standard methods, respond 2♣ with this hand, showing the longer suit first. Playing two-over-one game forcing, there isn't enough strength to bid 2♣ and force the partnership to the game level. Instead, compromise by showing the spade suit at the one level.

♠ J 8
♥ —
♦ Q 7 5 3
♣ K 9 8 6 4 3 2

Respond 1NT. Whether playing standard methods or two-over-one, this hand isn't strong enough to bid clubs at the two level. An advantage to playing two-over-one is that opener will not pass 1NT and might rebid a minor. Even if opener rebids 2♥, responder's 3♣ would be non-forcing.

THE SUBSEQUENT AUCTION

After the two-over-one response, the auction can proceed naturally. There is the added bonus that neither partner needs to worry about whether or not a particular bid is invitational or forcing, since all bids are forcing until at least game is reached. This can conserve bidding room for exploration on some auctions, since neither partner needs to jump to create a forcing sequence.

Here are some examples of how the auction might proceed when playing two-over-one game forcing:

West					East
♠ A J 8 7 3	WEST	NORTH	EAST	SOUTH	♠ K Q 4
♥ 9 4	1 ♠	Pass	2 ♣	Pass	♥ Q 3
♦ K J	3 ♣	Pass	3 ♠	Pass	♦ Q 8 2
♣ K 10 8 4	4 ♠	Pass	Pass	Pass	♣ A Q J 6 2

East's 2 ♣ response to West's opening bid is forcing to the game level. When West raises clubs, East can show spade support at the three level without fear of being passed. East's 3 ♠ bid leaves room for West to show some extra values if interested in slam. When West simply continues to the game level, East has nothing further to add, and the partnership rests comfortably in the best game.

West					East
♠ K Q J 9 3	WEST	NORTH	EAST	SOUTH	♠ 10 6
♥ K Q 9 7	1 ♠	Pass	2 ♦	Pass	♥ A J 8 3
♦ 5	2 ♥	Pass	3 ♥	Pass	♦ A K Q 10 3
♣ A 7 5	4 ♣	Pass	4 ♦	Pass	♣ 6 3
	4NT	Pass	5 ♥	Pass	
	6 ♥	Pass	Pass	Pass	

After West starts the bidding with 1 ♠, East makes a two-over-one response of 2 ♦, forcing to game. When West shows the second suit, East can raise to the three level, rather than jump to game, since East's bid is forcing. This gives West room to cuebid the ♣A and then use the Blackwood convention, after East cooperates by cuebidding the ♦ A. (See Chapter 6 for more on slam bidding.) The partnership reaches an excellent slam contract. If East had jumped to 4 ♥ over West's 2 ♥ rebid to make sure the partnership reached game, West might have been hesitant to move any higher. The raise to 3 ♥ gave the partnership room for exploration before committing to a slam contract.

West		East
♠ A 10 8 5 3		♠ Q 2
♥ Q J 3		♥ K 7 4
♦ 8 4		♦ A K J 9 5 3 2
♣ K Q 10		♣ 2

WEST	NORTH	EAST	SOUTH
1♠	Pass	2♦	Pass
2NT	Pass	3♦	Pass
3NT	Pass	Pass	Pass

Playing standard methods, East would have an uncomfortable rebid over 2NT, since 3 ♦ would not be forcing. East would have to choose between raising to 3NT with a singleton club or jumping to 4 ♦, bypassing 3NT. Playing two-over-one, East comfortably rebids 3 ♦ after West's 2NT bid, since the 2 ♦ response has already committed the partnership to game. Having emphasized the diamond suit, East is happy to respect West's decision to play in notrump.

West		East
♠ A J 8 5 3		♠ Q 2
♥ A Q 3		♥ K 7 4
♦ 8 4		♦ A K J 9 5 3 2
♣ Q 9 3		♣ 2

WEST	NORTH	EAST	SOUTH
1♠	Pass	2♦	Pass
2NT	Pass	3♦	Pass
3♥	Pass	5♦	Pass
Pass	Pass		

The bidding starts the same way as in the previous auction, but on the third round, West shows a concentration of values in the heart suit. This warns East away from 3NT and into 5 ♦. Had East rebid 3NT rather than 3 ♦, the partnership would have finished in a poor contract. The advantage of the two-over-one response being forcing to game is that East had no worry that 3 ♦ would be passed.

PRINCIPLE OF FAST ARRIVAL

The advantage of two-over-one game forcing is that the partnership can take its time searching for the best contract after the initial two-over-one response. As a corollary to this approach, once the partnership has agreed on a suitable strain, an immediate jump to the game level shows no interest in exploring for a slam contract. This is called the *principle of fast arrival*. With interest in a slam contract, the partnership continues to explore below the game level.

Here are examples:

West		East
♠ A J 9 8 7 4		♠ K Q 3
♥ K 3		♥ A Q 9 7 4
♦ 10 4		♦ Q 9 3
♣ A 7 6		♣ 8 4

WEST	NORTH	EAST	SOUTH
1 ♠	Pass	2 ♥	Pass
2 ♠	Pass	4 ♠	Pass
Pass	Pass		

East's two-over-one response shows a hand worth 13 or more points, enough to force to game. With nothing extra, East takes the partnership directly to game following West's rebid. This is the principle of fast arrival. East has no interest in searching for a slam.

West		East
♠ A J 9 8 7 4		♠ K Q 3
♥ K 3		♥ A Q 9 7 4
♦ 10 4		♦ A 9 3
♣ A 7 6		♣ 8 4

WEST	NORTH	EAST	SOUTH
1 ♠	Pass	2 ♥	Pass
2 ♠	Pass	3 ♠	Pass
4 ♣	Pass	4 ♦	Pass
4 ♥	Pass	4NT	Pass
5 ♥	Pass	6 ♠	Pass
Pass	Pass		

The auction starts the same way as in the previous deal. With interest in a slam contract, East raises to only 3 ♠ on the second round. This lets West know that East has bigger things in mind — otherwise, East would have simply jumped to game. West cooperates by cuebidding the ♣A and then the ♥K (see Chapter 6), and the partnership reaches a good slam contract.

West		East
♠ A K J 8 3		♠ 7 4
♥ K Q 9 4		♥ J 5
♦ K 7 2		♦ A J 9 3
♣ 6		♣ K Q J 10 7

WEST	NORTH	EAST	SOUTH
1 ♠	Pass	2 ♣	Pass
2 ♥	Pass	3NT	Pass
Pass	Pass		

After starting with a two-over-one response, East jumps to game after West's rebid. West has a nice hand, but East's fast arrival at 3NT shows no interest in going further. West passes, leaving the partnership in its best contract.

West		East
♠ 4		♠ A 10 9
♥ A Q J 9 2		♥ 8 4
♦ A J 10 5 3		♦ K Q 9
♣ 9 2		♣ A K 8 7 3

WEST	NORTH	EAST	SOUTH
1♥	Pass	2♣	Pass
2♦	Pass	2NT	Pass
3♦	Pass	4♦	Pass
4♥	Pass	4NT	Pass
5♥	Pass	6♦	Pass
Pass	Pass		

After West's 2♦ rebid, East might jump to 3NT, playing standard methods, to make sure the partnership reaches game. West wouldn't know whether to bid again or to leave the partnership in 3NT. Playing two-over-one, East can afford to rebid only 2NT, since that is a forcing bid. West has an opportunity to finish describing the hand by rebidding the five-card diamond suit, and the partnership will reach an excellent slam contract in diamonds.

HANDLING INTERFERENCE

If an opponent makes an overcall directly over the opening bid, then a two-over-one response by responder is no longer treated as forcing to game. The response is still forcing for at least one round, but responder may have fewer than 13 points. For example, consider the following hands for East after the auction starts like this:

WEST	NORTH	**EAST**	SOUTH
1♦	1♠	?	

♠ 9 4
♥ K Q 10 9 7 5
♦ A 7 6
♣ 10 5

East responds 2♥. North's overcall prevents East from showing the heart suit at the one level. With 11 points — 9 HCPs plus 2 for the six-card suit — there isn't enough to force the partnership to game, but East wants to show the heart suit. Even if the partnership plays two-over-one game forcing, it doesn't apply when an opponent overcalls. East can respond 2♥ without committing the partnership to game. If partner rebids 2NT, for example, East can make a non-forcing rebid of 3♥.

♠ 9 5
♥ K Q 10 9 7 5
♦ A K 6
♣ 10 5

East responds 2♥. East has enough to force to the game level — 12 HCPs plus 2 points for the six-card suit. A 2♥ response is forcing for one round, but it isn't forcing to game. If West rebids 2NT, for example, East can't afford to bid 3♦ or 3♥. West might pass. East has to make certain the partnership reaches game by jumping to 4♥.

If an opponent interferes after a two-over-one response, the partnership is still committed to the game level — unless it appears more profitable to double the opponents' contract. If partner will have another opportunity to bid, however, either player can pass to await developments.

For example, consider the following auctions:

West	WEST	NORTH	EAST	SOUTH	East
♠ A J 10 7 2	1♠	Pass	2♣	2♦	♠ K Q 3
♥ K J 3	Pass	Pass	2♠	Pass	♥ A 4 2
♦ 10 6 3	4♠	Pass	Pass	Pass	♦ 8 4
♣ K 6					♣ A 10 9 5 3

East's 2♣ response is forcing to game. When South interferes with 2♦, West can afford to pass, because East will have another opportunity to bid. West's pass is actually quite descriptive. It says that West doesn't have great support for responder's suit, doesn't want to rebid spades, doesn't want to double 2♦ for penalty and doesn't want to bid 2NT — with no stopper in the opponent's suit. When the bidding comes back to East, East can afford to show spade support by bidding 2♠. There is no need to jump, since the partnership is already forced to game. On hearing about the spade support, West can go directly to the game level. West uses the principle of fast arrival, showing nothing extra by going directly to 4♠. A raise to 3♠ by West would show interest in exploring further.

West	WEST	NORTH	EAST	SOUTH	East
♠ J 9 4	1♥	Pass	2♦	2♠	♠ Q 7 3
♥ A K Q 7 3	Pass	Pass	Dbl	Pass	♥ 4
♦ 4 2	Pass	Pass			♦ A K 9 5 3
♣ K 7 6					♣ A 8 4 2

East's 2♦ response commits the partnership to game — unless something better comes along. When South overcalls 2♠, West can pass to see what partner has to say. East's double suggests defending for penalty, and West is happy to comply. The penalty from 2♠ doubled is likely to be more than enough to compensate East–West for any contract they could make.

When Responder Is a Passed Hand

When responder has passed originally, a two-over-one response is no longer forcing to game. If responder didn't have enough to open the bidding, responder is unlikely to have enough to commit the partnership to game. In fact, since opener may open a little light in third or fourth position, responder's two-over-one isn't even 100% forcing for one round. Consider the following auctions:

West					East
♠ A Q 7 6 3	WEST	NORTH	EAST	SOUTH	♠ 4 2
♥ K Q 6 2			Pass	Pass	♥ A J
♦ 10	1♠	Pass	2♦	Pass	♦ K J 9 8 6 5 3
♣ J 7 4	2♥	Pass	3♦	Pass	♣ 10 5
	Pass	Pass			

Since East passed originally, the 2♦ response is no longer forcing to game. When East rebids the diamond suit, West can pass, leaving the partnership in partscore.

West					East
♠ A K 9 8 4	WEST	NORTH	EAST	SOUTH	♠ 7 3
♥ J 8 2			Pass	Pass	♥ A Q 10 7 3
♦ K 9 2	1♠	Pass	2♥	Pass	♦ Q 7 5
♣ 6 3	Pass	Pass			♣ Q 8 2

Having opened light in third position, West can pass East's two-over-one response. The partnership settles in partscore and should score a small plus.

1NT FORCING

Playing two-over-one game forcing requires that responder bid 1NT on all of those hands that are not strong enough to bid two-over-one. The 1NT response now covers a wide variety of hands ranging from 6 to 12 points, rather than the standard range of 6 to 10* points. This can make it difficult for the partnership to reach the best contract. Especially when the opening bid is in a major suit, responder has less room to bid a new suit at the one level. To compensate for this, partnerships playing two-over-one game forcing usually play that a 1NT response to a major suit is forcing, rather than invitational. A response of 1NT to a minor suit remains as an invitational response.

1NT forcing also can be used by partnerships that don't play two-over-one game forcing, but it's more commonly used in conjunction with a combination of five-card majors and two-over-one.

Responding 1NT Forcing

Playing two-over-one game forcing, East, as responder, would bid 1NT following a 1♠ bid by West, as opener, with each of the following hands:

♠ 8 3
♥ K 10 9 4
♦ Q J 7 3
♣ Q 10 5

This is a typical 1NT response whether playing standard methods or two-over-one. If the partnership is playing 1NT forcing, the difference is that East will never get to play in the 1NT contract. West is forced to bid again. This is a disadvantage of playing 1NT forcing, since 1NT might be the best contract for the partnership.

♠ 4
♥ Q J 9 6 5 4 2
♦ 8 3
♣ K 8 4

East would bid 1NT playing either standard methods or two-over-one. Here it's an advantage to play 1NT forcing, since West must bid again. East will get an opportunity to bid, planning to show the long, weak, heart suit later. Using standard methods, East might be left to play in 1NT.

*Assuming that opener may have a 12 point hand.

♠ 9 4
♥ A Q 4
♦ J 10 7 5
♣ K J 9 3

This hand would be too strong to respond 1NT in standard methods, and East would start with a new suit at the two level, 2♣. Playing a two-over-one game force, East isn't strong enough to bid a new suit at the two level and commit the partnership to game, so East would start with 1NT. Since this is now a forcing bid, East will have an opportunity to show extra strength after hearing West's rebid.

♠ K J 3
♥ Q 9 6 2
♦ K 7 6 2
♣ Q 4

This hand is worth a limit raise of West's major suit. Most partnerships prefer not to make an immediate limit raise with only three-card support. In standard methods, East would start by bidding a new suit, 2♦, intending to show spade support by rebidding 3♠ at the next opportunity. Playing two-over-one, East can't bid 2♦, since that would be forcing to game. Instead, East starts with 1NT. Since this is forcing, East will be able to show spade support and strength later.

The 1NT response is forcing, only when opener has started with a major suit. Consider the following hands for East, as responder, after West has opened bidding with 1♦:

♠ K 10 8
♥ Q J 7
♦ 10 4
♣ Q 9 7 6 2

This hand is a typical 1NT response. The 1NT response isn't forcing.

♠ 4 3
♥ K J 8 5
♦ K Q 8 6 3
♣ Q 5

East would bid 1♥, showing a four-card major suit. When West opens with a minor suit bid, East usually has a bid that can be made at the one level. It would be a different matter if the opening bid were 1♠. East wouldn't be able to show any suit at the one level and couldn't bid a new suit at the two level when playing a two-over-one game force. That's the reason 1NT forcing is used in response to major-suit openings, rather than minor-suit openings.

♠ 9 6 2
♥ A 8
♦ 7 5
♣ Q 10 8 7 6 3

East has to bid 1NT with an unbalanced hand. This is non-forcing, even if the partnership is playing 1NT forcing, since it's in response to a minor suit. Some hands are inconvenient no matter what methods the partnership uses.

♠ Q 4
♥ K 8 2
♦ J 5 3
♣ A J 10 8 2

This hand would be straightforward playing standard methods, since East could bid 2♣. It's awkward when playing two-over-one forcing, because East isn't strong enough to bid a new suit at the two level and must be content with a non-forcing 1NT. Some partnerships get around this by using a 2NT response to show a balanced hand of 11 or 12 points, or by not treating a 2♣ response to 1♦ as game forcing (see Exceptions to Two-Over-One Game Force in the Appendix). Most partnerships, however, accept that responder occasionally will hold a hand of 11 or 12 points for a 1NT response to 1♦.

This last situation will arise less frequently when the opening bid is 1♣. If responder can't bid a new suit at the one level, responder must have at least four clubs. Responder will usually be able to raise clubs to the appropriate level. The partnership may still treat the 1NT response to 1♣ as possibly showing up to 12 points, however, since responder may be reluctant to make a limit raise of clubs with only four-card support.

Opener's Rebid

When opener starts with one of a major suit and responder bids 1NT, opener has to bid again when playing 1NT forcing. This usually doesn't present a problem, since opener can rebid in exactly the same manner as if responder had made a standard 1NT response. The only exception is when opener holds a minimum balanced hand that would normally pass a 1NT response. Opener now has to bid again and may have to manufacture a bid on a three-card suit.

Here are examples for West, as opener, after the auction starts:

WEST	NORTH	EAST	SOUTH
1♥	Pass	1NT	Pass
?			

♠ J 8
♥ K J 10 8 6
♦ 6
♣ A K 10 5 2

West rebids 2♣. This is West's natural rebid. West would make the same rebid even if the 1NT response were not forcing.

♠ Q 5
♥ A Q J 10 7 5
♦ A Q 6
♣ 9 3

West rebids 3♥. The 1NT forcing response hasn't changed West's standard rebid.

♠ A Q 7
♥ K Q J 8 3
♦ K 9
♣ K 10 4

West raises to 2NT. This is the standard way to show a balanced hand worth 18 or 19 points. West's raise to 2NT invites East to bid game.

♠ A 8 4
♥ K 10 9 6 2
♦ A 6 5
♣ Q 3

West rebids 2♦. If 1NT weren't forcing, West would pass, leaving East to play in partscore. Because West is forced to make a rebid, a bid has to be manufactured in a three-card suit. West has already shown a five-card heart suit. A rebid of 2♥ would tend to show a six-card suit (but see next example). A raise to 2NT would show 18 or 19 points. Instead, West must treat the diamonds as though they are a four-card suit. East will be aware of this possibility.

♠ K 9 6 4
♥ A K J 6 3
♦ Q 4
♣ 9 2

West rebids 2♥. This is an awkward hand. A rebid of 2♠ would be a reverse, since it prevents East from returning to hearts, West's original suit, at the two level. Besides, East could have bid 1♠ with four cards in that suit, so there is no eight-card fit in spades. Rather than bid a two-card minor suit, West rebids the major, hearts. East will expect West to have a six-card suit, but it's the best that can be done. Hands like this are the reason some partnerships like to use the Flannery convention (see the Appendix).

♠ J 5
♥ Q J 9 5 3
♦ A J 5
♣ K 7 3

West rebids 2♣. With a choice of three-card minor suits, most players respond 2♣. This is similar to opening the bidding with a choice of three-card minors.

Responder's Rebid

After using 1NT forcing, responder will have an opportunity to bid again after hearing opener's rebid. If opener's rebid is 2♣ or 2♦, responder must be aware that opener may have been forced to bid a three-card suit.

Here are some examples of how East, the responder, handles the auction after the bidding has started:

WEST	NORTH	**EAST**	SOUTH
1♠	Pass	1NT	Pass
2♣	Pass	?	

♠ 5
♥ Q 10 7 3
♦ J 9 6 4
♣ K 8 6 5

East passes. Although the 1NT response was forcing on West, East isn't required to bid again unless West makes a jump shift or reverses. West may have only a three-card club suit, but a partscore contract of 2♣ looks like the best spot for East–West.

♠ 4
♥ J 10 8 7 5 4 2
♦ K 9 4
♣ J 3

East rebids 2♥. East has an opportunity to show the heart suit, having denied the strength for a two-over-one response. This is an advantage of playing 1NT forcing, since East will always get another chance to bid with an unbalanced hand.

In standard methods, East might have ended as declarer in 1NT.

♠ J 7
♥ K 10 9 7
♦ A Q 8 3
♣ J 6 2

East rebids 2NT. This shows a balanced hand of 11 or 12 points, inviting West to continue to game.

♠ K 6
♥ J 9 5 2
♦ Q 8 6 5
♣ Q 8 4

East rebids 2 ♠. This hand illustrates an important concept when giving preference between opener's suits. Although East has more clubs than spades, East should return to West's original suit unless East has at least two more cards in the second suit. West is guaranteed to hold at least five spades, so the partnership will be in a 5–2 fit at worst. West might have a three-card club suit, so passing risks playing in a 3–3 fit. Finally, by returning to 2 ♠, East gives West another chance to bid. West could have 17 or 18 points, not quite enough for a jump shift, and might welcome the opportunity to take another bid.

♠ A J 4
♥ K Q 3
♦ 9 7 4 2
♣ J 10 5

East jumps to 3 ♠. This shows the values for a limit raise in West's major suit but with only three-card support. Some partnerships might make an immediate jump raise to 3 ♠, but most partnerships prefer to have four-card support for a direct limit raise. Playing 1NT forcing together with two-over-one is an improvement over standard methods in this regard, since East doesn't have to start with a new suit response, such as 2 ♦.

♠ 8 2
♥ 6 5 3
♦ A Q 5
♣ K J 8 6 3

East raises to 3 ♣. With a hand of invitational strength, East can raise West's second suit. East should have five cards to raise West's minor suit, since West may have been forced to bid a three-card suit.

♠ 6
♥ 10 8 4
♦ A K J 10 7 5
♣ Q 9 3

East jumps to 3 ♦. This shows a good six-card suit with just under the strength for a two-over-one response. It's an invitational bid, and West can pass with a minimum hand. With a weaker hand, East would rebid only 2 ♦.

♠ K J 4
♥ 9 2
♦ A 7 5
♣ Q J 10 5 3

Jump to 4 ♠. East was planning to show a limit raise with three-card support by bidding 3 ♠ on the second round. West's 2 ♣ rebid improves the partnership's prospects of making a game contract, since the hands are likely to fit well together. East can revalue the hand as worth taking a chance on going all the way to game.

Handling Interference

If there is an overcall or takeout double of the opening bid, responder's 1NT is no longer treated as forcing. It becomes a natural response showing 6 to 10 points.

For example, suppose East holds the following hands after the auction has started:

WEST	NORTH	**EAST**	SOUTH
1♥	1♠	?	

♠ K J 9
♥ J 5
♦ K 10 8 4
♣ J 10 7 3

East responds 1NT. After the overcall, 1NT becomes a natural response. West can pass with a minimum-strength balanced hand.

♠ 8 6
♥ 10 4
♦ A J 10 8 7 4
♣ A 10 3

East responds 2♦. If North hadn't interfered, East would have responded 1NT, since there isn't enough strength for a two-over-one response. After the overcall, a two-over-one response is no longer forcing to game, so East can bid a new suit at the two level with as few as 10 or 11 points.

♠ 7 6 3 2
♥ Q 5
♦ K J 4
♣ 9 8 4 2

East passes. Although East would respond 1NT if North had passed, there is no need to bid after the overcall. With no strength in the opponent's suit, this isn't a good hand to be playing in a notrump contract from East's side. With a strong hand, West will get another opportunity to bid.

If an opponent interferes after responder has bid 1NT forcing, opener is no longer forced to bid. Responder makes a normal rebid if room is available but has other options. Opener can pass with a minimum-strength hand or double the opponent's contract for penalty.

For example, suppose West holds the following hands after the auction has started:

WEST	NORTH	EAST	SOUTH
1♠	Pass	1NT	2♦
?			

♠ A Q J 9 4
♥ K Q 10 5
♦ 9
♣ Q 8 4

West rebids 2♥. South's overcall hasn't prevented West from making a normal rebid to show a second suit.

♠ K J 9 6 4
♥ A J 4
♦ J 5
♣ K 7 2

West passes. If South hadn't interfered, West would have had to rebid 2♣ on a three-card suit, since East's 1NT response is forcing. South's overcall gives West a chance to pass and show a minimum-strength hand.

♠ A K 8 4 2
♥ A 5
♦ K J 10 8
♣ 7 6

West doubles. This double is for penalty, suggesting that South has picked an inopportune time to enter the bidding.

♠ K Q 9 7 5
♥ K 5
♦ 10 6
♣ A J 8 3

West passes. South's bid prevents West from showing the club suit at the two level. West doesn't have enough strength to bid 3♣, since that might get the partnership too high if East has a weak hand and no fit. The best choice is to pass.

1NT by a Passed Hand

When responder passed originally, a 1NT response to a major suit is still intended as forcing, but opener can pass if game is very unlikely.

For example, suppose West holds the following hands after the auction has started:

WEST	NORTH	EAST	SOUTH
		Pass	Pass
1♥	Pass	1NT	Pass
?			

♠ A K 4
♥ Q 10 9 7 5
♦ Q 5
♣ 9 6 3

West passes. West has opened light in third position. There's no reason to expect that the partnership can make a game contract once East passed originally. It's unlikely that the partnership has a better contract than 1NT. Rebidding 2♣ could get the partnership into trouble.

♠ 6 4
♥ K Q 10 7 5
♦ 10 7
♣ A Q 10 2

West rebids 2♣. With a minimum-strength hand, it's unlikely that the partnership can make a game contract after East passed on the first round. Nonetheless, West should make a natural rebid of 2♣ to show an unbalanced hand and let East pick the best spot to play. Note that with only three clubs (a balanced hand), West would probably pass 1NT.

♠ A Q 5
♥ A K J 10 8 4
♦ 8
♣ J 7 4

West rebids 3♥. Although East is a passed hand, a game is still possible. West should make a standard rebid to show a medium-strength hand with a six-card or longer heart suit.

Sample Auctions

Once responder starts with 1NT forcing, the auction can proceed in many different directions. Here are examples.

West
♠ K Q 10 8 3
♥ A 8 5
♦ K 9 3
♣ 6 4

WEST	NORTH	EAST	SOUTH
1♠	Pass	1NT	Pass
2♦	Pass	2♠	Pass
Pass	Pass		

East
♠ J 5
♥ 10 7 4
♦ Q J 6
♣ K 10 8 7 3

East's 1NT response is forcing, so West can't pass. With a five-card spade suit and no second four-card or longer suit, West rebids the three-card diamond suit. East is careful to give preference back to the major suit. The partnership is assured of playing in a 5–2 fit. 2♦ would not have been a comfortable spot. Playing standard methods, the partnership would have rested in 1NT, but 2♠ is also a reasonable contract.

West	WEST	NORTH	EAST	SOUTH	East
♠ A J 9 7 4	1♠	Pass	1NT	Pass	♠ 5
♥ J 6	2♣	Pass	2♥	Pass	♥ K 10 9 7 5 3
♦ Q 9 5	Pass	Pass			♦ J 10 8 6
♣ A 9 3					♣ J 6

Playing standard methods, East might have been left to play in 1NT. Using 1NT forcing, East gets an opportunity to show the heart suit on the second round. West has no reason to expect that there is a better spot than 2 ♥, if East has a weak hand with a long heart suit.

West	WEST	NORTH	EAST	SOUTH	East
♠ 9 3	1♥	Pass	1NT	Pass	♠ A 10 6
♥ Q J 9 5 2	2♣	Pass	3♥	Pass	♥ K 10 4
♦ K 3	4♥	Pass	Pass	Pass	♦ Q 10 8 2
♣ A K J 5					♣ Q 9 3

East isn't strong enough to make a game-forcing two-over-one response and doesn't want to make a limit raise with only three-card support. East starts with a forcing 1NT and then shows three-card heart support and 11 or 12 points by jumping on the second round. With a little extra, West accepts the invitation.

West	WEST	NORTH	EAST	SOUTH	East
♠ A Q J 9 7 4	1♠	Pass	1NT	Pass	♠ K 8
♥ K 5	2♠	Pass	3♠	Pass	♥ A 9 7 4
♦ 10 8 3	Pass	Pass			♦ 5 4 2
♣ Q 5					♣ K J 7 3

West's 2 ♠ rebid after the forcing 1NT response shows a six-card suit, so East can afford to raise with a doubleton as an invitational bid. With a minimum-strength hand, West declines the invitation.

West	WEST	NORTH	EAST	SOUTH	East
♠ A Q 9 8 2	1♠	Pass	1NT	Pass	♠ 3
♥ Q J 10 6	2♥	Pass	4♥	Pass	♥ K 9 8 7 4
♦ Q 3	Pass	Pass			♦ A J 10 5
♣ K 5					♣ Q 6 2

East doesn't have enough to make a two-over-one response and starts with 1NT. On hearing West's rebid, East revalues the hand and decides that it is worth a shot at game.

West	WEST	NORTH	EAST	SOUTH	East
♠ A K Q 8 5	1♠	Pass	1NT	Pass	♠ 10 6
♥ Q 5	2♦	Pass	2♠	Pass	♥ K J 9 3
♦ K Q 10 7 3	3♦	Pass	3NT	Pass	♦ J 9 2
♣ 5	Pass	Pass			♣ Q J 10 8

West doesn't have enough to jump shift after East's 1NT response, but when East gives preference back to spades, West bids again to show the 5–5 hand pattern. With strength in the other suits, East presses on to a reasonable 3NT contract.

West	WEST	NORTH	EAST	SOUTH	East
♠ Q 6 2	1♥	Pass	1NT	Pass	♠ 9 5
♥ K Q 8 6 4	2♦	Pass	3♣	Pass	♥ 7 2
♦ A J 8 3	Pass	Pass			♦ K 4 2
♣ 5					♣ A Q J 10 8 3

East can't afford to commit the partnership to game with a two-over-one response. Once West rebids 2♦, East has a good enough suit to bid it invitationally at the three level. With a minimum, West goes no further.

West	WEST	NORTH	EAST	SOUTH	East
♠ A J 8 7 3	1♠	Pass	1NT	Pass	♠ 5
♥ K 8 6	2♦	Pass	Pass	Pass	♥ J 10 7 3
♦ A 10 3					♦ K 9 4
♣ 6 2					♣ Q 9 7 6 3

Every convention has its drawbacks, and on these hands, East–West wind up playing in their 3–3 fit. 1NT would probably be a better contract, but 2♦ will prove interesting. West can't pass the 1NT forcing response, and East can't afford to bid beyond 2♦ in search of a better spot.

SUMMARY

If the partnership agrees to play two-over-one game forcing, a response at the two level in a new suit is forcing to game. This doesn't apply if responder is a passed hand or if the opponents interfere over the opening bid. Once responder has made a game-forcing two-over-one response, the partnership bidding can proceed slowly to find the best game or slam contract, since all bids are forcing until game is reached. Once the partnership has agreed on the strain, a jump to game usually indicates no interest in further investigation — the principle of fast arrival. With interest in slam, or uncertainty about the best strain, the bidding can be prolonged.

When the partnership plays two-over-one game forcing, a 1NT response has to be used with a greater range of hands than when using standard methods. To compensate, most partnerships play 1NT forcing when the opening bid is a major suit. Playing 1NT forcing, opener must bid again after a response of 1NT to an opening bid of 1 ♥ or 1 ♠, unless responder is a passed hand or the opponents have interfered in the auction. With a minimum-strength balanced hand, opener will have to rebid in a three-card minor suit, and responder will need to allow for this possibility.

If opener makes a minimum-strength rebid at the two level — a rebid of the original suit or a new suit that is lower-ranking than the original suit — responder rebids as follows:

Responder's Rebid after a Forcing 1NT and a Minimum Rebid by Opener

- Pass, to play in opener's last bid suit — remembering that a minor-suit rebid by opener may be only three cards.

- Return to the two level of opener's major suit. This will usually show only two-card support, since responder could raise immediately with three-card support.

- Bid a new suit, without a jump. This shows a five-card or longer suit with a weak hand and is non-forcing.

- Bid three of opener's major suit. This is invitational, showing a hand of limit-raise strength with only three-card support — or two-card support if opener has rebid the major suit.

- Raise opener's second suit. This is invitational. If opener's second suit is a minor, responder will usually have five-card support.

- Bid 2NT. This is invitational, showing 11 or 12 points with strength in the unbid suits.

- Bid a new suit with a jump. This is invitational, showing a good six-card or longer suit with less than the strength for a game-forcing two-over-one response.

- Jump to game. This occurs if responder revalues the hand as being worth going to game after hearing opener's response.

NOTE: See the Appendix (pages 360–361) for a discussion of these supplemental conventions and/or treatments.

Exceptions to Two-Over-One Game Force

Constructive Raises

Note: The following exercises illustrate the methods outlined in the summary.

Exercise One — Two-Over-One Game Forcing

West opens the bidding 1 ♥. What does East respond with each of the following hands?

1) ♠ K 10 6	2) ♠ Q J 7 6 3	3) ♠ 5 2
♥ J 6	♥ 9 3	♥ Q 9 4
♦ Q 10 8 5 3	♦ K 7	♦ 7 6 3
♣ Q 9 5	♣ A Q J 2	♣ A J 8 6 2
4) ♠ J 7 2	5) ♠ K 9 8 5	6) ♠ 10 3
♥ 4	♥ 10 6	♥ 6
♦ A K J 7 4	♦ A K J 6 3	♦ A J 5 3
♣ Q 10 8 4	♣ K 5	♣ K J 10 6 3 2

Exercise One *Answer* — Two-Over-One Game Forcing

1) 1NT. This is the same bid East would make whether or not the partnership plays two-over-one. The only difference is that East knows West will bid again since the 1NT response is forcing. That will be too bad if 1NT is the best possible contract on this deal, but it's the price that must be paid for using this convention.

2) 1♠. No reason for East not to make a natural response. 1♠ is forcing.

3) 2♥. Playing five-card majors, East should raise with three-card support.

4) 1NT. Playing natural methods, East could respond 2♦. Playing two-over-one, a response of 2♦ would be forcing to game. East isn't quite strong enough for that and must settle for 1NT. The good news is that West will bid again, giving East an opportunity to further describe the hand.

5) 2♦. East has enough to commit the partnership to game and makes a natural response, bidding the longest suit first.

6) 1NT. Unless the partnership is playing that a response of 2♣ followed by 3♣ is non forcing, East has to make a forcing 1NT response. East will have an opportunity to show the club suit after West makes a rebid.

Exercise Two — Opener's Rebids

What call does West make with the following hands after the auction goes as shown?

1) ♠ A K J 8 7 3
   ♥ 10 5
   ♦ Q J 9
   ♣ J 8

WEST	NORTH	EAST	SOUTH
1 ♠	Pass	2 ♥	Pass
2 ♠	Pass	3 ♣	Pass
?			

2) ♠ K J 8 6 2
   ♥ A Q 8 3
   ♦ 9 4
   ♣ Q 5

WEST	NORTH	EAST	SOUTH
1 ♠	Pass	2 ♦	Pass
2 ♥	Pass	2NT	Pass
?			

3) ♠ 8 6
   ♥ K Q 10 8 6 2
   ♦ 9 4
   ♣ A K 5

WEST	NORTH	EAST	SOUTH
1 ♥	Pass	2 ♦	Pass
2 ♥	Pass	3 ♥	Pass
?			

4) ♠ K 10 8 7 4
   ♥ J 8 3
   ♦ K 4
   ♣ A 7 5

WEST	NORTH	EAST	SOUTH
		Pass	Pass
1 ♠	Pass	2 ♥	Pass
?			

5) ♠ 10 6
   ♥ K Q 10 8 5
   ♦ A Q J 3
   ♣ 5 4

WEST	NORTH	EAST	SOUTH
1 ♥	1 ♠	2 ♣	Pass
2 ♦	Pass	3 ♣	Pass
?			

Exercise Two *Answer* — Opener's Rebids

1) 4♠. East's 2♥ response committed the partnership to at least game. East's 3♠ bid is forcing, leaving room to explore slam possibilities. With nothing to add to the conversation, West settles for 4♠.

2) 3NT. The 2NT bid is forcing once East started with a two-over-one. West has shown a five-card spade suit and a four-card heart suit. If East doesn't want to support either of these suits, notrump looks like the spot.

3) 4♣. After the 2♦ response, the partnership is committed to at least game. East's 3♥ bid shows interest in a slam. With a minimum hand and heart support, East could have jumped to 4♥. West should co-operate with East by cuebidding 4♣ (see Chapter 6). The first-round control of clubs may be what East needs to know about before bidding a slam.

4) Pass. Since East passed originally, the 2♥ response is not forcing. With a light opening bid, there's no need for West to bid again. Hearts should be a satisfactory trump suit.

5) Pass. After the interference, East's 2♣ bid is not game forcing. The 3♣ bid is only invitational so, with nothing else to say, West should stop in partscore.

Exercise Three — Principle of Fast Arrival

What does East call with each of the following hands after the auction goes as shown?

1)	WEST	NORTH	**EAST**	SOUTH	♠ A 4
	1♥	Pass	2♦	Pass	♥ Q 7 5
	2♥	Pass	?		♦ A K J 9 7 5
					♣ 6 4

2)	WEST	NORTH	**EAST**	SOUTH	♠ K Q 7
	1♠	Pass	2♣	Pass	♥ 8 4 3
	2♠	Pass	?		♦ 10 3
					♣ A Q J 8 5

3)	WEST	NORTH	**EAST**	SOUTH	♠ K 2
	1♥	Pass	2♣	Pass	♥ 7 3
	2♦	Pass	?		♦ K Q 8 3
					♣ A J 9 7 5

4)	WEST	NORTH	**EAST**	SOUTH	♠ K Q 10
	1♥	Pass	2♣	Pass	♥ 3
	2♥	Pass	?		♦ Q J 10 5
					♣ K Q 9 7 3

5)	WEST	NORTH	**EAST**	SOUTH	♠ 9 3
	1♠	Pass	2♣	Pass	♥ A J 6
	2♥	Pass	?		♦ K Q 3
					♣ A K 9 8 5

Exercise Four — 1NT Forcing

What does West respond with each of the following hands, when East opens the bidding 1♥ and South passes?

1) ♠ K J 4
♥ 9 3
♦ A J 10 7
♣ Q 10 6 3

2) ♠ 10 8 3
♥ 6
♦ K J 8 7 6 2
♣ K 9 4

3) ♠ J 6 2
♥ A 10 4
♦ J 4 3
♣ K Q 6 2

Exercise Three *Answer* — Principle of Fast Arrival

1) 3♥. The 2♦ response by East committed the partnership to at least game. There still could be a slam, if West has a good heart suit and first- or second-round control of clubs. East should raise to the three level to leave room to explore. West may be able to cuebid 4♣. If not, East can settle for game.

2) 4♠. If West has a minimum opening bid, East has no interest in going beyond game. By jumping to game, East uses the principle of fast arrival to send that message to West.

3) 3♦. East can't be certain that the best contract is 5♦. The partnership might still belong in 3NT, 4♥ — if West has six of them — or even 6♦. East should raise to 3♦, and see what partner has to say next.

4) 3NT. Without a fit in West's suit and strength in all of the other suits, East jumps to game in notrump. By using the principle of fast arrival, West gets the message that East doesn't have much interest in any other contract. By bidding 2NT first and then 3NT, East would be indicating interest in other contracts.

5) 2NT. No need to jump to 3NT when there is the possibility of bigger things. East leaves room for West to make a further descriptive bid. West might rebid 3♥, for example, showing a five-card suit, and slam might be possible.

Exercise Four *Answer* — 1NT Forcing

1) 1NT. Playing standard methods, West would be too strong for 1NT. Playing two-over-one, a 1NT response is forcing, so West will have an opportunity to show additional strength on the rebid.

2) 1NT. The forcing 1NT response doesn't promise a balanced hand.

3) 1NT. West has enough strength for a limit raise in hearts but only three-card support. West should start with a forcing 1NT response, planning to bid 3♥ at the next opportunity.

Exercise Five — Opener's Rebid after 1NT Forcing

What does West rebid with the following hands after the auction shown?

WEST	NORTH	EAST	SOUTH
1♠	Pass	1NT	Pass
?			

1) ♠ Q J 9 7 5 3
   ♥ J 4
   ♦ A 7 3
   ♣ K J

2) ♠ K Q 9 8 3
   ♥ 4
   ♦ A J 8 4 2
   ♣ Q 3

3) ♠ A 10 8 7 3
   ♥ Q 5
   ♦ K 7 2
   ♣ A 9 3

4) ♠ A Q J 8 3
   ♥ K J 7
   ♦ A J 6
   ♣ Q 4

5) ♠ A Q J 7 4
   ♥ A 9 4
   ♦ 10 7 3
   ♣ J 5

6) ♠ A K Q 9 6
   ♥ 8
   ♦ K 6 4
   ♣ A K 10 3

Exercise Six — Responder's Rebid after 1NT Forcing

What does East rebid with the following hands after the auction shown?

WEST	NORTH	EAST	SOUTH
1♠	Pass	1NT	Pass
2♦	Pass	?	

1) ♠ J 2
   ♥ 10 7 4 2
   ♦ K 7 3
   ♣ Q 9 4 2

2) ♠ 8
   ♥ A 6 4
   ♦ J 9 7 4
   ♣ J 10 7 6 3

3) ♠ 7 3
   ♥ K Q 10 9 5
   ♦ 7 5
   ♣ Q 8 6 2

4) ♠ 9 7
   ♥ K Q 9 8
   ♦ J 6 5
   ♣ A Q 7 5

5) ♠ K 10 5
   ♥ A J 5 3
   ♦ Q 8
   ♣ J 7 4 3

6) ♠ 8
   ♥ A Q J 9 8 5
   ♦ J 6 4
   ♣ Q 9 4

Exercise Five *Answer* — Opener's Rebid after 1NT Forcing

1) 2♠. West has an opportunity to show the sixth spade. This is the same rebid West would make if 1NT were not a forcing response.

2) 2♦. West should make a natural rebid, showing the second suit.

3) 2♣. If the 1NT response were not forcing, West could pass. Using this convention, however, West has to manufacture a rebid. With no four-card suit, West bids 2♣ on the three-card suit. West can't raise to 2NT, since East might have a very weak hand.

4) 2NT. With a balanced hand too strong to open 1NT, West raises to 2NT. That bid shows this type of hand.

5) 2♦. Ugly, but West doesn't want to rebid 2♠ with only a five-card suit or bid 2♣ with a doubleton. 2♦ is the lesser of evils.

6) 3♣. A response of 2♣ could be passed. Here West has enough to commit the partnership to game by making a jump shift.

Exercise Six *Answer* — Responder's Rebid after 1NT Forcing

1) 2♠. West has at least five spades but could have only a three-card diamond suit. East should put the partnership in its seven-card fit. That also gives West another opportunity to bid with a medium-strength hand.

2) Pass. Even if West has only three diamonds, this looks like the best spot for the partnership.

3) 2♥. This shows a five-card or longer heart suit but not enough to respond 2♥ initially. West can pass or return to 2♠ with good spades and a singleton or void in hearts.

4) 2NT. This is an invitational bid, showing 11 or 12 points.

5) 3♠. This shows a limit raise in spades with only three-card support.

6) 3♥. This is highly invitational, but West can pass with a minimum and no fit. It shows the type of hand where East would respond 2♥, if the partnership weren't playing two-over-one game forcing.

Exercise Seven — The Subsequent Auction

What call does West make with the following deals after the auction goes as shown?

1)
♠ K J 9 6 2	**WEST**	NORTH	EAST	SOUTH
♥ 10 6	1♠	Pass	1NT	Pass
♦ A Q 8 3	2♦	Pass	2♥	Pass
♣ K 5	?			

2)
♠ A 2	**WEST**	NORTH	EAST	SOUTH
♥ A Q 10 7 4	1♥	Pass	1NT	Pass
♦ 6 3	2♣	Pass	3♥	Pass
♣ K J 10 4	?			

3)
♠ Q 3	**WEST**	NORTH	EAST	SOUTH
♥ A Q 9 8 4	1♥	1♠	1NT	Pass
♦ K 8 2	?			
♣ Q 9 5				

4)
♠ A J 10 8 3	**WEST**	NORTH	EAST	SOUTH
♥ J 5	1♠	Pass	1NT	Pass
♦ K Q 9 4	2♦	Pass	2NT	Pass
♣ A 6	?			

5)
♠ K J 2	**WEST**	NORTH	EAST	SOUTH
♥ A Q 10 7 5	1♥	Pass	1NT	Pass
♦ 9 3	2♣	Pass	3♣	Pass
♣ Q 5 4	?			

Exercise Seven *Answer* — The Subsequent Auction

1) Pass. East shows a weak hand with five or more hearts. Looks like this is the best partscore. East hasn't shown support for either of West's suits.

2) 4♥. East shows a hand of limit-raise strength with only three-card support for hearts. With more than a minimum, West accepts the invitation.

3) Pass. When the opponents interfere, the 1NT response is no longer forcing.

4) 3NT. East shows 11 or 12 points and strength in the unbid suits. West accepts the invitation.

5) Pass. East's raise is invitational, showing 11 or 12 points. With a minimum opening, West doesn't want to get any higher. West should not worry about the clubs; East knows West could have a three-card suit.

Bid and Play — Two-Over-One Game Forcing

(E-Z Deal Cards: #8, Deal 1 — Dealer, North)

Suggested Bidding

WEST	NORTH	EAST	SOUTH
	1♠	Pass	2♦
Pass	2♠	Pass	3♠
Pass	4♣	Pass	4NT
Pass	5♥	Pass	5NT
Pass	6♣	Pass	6♠
Pass	Pass	Pass	

Playing two-over-one game forcing, South starts by responding 2♦ to North's 1♠ opening. When North rebids spades, South's raise to the three level is still forcing and leaves room for investigating slam. Having agreed on the trump suit, North is able to show some values in clubs (see cuebidding in Chapter 6) and it's now safe for South to use the Blackwood convention (see Chapter 5) to check for the number of aces and kings. When North shows two aces but no kings, South bids the excellent slam.

Dealer: North
Vul: None

♠ A Q 10 8 6 5
♥ 7 3
♦ 10 2
♣ A Q 3

♠ 2
♥ Q 10 5 2
♦ K 7 6 5 3
♣ J 10 9

```
   N
W     E
   S
```

♠ J 9 3
♥ J 9 8 6 4
♦ 4
♣ K 8 6 2

♠ K 7 4
♥ A K
♦ A Q J 9 8
♣ 7 5 4

If North–South weren't playing two-over-one game forcing, South would have a dilemma after North's 2♠ rebid. A raise to 3♠ would be invitational and would risk missing a game contract. A jump to 4♠ would give up on the possibility of a slam contract. South can't conveniently show the spade support in any other manner, and the partnership might get too high if South raises to 5♠ as a slam try or uses the Blackwood convention.

Suggested Opening Lead

East is on lead and might try leading the singleton diamond, hoping for a ruff. This isn't likely to be an effective lead, since South's 5NT bid is a grand slam try, presumably showing that North–South have all of the aces. It's unlikely that East can get a ruff before trumps are drawn. However, it may work if declarer is careless.

Another choice would be to lead a heart, trying to establish a trick if West has the ♥ K and hoping to get another trick, such as the ♦ K. A club lead also could be effective in establishing a trick if partner holds the ♣ Q, but it looks a little more dangerous once North has shown values in clubs.

Suggested Play

Declarer has no losers in spades (unless East has all four trumps), no losers in hearts, one loser in diamonds and two losers in clubs. North's plan should be to draw trumps and then establish the diamond suit. The club losers can be discarded on the extra diamond winners in dummy. There's no need to take the club finesse.

If the opening lead is a heart or a club, declarer has no difficulty. After winning the first trick, declarer can draw all of the trumps and try the diamond finesse. Even though the finesse loses to West's ♦ K, the remaining diamonds in dummy are winners and can be used to discard all of North's losers.

If the opening lead is a diamond, North should be careful. A successful diamond finesse would result in an overtrick, but if the diamond finesse loses, the defenders may be able to get a diamond ruff. North should play safe by winning the first trick with the ♦ A, drawing trumps and then driving out the ♦ K.

Suggested Defense

The defenders can't defeat 6♠ if declarer is careful. If East leads the singleton diamond and declarer takes the finesse, West should return a diamond to give East a ruff.

If South were declarer in 6NT, West could defeat the contract by leading the ♣ J. South can't take 12 tricks in notrump without losing a trick to the ♦ K, and then the defenders can take any established club winners.

Hand Variation of Deal 1 — Looking for Controls

Instructions

To construct a variation of the previous hand, make the following changes:

From the North hand, take the ♥3, ♦2, ♣A and ♣Q and give them to West.

From the West hand, take the ♥Q, ♦K, ♣J and ♣10 and give them to North.

Suggested Bidding

WEST	NORTH	EAST	SOUTH
	1♠	Pass	2♦
Pass	2♠	Pass	3♠
Pass	4♠	Pass	Pass
Pass			

Again, playing two-over-one game forcing, South starts by responding 2♦ to North's 1♠ opening. When North rebids spades, South's raise to the three level is still forcing and leaves room for investigating slam. With no first-round control outside of the trump suit, North might simply sign off in 4♠.

In an experienced partnership, North might cuebid 4♦, showing a control in the

```
Dealer: North    ♠ A Q 10 8 6 5
Vul: None        ♥ Q 7
                 ♦ K 10
                 ♣ J 10 3
♠ 2                        ♠ J 9 3
♥ 10 5 3 2     ┌─────┐     ♥ J 9 8 6 4
♦ 7 6 5 3 2    │N    │     ♦ 4
♣ A Q 9        │W   E│     ♣ K 8 6 2
               │  S  │
               └─────┘
                 ♠ K 7 4
                 ♥ A K
                 ♦ A Q J 9 8
                 ♣ 7 5 4
```

diamond suit, but denying first-round control in clubs. South might make another slam try by cuebidding 4♥, but North, having nothing further to cuebid, would sign off in 4♠. South now passes, since the partnership doesn't have a first- or second-round control of the club suit.

The auction would go like this:

WEST	NORTH	EAST	SOUTH
	1♠	Pass	2♦
Pass	2♠	Pass	3♠
Pass	4♦	Pass	4♥
Pass	4♠	Pass	Pass
Pass			

Playing two-over-one game forcing allows South to show interest in slam without getting the partnership too high, when there is a critical weakness in one of the suits.

Suggested Opening Lead

When the opponents have been bidding strongly but stop below the slam level, it is usually because there is a weakness in one of the suits. In this auction, neither opponent bid clubs, so East should choose the unbid suit and lead the ♣2.

Suggested Play

If East leads a club, there is nothing declarer can do to prevent the defenders from taking the first three tricks. After that, declarer has all of the remaining tricks. If East doesn't lead a club, declarer can take all 13 tricks by discarding the club losers on dummy's extra diamond winners, after drawing trumps.

Suggested Defense

After listening to the auction, East should lead a club. This allows West to win the ♣A, ♣Q and then return a club to East's ♣K. It is unlikely that declarer has any losers outside of the trump suit. Without the ♦K, North wouldn't have enough to open the bidding at the one level. East's best hope is to lead the last club and hope that West holds the ♠10. If West can ruff the fourth round of clubs with the ♠10 — an uppercut — East's ♠J will be promoted into a winner.

North holds the ♠10, so there's nothing the defenders can do to defeat the contract, but congratulations to East if the defender tried for the uppercut. Exchange North's ♠10 and West's ♠2 to see how this could be the winning defense!

Bid and Play — The Principle of Fast Arrival

(E-Z Deal Cards: #8, Deal 2 — Dealer, East)

Suggested Bidding

WEST	NORTH	EAST	SOUTH
		1♠	Pass
2♦	Pass	2♠	Pass
4♠	Pass	Pass	Pass

After East's 1♠ opening, West makes a two-over-one response to show the diamond suit and create a game forcing situation. After East makes a minimum rebid in spades, West has nothing extra to suggest the possibility of a slam. West should use the principle of fast arrival and take the partnership directly to 4♠. East has no reason to override partner's decision and bid any higher.

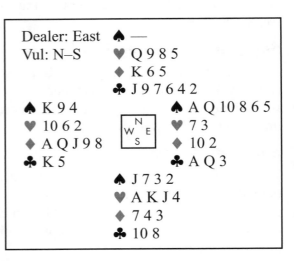

Dealer: East
Vul: N–S

♠ —
♥ Q 9 8 5
♦ K 6 5
♣ J 9 7 6 4 2

♠ K 9 4
♥ 10 6 2
♦ A Q J 9 8
♣ K 5

♠ A Q 10 8 6 5
♥ 7 3
♦ 10 2
♣ A Q 3

♠ J 7 3 2
♥ A K J 4
♦ 7 4 3
♣ 10 8

Notice that East has the same hand as North in Deal 1. The first three bids are identical. The difference comes with responder's rebid.

Suggested Opening Lead

South is on lead. South would start with the ♥A, top of a broken sequence — or the ♥K, if the partnership leads the king from ace–king.

Suggested Play

This appears to be an easy contract, but declarer should always be cautious when things look straightforward. The only apparent losers are two hearts and a potential diamond loser. Declarer may even be able to make an overtrick by taking a finesse for the ♦ K, after drawing trumps.

Declarer should be careful, however, of assuming that the four missing trumps will divide 2–2 or 3–1. Sometimes, they divide 4–0. The presence of the ♠9 in dummy provides the opportunity for a safety play in the trump suit to guard against a 4–0 break. Suppose the defenders start with three rounds of hearts, and declarer trumps the third round. Declarer should start the trump suit by playing the ♠A or the ♠Q from the East hand. If both defenders follow suit, the suit has broken 2–2 or 3–1, and declarer can finish drawing trumps and try the diamond finesse.

North shows out on the first round of spades. Having discovered that South holds all four spades, including the ♠J, East can now play a low spade toward dummy and finesse with the ♠9. Declarer then plays dummy's ♠K, comes back to the East hand with a club and draws South's last trump. Now declarer can try the diamond finesse, which loses to North's ♦K.

If North had held all four spades, South would discard on the first round of spades. Declarer could play a spade to dummy's ♠K and then finesse against North's ♠J. By first leading a high spade from the East hand, declarer can guard against either opponent holding all four trumps.

If declarer starts by leading a spade to dummy's ♠K, South can no longer be prevented from getting a trump trick. When the diamond finesse loses, declarer loses four tricks. Unlucky, but avoidable.

Suggested Defense

The defenders are entitled to two heart tricks and one diamond trick with North's ♦ K. South will have to wait anxiously to see how declarer handles the spade suit. South might get a trick with the ♠J, if declarer isn't very careful.

Bid and Play — One Notrump Forcing

(E-Z Deal Cards: #8, Deal 3 — Dealer, South)

Suggested Bidding

WEST	NORTH	EAST	SOUTH
			Pass
1♠	Pass	1NT	Pass
2♦	Pass	3♠	Pass
4♠	Pass	Pass	Pass

After South's pass, West opens the bidding 1♠, and North passes. East has enough strength for a limit raise but only three-card support. Playing 1NT forcing, East responds 1NT. West makes a natural rebid of 2♦, and now East can make an invitational jump to 3♠. West has enough to accept the invitation.

East–West must be careful to play in their eight-card major-suit fit, rather than their eight-card minor-suit fit. The partnership can make 4♠, but not 5♦, since they have to lose two heart tricks and one diamond trick.

```
Dealer: South    ♠ 5
Vul: E–W         ♥ Q J 10 5
                 ♦ 8 6 4
                 ♣ K 9 4 3 2
      ♠ K Q 10 6 3          ♠ A 7 2
      ♥ 7 4 2       N       ♥ A 8 3
      ♦ K Q 10 5  W   E     ♦ J 7 3 2
      ♣ A           S       ♣ Q 6 5
                 ♠ J 9 8 4
                 ♥ K 9 6
                 ♦ A 9
                 ♣ J 10 8 7
```

Suggested Opening Lead

North is on lead and should start with the ♥Q. Against suit contracts, it's safer to lead from a sequence than to lead away from an honor. Since neither clubs nor hearts have been bid by the opponents, choose the safer lead.

Suggested Play

Declarer has two heart losers and one diamond loser, but the contract should be secure, provided there isn't a loser in the trump suit. If the missing trumps are divided 3–2, there won't be a problem. If the trumps are 5–0 or if North holds four trumps, there's not much that can be done. West should concentrate on safeguarding the contract if South holds four trumps.

After winning the ♥A, there are no sure entries left in dummy except for the ♠A. If declarer starts the trump suit by playing the ♠A and then a spade to the ♠K or the ♠Q, it will be too late to do anything if South started with four spades including the ♠J. West can't get back to dummy to finesse the spade.

Instead, after winning the ♥A, South should play a spade to the ♠K or the ♠Q and then a spade to dummy's ♠A. If the trumps divide 3–2, West can draw the remaining trump and drive out the ♦A to make the contract. When it turns out that South has four spades, declarer is in the right hand to lead the third round of spades and take a finesse against the ♠J. The last trump is drawn, and declarer loses only two heart tricks and one diamond trick.

Suggested Defense

After an initial heart lead, the defenders are entitled to two heart tricks and one diamond trick. Their only hope for a fourth trick is in the spade suit. If declarer handles the trump suit carefully, the contract can't be defeated. If declarer is careless, the defenders have a chance.

Suppose declarer leads the ♠A, after winning the ♥A, and then plays a spade to the ♠K or ♠Q, getting the bad news. Declarer might try to recover by leading the ♦K, hoping to drive out the ♦A and create an entry to dummy with the ♦J. South must be careful to let declarer win the first diamond trick and then take the second trick with the ♦A. Now declarer can't get to dummy without giving South a trump trick.

Bid and Play — More One Notrump Forcing

(E-Z Deal Cards: #8, Deal 4 — Dealer, West)

Suggested Bidding

WEST	NORTH	EAST	SOUTH
Pass	1♠	Pass	1NT
Pass	2♣	Pass	2♥
Pass	Pass	Pass	

After West's pass, North has a standard opening bid of 1♠. When East passes, South doesn't have enough to respond 2♥. That would be a two-over-one response committing the partnership to game. Instead, South starts with a 1NT-forcing response.

West passes again — the diamonds are too weak to risk a vulnerable overcall — and North must bid. With a

Dealer: West
Vul: Both

```
              ♠ A K 9 7 2
              ♥ 9 2
              ♦ K 10 5
              ♣ K 8 3
♠ Q 6                      ♠ J 8 5 4
♥ K 10 4       N           ♥ A 8
♦ Q 8 6 4 2   W   E        ♦ J 9 3
♣ Q 10 7       S           ♣ A J 6 4
              ♠ 10 3
              ♥ Q J 7 6 5 3
              ♦ A 7
              ♣ 9 5 2
```

minimum-strength hand and only five spades, North has to bid a three-card suit, 2♣. Now South has an opportunity to show the long heart suit by bidding 2♥. When the auction comes back to the opening bidder, North passes. South's bidding shows a weak hand with a five-card or longer heart suit. With a hand of invitational strength, South could have jumped to 3♥.

Neither East nor West has the right type of hand to enter the auction, especially when vulnerable. They may be able to make 3♦, but getting into the bidding is not easy. They will generally be better off trying to defeat 2♥.

Holding a minimum-strength balanced hand, North would probably pass South's 1NT response, if the partnership weren't playing 1NT forcing. 1NT would prove to be a poor contract after a diamond lead from West. South would likely be defeated two or three tricks.

Suggested Opening Lead

West has a difficult choice of leads. Against this type of auction, where North has not shown a fit with South's hearts, the unbid suit usually works well. West might lead the ♦4, fourth highest.

Suggested Play

Declarer has no losers in spades or diamonds, but has three potential losers in clubs if East holds the ♣A. South would like to restrict the trump losers to two in order to make the contract. Missing the ♥A, the ♥K and the ♥10, declarer's best plan is to lead hearts twice from dummy toward the ♥Q and the ♥J, hoping East holds either the ♥A or the ♥K and that the suit is divided 3–2.

Declarer should win the first trick with dummy's ♦K and lead a heart. When East follows with a low heart, declarer should play the ♥J or the ♥Q to drive out West's high honor. If West leads another diamond, South wins the ♦A, crosses to dummy with a spade and leads another heart. East wins this trick with the ♥A, and the defense is helpless. If East leads a diamond, declarer ruffs low, draws the last trump and can try leading toward the ♣K for an overtrick. If East returns a spade, declarer can win in dummy, ruff a diamond to get back to the South hand and draw the last trump.

There is some danger on this deal that West might be able to get a trick with the ♥10. Suppose, for example, declarer wins the first trick with the ♦A and leads a spade to dummy. Declarer leads a heart toward the ♥J, and West wins this trick with the ♥K. West might lead another spade. Declarer wins this in dummy and leads another heart toward the ♥Q. East wins this trick with the ♥A and can lead a third round of spades. Now South can't prevent West from getting a trick with the ♥10. If South ruffs low, West overruffs. If South ruffs with the ♥Q, West gets the ♥10 later. If South tries discarding clubs, West can also discard clubs, and East can eventually lead the ♣A and another club to promote West's ♥10.

The same danger exists if South wins the first trick with the ♦A and crosses to dummy with the ♦ K. When the first heart loses to West's ♥ K, West might lead a third round of diamonds. South ruffs, crosses to dummy with a spade and leads another heart. East wins the ♥ A and leads another spade. Now declarer can't get safely back to the South hand without giving the defenders an opportunity to get a trick with the ♥ 10.

While the defenders may not see the possibility of promoting West's ♥ 10, declarer makes it even more difficult by winning the first diamond in dummy and leading a heart right away.

Suggested Defense

Can the defenders always defeat 2 ♥ ? As mentioned above, declarer may give the defenders an opportunity to get a trick with West's ♥ 10, if the first trick isn't won with dummy's ♦ K. Even if declarer does this, however, the defenders can prevail — but it's not easy.

Suppose declarer wins the first trick with dummy's ♦ K and leads a heart to the ♥ J and West's ♥ K. West could now switch to the ♣ Q or ♣ 10 to trap dummy's ♣ K. Once the defenders have taken three club tricks, East can lead a fourth round to promote West's ♥ 10 as a winner. Will East–West be able to find this defense? Probably yes, since declarer is known to hold the ♦ A and has a limited point count.

APPENDIX

The Convention Card

Other Conventions

Glossary of Terms

THE CONVENTION CARD

For a club or tournament game, both members of a partnership are expected to have a completed convention card describing the general style and the conventional bids they have agreed to use. Both cards must be identical.

Writing down the conventions is useful to make sure that both partners are playing the same methods. When playing with an unfamiliar partner, the convention card gives the partnership a chance to discuss the methods that will be used. Its real purpose, however, is for the benefit of the opponents. As they sit down at each table, the players can look at their opponents' convention cards to familiarize themselves with the partnership's methods. It isn't necessary to ask a lot of questions about the methods being used by the opponents. The players need to look only at the information each feels might be relevant. A player can look at an opponent's convention card any time during the auction, when it is that player's turn to call, and at any time during the play, when it is that player's turn to play. A player is not allowed to look at a personal convention card during the bidding for a reminder of what the partnership has decided to play. The convention card is for the benefit of the opponents.

The ACBL has developed a classification system for all conventional bids. The purpose is to allow some events to be restricted to a subset of all possible conventions. In this way, inexperienced players don't have to play against complex systems and conventions which would put them at a distinct disadvantage. For example, some games for beginners are restricted to only those conventions on the ACBL Limited Convention Chart, which includes such favorites as Stayman, Blackwood and Gerber. As players become more familiar with handling a wider variety of conventions, they can move into games with fewer and fewer restrictions powered by the ACBL General Convention Chart and the ACBL Mid-Chart. Only in the last stages of some NABC championships are the restrictions lifted to permit nearly all of the recognized conventions. These games use the ACBL Superchart.

Convention cards come in different formats and colors, depending on the type of game in which they are being used. Periodically, the design of these cards is changed to reflect new regulations.

There are three types of convention cards currently in use:

- **General Convention Card** — The most common format is the white General Convention Card, designed to cover the widest variety of conventions. This can be used at virtually any level of competition — provided only allowable conventions are used.

- **Standard American Yellow Card** — The ACBL Standard American Yellow Card (SAYC) is pre-filled with many popular conventions, and it is designed for games where everyone plays the same methods. It is popular among players on the Internet.

- **"Fat Free" Simplified Card** — The simplified convention card (Form SS4) is affectionately know as the "Fat Free" Card. It is streamlined and perfect for both newer players and those who play less complicated systems.

ACBL CONVENTION CARD

Left side of convention card

not actual size

SPECIAL DOUBLES	NOTRUMP OVERCALLS
After Overcall: Penalty☐ _____	**Direct:** ____to____Systems on☐
Negative☐ thru_____	Conv.☐ _____
Responsive☐ : thru _____ Maximal☐	**Balancing:** _____to_____
Support: Dbl.☐ thru _____ Redbl☐	Jump to 2NT: Minors☐ 2 Lowest☐
Card-showing☐ Min. Offshape T/O☐	Conv.☐ _____

DEFENSE VS NOTRUMP

SIMPLE OVERCALL	vs:
1 level_____to_____HCP (usually)	2♣ _____ _____
often 4 cards☐ very light style☐	2♦ _____ _____
Responses	2♥ _____ _____
New Suit: Forcing☐ NFConst☐ NF☐	2♠ _____ _____
Jump Raise: Forcing☐ Inv.☐ Weak☐	Dbl: _____
	Other_____

JUMP OVERCALL	OVER OPP'S T/O DOUBLE
Strong☐ Intermediate☐ Weak☐	New Suit Forcing: 1 level☐ 2 level☐
	Jump Shift: Forcing☐ Inv.☐ Weak☐

Redouble implies no fit☐

OPENING PREEMPTS	2NT Over	Limit+	Limit	Weak
Sound Light Very Light	Majors	☐	☐	☐
3/4-bids ☐ ☐ ☐	Minors	☐	☐	☐
Conv./Resp. _____	Other_____			

DIRECT CUEBID	VS Opening Preempts Double Is
OVER: Minor Major	Takeout☐ thru _____ Penalty☐
Natural ☐ ☐	Conv. Takeout: _____
Strong T/O ☐ ☐	Lebensohl 2NT Response☐
Michaels ☐ ☐	Other: _____

SLAM CONVENTIONS Gerber☐ : 4NT: Blackwood☐ RKC☐ 1430☐

vs Interference: DOPI☐ DEPO☐ Level: _____ ROPI☐

LEADS (circle card led, if not in bold)	DEFENSIVE CARDING
versus Suits	versus Notrump		vs SUITS vs NT

LEADS	versus Suits		versus Notrump		DEFENSIVE CARDING
	X x	x x x **X**	**X** x	**X** x x x	Standard: ☐ ☐
	x x **X**	x x x x **X** x	**X** x x	x x x x **X** x	Except ☐
	A K x	**T** 9 x	A **K** J x	A **Q** J x	
	K Q x	K **J** T x	A **J** T 9	A **T** 9 x	
	Q J x	K **T** 9 x	**K** Q J x	K **Q** T 9	Upside-Down:
	J T 9	Q **T** 9 x	**Q** J T x	Q **T** 9 x	count ☐ ☐
	K Q T 9		**J** T 9 x	**T** 9 x x	attitude ☐ ☐

LENGTH LEADS:

			FIRST DISCARD		
4th Best	vs SUITS☐ vs NT☐		Lavinthal	☐	☐
3rd/5th Best	vs SUITS☐ vs NT☐		Odd/Even	☐	☐
	Attitude vs NT☐		_____	☐	☐

OTHER CARDING

Primary signal to partner's leads

	OTHER CARDING		
Attitude☐ Count☐ Suit preference☐	Smith Echo	☐	☐
	Trump Suit Pref.	☐	
	Foster Echo	☐	☐

SPECIAL CARDING ☐   PLEASE ASK

ACBL CONVENTION CARD

NAMES _____

GENERAL APPROACH

Two Over One: Game Forcing ☐   Game Forcing Except When Suit Rebid ☐
VERY LIGHT: Openings ☐   3rd Hand ☐   Overcalls ☐   Preempts ☐
FORCING OPENING: 1♣ ☐   2♣ ☐   Natural 2 Bids ☐   Other ☐ _____

NOTRUMP OPENING BIDS

1NT
_____ to _____
_____ to _____
5-card Major common ☐
System on over _____
2♣ Stayman ☐ Puppet ☐
2♦ Transfer to ♥ ☐
    Forcing Stayman ☐
2♥ Transfer to ♠ ☐
2♠ _____
2NT

3♣ _____
3♦ _____
3♥ _____
3♠ _____

4♦, 4♥ Transfer ☐
Smolen ☐
Lebensohl ☐ (_____ denies)
Neg. Double ☐: _____
Other: _____

2NT _____ to _____
    Puppet Stayman ☐
Transfer Responses:
    Jacoby ☐   Texas ☐
3♠ _____

3NT _____ to _____

Conventional NT Openings
_____

MAJOR OPENING

Expected Min. Length	4	5
1st/2nd	☐	☐
3rd/4th	☐	☐

RESPONSES

Double Raise: Force ☐ Inv. ☐ Weak ☐
After Overcall: Force ☐ Inv. ☐ Weak ☐
Conv. Raise: 2NT ☐ 3NT ☐ Splinter ☐
Other: _____
1NT: Forcing ☐   Semi-forcing ☐
2NT: Forcing ☐ Inv. ☐ _____ to _____
3NT: _____ to _____
Drury ☐: Reverse ☐ 2-Way ☐ Fit ☐
Other: _____

MINOR OPENING

				NF
Expected Min. Length	4	3	0–2 Conv.
1♣	☐	☐	☐	☐
1♦	☐	☐	☐	☐

RESPONSES

Double Raise: Force ☐ Inv. ☐ Weak ☐
After Overcall: Force ☐ Inv. ☐ Weak ☐
Forcing Raise: J/S in other minor ☐
Single raise ☐ Other: _____
Frequently bypass 4+ ♦ ☐
1NT/1♣ _____ to _____
2NT Forcing ☐ Inv. ☐ _____ to _____
3NT: _____ to _____
Other _____

DESCRIBE   RESPONSES/REBIDS

2♣ _____ to _____ HCP _____
Strong ☐   Other ☐
2♦ Resp: Neg ☐   Waiting ☐

2♦ _____ to _____ HCP _____
Natural: Weak ☐ Intermediate ☐ Strong ☐ Conv. ☐ | 2NT Force ☐ New Suit NF ☐

2♥ _____ to _____ HCP _____
Natural: Weak ☐ Intermediate ☐ Strong ☐ Conv. ☐ | 2NT Force ☐ New Suit NF ☐

2♠ _____ to _____ HCP _____
Natural: Weak ☐ Intermediate ☐ Strong ☐ Conv. ☐ | 2NT Force ☐ New Suit NF ☐

OTHER CONV. CALLS: New Minor Forcing: ☐   2-Way NMF ☐
Weak Jump Shifts: In Comp. ☐   Not in Comp. ☐ _____
4th Suit Forcing: 1 Rd. ☐ Game ☐ _____

Right side of convention card

not actual size

Items appearing in grey are blue on the actual convention card.

ACBL SAYC

<table>
<tr><td>

SPECIAL DOUBLES (Describe)

Negative ——→ **2♠**

SIMPLE OVERCALL

___ **8** ___ to ___ **16** ___ HCP

Cuebid is: One-Round Force

JUMP OVERCALL

Preemptive _____

OVER OPP'S TAKEOUT DOUBLE

New Suit Force 1-level

Other **2NT = Limit Raise or**
Better over Majors & Minors

OPENING PREEMPTS

3-bids [X] *Sound*   [X] *Light*
equal or unfavorable vul.   favorable vul.

Psychics: Very Rare

</td><td>

DIRECT NT OVERCALLS

1NT __ **15** __ to __ **18** __ HCP

2♣ = Stayman

Other **Other Systems Off**

Unusual 2 NT = 2 Lowest Unbid

OVER OPPONENT'S NT

2♣ shows ♣   2♦ shows ♦
2♥ shows ♥   2♠ shows ♠

VS. OPP'S OPENING PREEMPTS

Dbl. Is   Takeout   Wk. 3s Takeout
Wk. 2s   ☐

2 NT/ Weak 2 = 16–19 HCP Bal.

DIRECT CUEBID

Two Suits [X] __ **Michaels** __
(5-5) or Longer

Natural [X] **In either suit if**
opponents have bid 2 suits

</td></tr>
</table>

Left side of SAYC

not actual size

SLAM CONVENTIONS

Gerber [X] __ **Over 1 NT & 2NT openings, responses, rebids** __

Blackwood [X]   Grand Slam Force [X]

After Interference over 4♣ or 4 NT [X] **Double = 0,**
Pass = 1, Next Suit = 2, Etc.

Defenses vs. Opp's Conventions __ **SOS Redoubles** __

DEFENSIVE CARD PLAY

Opening lead vs. SUITS: 4th best [X]

K Q x   Q J x   J 10 x   10 9 x   K J 10 x   K 10 9 x   Q 10 9 x
x x x   x x x x   x x x x x   A K x

Opening lead vs. NT: 4th best [X]

A K J x   A Q J x   A J 10 9   A 10 9 8   K Q J x   K Q 10 9
K J 10 9   K 10 9 8   Q J 10 x   Q 10 9 8   J 10 9 x   10 9 8 x
x x x   x x x x   x x x x x

A high discard encourages; low discourages.
Standard Count Signals

ACBL SAYC

Names _____ Pair # _____

ACBL STANDARD YELLOW CARD

Strong Forcing Opening: 2♣

NOTRUMP OPENING BIDS

1 NT __15__ to __17__ HCP   2 NT __20__ to __21__ HCP

2♣ Non-Forcing Stayman   3 NT __25__ to __27__ HCP

Transfers: Jacoby for majors over 1, 2 and 3 NT (on over dbls.)

2♠ forces 3♣ (for signoff in either minor)

1 NT - 3♣/3♦ Is Game Invitational; 1 NT - 3♥/3♠ Is Slam Invitational

---

MAJOR OPENINGS
Normally Five-Card Majors

RESPONSES:
2 NT = Forcing Raise (Jacoby)
Double Raise = Limit (10-11 pts.)
Double Raise = Preemptive
Over Double

Be Courteous –
Opponents May Just
Be Friends We
Haven't Met Yet!

MINOR OPENING
Length Promised

	3+
1♣	X
1♦	X

RESPONSES:
Double Raise = Limit (10-12 pts.)
Double Raise = Preemptive
Over Double

1 NT/1♣ or 1♦ __6__ to __10__ HCP

2 NT/1♣ or 1♦ __13__ to __15__ HCP

3 NT/1♣ or 1♦ __16__ to __18__ HCP

Right side of SAYC

not actual size

Describe __22+ Balanced Points or 9+ Tricks__

2♣ STRONG   Conventional Response __2♦ Artificial,__

__May be waiting lacking a good suit__

__5__ to __11__ HCP __Normally a good 6 card suit__

2♦ WEAK   __RONF__

2♥ WEAK   Conventional Response: 2 NT X   __if maximum__

2♠ WEAK   __requests feature__

OTHER CONVENTIONS

OTHER DOUBLES
(Supplement to Chapter 2)

Responsive Double

When West makes a takeout double and North raises South's opening bid, a double by East is treated as a penalty double in standard methods. West's takeout double already asked East to pick the trump suit, so there doesn't appear to be much sense in having East's double also be for takeout. Nonetheless, since North–South have presumably found a fit, it's not often that East would want to double for penalty. As a result, some partnerships prefer to use the double for takeout in this situation. This is known as a responsive double.

For example:

West		WEST	NORTH	EAST	SOUTH		East
♠ K J 8 3					1♦		♠ Q 6 4 2
♥ K 8 5		Double	2♦	Double	Pass		♥ Q 7 4 2
♦ 5 2		2♠	Pass	Pass	Pass		♦ J 3
♣ A J 6 3							♣ K 10 2

After West's takeout double, North raises partner's suit to the two level. East has enough to compete, but doesn't want to guess which suit to bid. Instead, East makes a responsive double. This acts like a takeout double, asking West to pick a suit. When West bids 2♠, East can pass in the knowledge that the partnership has found it's eight-card fit. If the partnership weren't using responsive doubles, East might have chosen to bid 2♥, and the partnership would have wound up in a seven-card fit.

Like the negative double, the partnership needs to agree on the level through which the responsive double applies. A common agreement is that a double is responsive if responder raises opener's suit anywhere up to and including the level of 4♦.

The partnership also needs to discuss all of the situations in which responsive doubles are used and what they promise in each situation. Most partnerships would also use them when the opening bid is a weak two-bid and responder raises after a takeout double. Some partnerships use them after partner has made an overcall and responder raises opener's suit. For example:

WEST	**NORTH**	EAST	SOUTH
1♦	1♠	3♦	Double
Pass	?		

Playing responsive doubles in this situation, South would be promising support for hearts and clubs — probably with some tolerance for spades as well, in case North doesn't like either of South's suits. If the partnership doesn't use the convention in this manner, South's double would be for penalty.

Maximal Double

Consider both of the following hands for West after the auction has started:

WEST	NORTH	EAST	SOUTH
1♠	2♥	2♠	3♥
?			

a) ♠ A K J 8 4　　b) ♠ K Q 10 8 6 3
♥ 6 3　　　　　　♥ 6 3
♦ A Q 7 2　　　　♦ A 7 2
♣ K 5　　　　　　♣ K 5

With the first hand, West has a medium-strength hand and would like to invite partner to bid game with the upper range for a raise to 2♠. Without the interference from the opponents, West would have invited game by freely raising to 3♠, or bidding a new suit as a game try. With the second hand, West has a minimum-strength hand, but would like to compete to 3♠ without having partner treat it as a game invitation. The opponents' bidding, however, has left only 3♠ available for both types of hands.

In this situation, some partnerships use a double to show the first type of hand — extra strength and game-invitational. This is referred to as a maximal double. East can retreat to 3♠ with a minimum raise, jump to

4♠ with a maximum raise or pass the double with a good hand for defending 3♥. Using this convention, an immediate 3♠ bid by West would show the second type of hand — a competitive, but non-invitational, raise.

The partnership needs to agree on exactly when this convention is used. The standard agreement is that a maximal double is used only when no bidding room has been left by the opponents to make any other form of game try. Using this agreement, a double by West would be for penalty in the above auction, if the opponents were competing either in clubs or diamonds, since there would still be room available for West to bid something other than 3♠ with an invitational-strength hand.

Some partnerships also use this convention after their side has overcalled.

For example:

WEST	NORTH	EAST	SOUTH
	1♥	1♠	2♥
2♠	3♥	Double	Pass
?			

With this agreement, East's double would be a game try, rather than a penalty double. With no interest in game, East could compete by bidding 3♠ immediately.

Support Double

When there is an overcall on opener's right after partner has responded in a suit, some partnerships like to use a double by opener to show exactly three-card support for responder's suit. This is called a support double.

For example, consider the following hands after the auction starts like this:

WEST	NORTH	EAST	SOUTH
1♦	Pass	1♥	1♠
?			

♠ Q 5 2   East could have a four-card suit to respond 1♥,
♥ 10 7 3   so raising on three-card support might get the
♦ A K J 6 3   partnership to a poor contract. Rebidding 1NT or
♣ K 5   2♦, however, might result in missing a heart fit
               if partner has five or more. For example, North
               might bid 2♠ and East might not have enough
to bid higher without knowing there is some support for hearts. Using
support doubles, West would double with this hand. With five or more
hearts, East would now know there is a fit and could compete effectively.
With only four hearts, East could pick another contract, perhaps diamonds
or notrump.

♠ Q 5   With four-card support, West would raise to 2♥
♥ 10 7 3 2   right away. Holding a four-card suit, East would
♦ A K J 6 3   know the partnership had an eight-card fit and
♣ K 5   could compete to the appropriate level.

♠ Q 5 2   With two or fewer hearts, West does something
♥ 10 7   other than raise or double. West can pass, bid
♦ A K J 6 3   notrump or rebid diamonds. Whatever West
♣ K 5 2   chooses to do, East will now know that partner
               doesn't have support for hearts.

Use of support doubles requires a lot of discussion by the partnership.
Both partners must be clear on the level through which they apply and
the exact circumstances in which they are used.

For example, if South had made a takeout double in the above auction, some partnerships would treat a redouble as showing three-card
support for hearts.

Lebensohl in Response to a Takeout Double of a Weak Two-Bid

The use of 2NT as a transfer to 3♣, when an opponent has overcalled
partner's opening 1NT bid, is the lebensohl convention. A variation of
this convention is sometimes used when responding to partner's takeout
double, after the opponent's have opened a weak two-bid. Consider the

following hands for West after the auction has started:

WEST	NORTH	EAST	SOUTH
	2♠	Double	Pass
?			

a) ♠ J 4 2   b) ♠ 10 8 5
   ♥ J 8 7 3   ♥ Q J 6 3
   ♦ 10 8 3   ♦ K 9
   ♣ J 6 4   ♣ Q 9 8 4

Using standard methods, West would bid 3 ♥ with both hands. On the first hand, West hopes partner won't bid any more, since West is unlikely to make even 3 ♥, unless East has an extremely strong hand.

With the second hand, West would be happy if East continued to game with a little extra strength, since West has almost enough to immediately jump to game in response to East's double of 2♠. Unfortunately, East won't know which of these hands West holds, so East may bid too much or too little.

To resolve this, some partnerships use the lebensohl convention in this situation. A response of 2NT is artificial, asking opener to bid 3 ♣. Responder can now pass or bid 3 ♦ or 3 ♥ to show a weak hand. By inference, an immediate bid of a new suit at the three level by responder shows a hand with some values, inviting opener to continue to game with a little extra.

The use of the lebensohl convention requires some discussion by the partnership before using it, since there are a number of possible variations.

OVERCALLS
(Supplement to Chapter 3)

Jump Cuebid in Response to an Overcall

After partner makes an overcall, a cuebid of the opponent's suit is commonly used as a forcing bid. It usually shows support for partner's suit and at least game-invitational strength. When a new suit isn't played as forcing, it's necessary to start with a cuebid to prevent partner from passing. Thus, partner can't be sure if the cuebid guarantees support for the overcalled suit. To avoid this situation, some partnerships use a jump cuebid in the opponent's suit to show a hand with four-card or longer support and at least invitational strength.

For example:

WEST	NORTH	**EAST**	SOUTH
	1♣	1♥	Pass
3♣	Pass	?	

West's jump cuebid to 3♣ shows four-card support for hearts and game-invitational strength. This still allows West to make a single raise to 2♥ with 6 to 10 points and to use a jump raise to 3♥ as preemptive. With a hand of game-invitational strength or better but less than four-card support, West can start with the more standard cuebid of 2♣.

Fit-showing Jump

In competitive situations, there's usually little opportunity to use a jump shift to show a strong hand. Many partnerships prefer to use a jump in a new suit as a fit-showing jump. It shows at least nine cards in the two suits — West's suit and the suit in which East jumps — and a hand of invitational strength. Usually, East will have at least four-card support for West's suit and five or more cards in the suit in which East jumps.

Here's an example:

WEST	NORTH	**EAST**	SOUTH
1♥	2♣	?	

Playing fit-showing jumps in competition, East could now jump to 3 ♦ with this hand:

♠ 7 4
♥ Q 10 8 5
♦ A Q J 7 3
♣ 9 3

It's rather like making a limit raise to 3 ♥ while showing the diamonds along the way. West can sign off by bidding 3 ♥, or accept the invitation by jumping to 4 ♥. The information about the diamond suit may help West make the best decision.

Fit-showing jumps can be used in other situations.

For example, consider this auction:

WEST	NORTH	**EAST**	SOUTH
Pass	Pass	1 ♣	Pass
2 ♥	Pass	?	

Having passed originally, West can't have enough to make a normal jump shift. Most partnerships would use this sequence by West to show a hand with hearts, but also a fit with clubs and game-invitational strength. With a minimum hand, East can pass or return to 3 ♣. With extra strength, East can get the partnership to game.

There's also this type of auction:

WEST	NORTH	EAST	SOUTH
1 ♦	Double	2 ♠	Pass
?			

Again, East's jump to 2 ♠ isn't useful as a strong jump shift. With a strong hand, East could start with a redouble. Some partnerships use East's 2 ♠ as a fit-showing jump. The partnership should discuss this, however, since many players prefer to use a jump in a new suit after a takeout double as a preemptive bid, showing a long suit and a weak hand.

Conventional Defenses to an Opponent's 1NT Opening Bid

Ripstra

Ripstra is similar to Landy, except that a player would overcall the better minor, rather than 2 ♣, as takeout for the major suits.

For example, suppose West has this hand when South opens 1NT:

♠ K Q 8 7   Playing Landy, West would bid 2♣, asking East
♥ A J 10 8 5   to pick a major suit. Playing Ripstra, West would
♦ 10 9 3   bid 2♦, asking East to bid a major suit. The ad-
♣ 5   vantage of Rispstra is that partner has the option of
               passing, leaving West to play in the better minor
suit, when holding no fit for either major suit. The disadvantage is that
West can no longer overcall either 2♣ or 2♦ as a natural bid. Ripstra
was invented by Joseph Ripstra of Wichita, Kansas, a former president
of the ACBL.

Becker

Becker uses an overcall of 2♣ to show both minor suits and an overcall of 2♦ to show both major suits.

For example, suppose West holds these two hands:

a)   ♠ 8   b)   ♠ K Q 8 7
     ♥ 9 4   ♥ A J 10 8 5
     ♦ K Q 10 8 3   ♦ 10 9 3
     ♣ A J 10 8 3   ♣ 5

Playing Becker, West would overcall 2♣ with the first hand. With a
preference for clubs, East would pass; with a preference for diamonds,
East would bid 2♦.

With the second hand, West would bid 2♦, asking East to pick a
major suit.

Brozell

Brozell was invented by Bernard Zeller and uses the following agreements over an opponent's 1NT opening bid:

- Double shows a one-suited hand. Partner can pass to defend
  or bid 2♣ to discover which suit the doubler holds. The doubler would then pass with clubs or bid another suit at the two
  level.

- 2♣ shows hearts and clubs.
- 2♦ shows hearts and diamonds.
- 2♥ shows hearts and spades.
- 2♠ shows spades and a minor suit. Partner can bid 2NT to find which minor is held.
- 2NT shows clubs and diamonds.

For example, suppose West holds the following hands after a 1NT opening bid when playing Brozell:

a)		b)		c)	
♠	8 3	♠	K Q 8 7	♠	A J 9 8 5
♥	K 7 5	♥	A J 10 8 5	♥	8 6
♦	A Q J 9 8 3	♦	10 9 3	♦	K Q 8 7 3
♣	9 2	♣	5	♣	7

With the first hand, West would double the 1NT bid. East would bid 2♣ to show a willingness to play in West's suit. West would then bid 2♦.

With the second hand, West would bid 2♥, showing hearts and spades.

With the third hand, West would bid 2♠, showing spades and a minor.

With no support for spades, East could bid 2NT, and West would now bid 3♦.

DONT

DONT (<u>D</u>isturb <u>O</u>pponent's <u>N</u>o<u>t</u>rump) was devised by Marty Bergen and uses a scheme similar to Brozell:

- Double shows a one-suited hand, usually not spades.
- 2♣ shows clubs and another suit.
- 2♦ shows diamonds and a major suit.
- 2♥ shows hearts and spades.
- 2♠ shows spades.

Using DONT, suppose West holds the following hands after South's opening bid of 1NT:

a) ♠ 8 3
♥ K 7 5
♦ A Q J 9 8 3
♣ 9 2

b) ♠ K Q 8 7
♥ A J 10 8 5
♦ 10 9 3
♣ 5

c) ♠ A J 9 8 5
♥ 8 6
♦ K Q 8 7 3
♣ 7

With the first hand, West would double 1NT. East can bid 2♣ to play in West's suit, and West would then bid 2♦.

With the second hand, West would bid 2♥, showing hearts and spades.

With the third hand, West would bid 2♦, showing diamonds and a major. With no support for diamonds, East could bid 2♥, looking for West's major suit, and West would then bid 2♠.

Cappelletti (Hamilton, Pottage)

Cappelletti was invented by Mike Cappelletti, an expert from the Washington area. (It's sometimes known as Hamilton or Pottage.) It uses the following scheme over the opponent's 1NT:

- Double is for penalty.
- 2♣ shows a one-suited hand.
- 2♦ shows hearts and spades.
- 2♥ shows hearts and a minor suit.
- 2♠ shows spades and a minor suit.

For example, suppose West holds the following hands after a 1NT opening bid by South when playing Cappelletti:

a) ♠ 8 3
♥ K 7 5
♦ A Q J 9 8 3
♣ 9 2

b) ♠ K Q 8 7
♥ A J 10 8 5
♦ 10 9 3
♣ 5

c) ♠ A J 9 8 5
♥ 8 6
♦ K Q 8 7 3
♣ 7

With the first hand, West would bid 2♣, showing a one-suited hand. East would be expected to bid 2♦, unless holding a long club suit. West would now pass, to confirm diamonds as the suit.

With the second hand, West would bid 2♦, showing hearts and spades.

With the third hand, West would bid 2♠, showing spades and a minor. With no support for spades, East could bid 2NT, and West would now bid 3♦.

Astro

The Astro convention is named after its co-inventors, Paul <u>A</u>llinger, Roger <u>S</u>tern and Larry <u>R</u>osler. It uses the following approach:

- 2♣ shows hearts and a minor suit.
- 2♦ shows spades and another suit.

For example, suppose West holds the following hands after South's opening bid of 1NT:

	a)		b)	
	♠	5	♠	K Q 8 7
	♥	K Q 10 7 5	♥	A J 10 8 5
	♦	6 3	♦	10 9 3
	♣	A J 10 9 2	♣	5

With the first hand, West would bid 2♣, showing hearts and a minor suit. With support for hearts, East can bid 2♥. Without support for hearts, East bids 2♦. With this hand, West would now bid 3♣, showing the minor suit.

With the second hand, West would overcall 2♦, showing spades and another suit. With support for spades, East would bid 2♠. Otherwise, East can bid 2♥, looking for West's second suit. West would now pass, leaving the partnership in a heart partscore.

TWO-SUITED OVERCALLS
(Supplement to Chapter 4)

Defense to Strong Club (Mathe)

When the opponents use an artificial 1♣ as their strong opening bid — for example, a Precision club — many players like to use an artificial defense, which allows them to compete with two-suited hands. One of the most popular is Mathe, named after Lew Mathe, a world champion and former ACBL president:

- Double shows both major suits.

- 1NT shows both minor suits.

All other bids are natural. For example, suppose North opens the bidding 1♣, which is alerted as being artificial and showing a strong hand, and East holds the following hands:

a)	♠ Q J 10 8 6	b)	♠ 8
	♥ K Q 9 7 5		♥ 7 3
	♦ 8		♦ Q J 10 8 6
	♣ 7 3		♣ K Q 9 7 5

Playing Mathe, East could double with the first hand to show both major suits.

With the second hand, East could bid 1NT, showing both minor suits.

Leaping Michaels

An extension to the Michaels cuebid can be used when the opponents open with a weak 2♥ or 2♠ bid. Since a cuebid wouldn't immediately identify the minor suit held, some players use this approach:

- A jump to 4♣ shows at least five clubs and five cards in the unbid major.

- A jump to 4♦ shows at least five diamonds and five cards in the unbid major.

- A three-level cuebid shows both minor suits.

This variation is referred to as leaping Michaels. For example, suppose the auction starts:

WEST	NORTH	EAST	SOUTH
	2♠	?	

♠ 8 3
♥ K Q J 9 4
♦ 7
♣ A K J 6 2

Jump to 4♣. This shows at least five clubs and five hearts. Most partnerships play this as a game-forcing bid, although some allow the 4♣ bid to be passed.

Unusual Over Unusual

When an opponent makes a two-suited overcall, such as Michaels or the unusual notrump, it takes away some of the bidding room. To compensate, some partnerships use the following approach, commonly referred to as unusual over unusual:

- Double is penalty-oriented, showing interest in defending against the opponents' eventual contract.
- A raise of partner's suit at the cheapest available level is invitational, not forcing.
- A bid of the suit not shown by partner or by the opponent's bid is invitational, not forcing.
- A cuebid of the lower-ranking of the suits shown by the opponent's bid shows the lower-ranking of the other two suits and is forcing for one round.
- A cuebid of the higher-ranking of the suits shown by the opponent's bid shows the higher-ranking of the other two suits and is forcing for one round.

This is more easily explained with some sample hands after the auction begins as follows, and East holds these hands:

WEST	NORTH	EAST	SOUTH
1♦	2♦	?	

♠ Q J 8 3
♥ K 10 9 5
♦ 8 3
♣ A 7 4

Double. North's Michaels cuebid shows both major suits. Double shows that East would like to defend for penalty when the North–South partnership finds a resting place.

♠ 8 5
♥ J 4
♦ K J 9 7 2
♣ A 8 3 2

Raise to 3 ♦. A raise of partner's suit to the cheapest available level is competitive. It doesn't show much more than a raise to the two level.

♠ 9 2
♥ 7 5 2
♦ Q 7
♣ A Q J 8 7 5

Bid 3 ♣. A bid of the suit that hasn't been shown by partner or the opponent's cuebid is simply competitive. 3 ♣ here would be non-forcing.

♠ A 8 3
♥ 7 5
♦ J 9 4
♣ A K J 8 3

Cuebid 2 ♥. A cuebid of the lower-ranking of the suits shown by the opponent — hearts in this situation — shows the lower-ranking of the other two suits — clubs and diamonds — and is forcing for one round. Since 3 ♣ would be non-forcing, East cuebids 2 ♥ to show a strong hand with clubs.

♠ 9 4
♥ A 8 4
♦ A Q J 8 6
♣ K 7 3

Cuebid 2 ♠. A cuebid of the higher-ranking of the suits shown by the opponent's bid — spades in this auction — shows the higher-ranking of the other two suits. In this case, it shows strong support for partner's minor suit and a hand of at least invitational strength. An immediate raise to 3 ♦ would be competitive.

Since there are variations of this approach that can be used, the partnership should discuss the convention beforehand.

BLACKWOOD AND GERBER
(Supplement to Chapter 5)

Key Card Blackwood

The king of the trump suit is usually as important as an ace when it comes to bidding slams. If a king in a side suit is missing, it might be possible to avoid a loser in the suit. If the king of the trump suit is missing, it's important to deal with it. For this reason, many players decide to treat the king of the trump suit as an ace when responding to Blackwood. Instead of there being four key cards when responding to 4NT — the four aces — there are now five key cards — the four aces and the king of trump. This requires a change to the responses:

5♣   Zero or four key cards

5♦   One or five key cards

5♥   Two key cards

5♠   Three key cards

This variation is referred to as Key Card Blackwood, but it isn't used by many players. A much more popular variation is Roman Key Card Blackwood.

Roman Key Card Blackwood

This version of Blackwood assumes that there are five key cards: the four aces and the king of the trump suit. It also takes into consideration another critical card, the queen of the trump suit. The most popular variation uses the following responses to 4NT:

5♣   Zero or three key cards

5♦   One or four key cards

5♥   Two key cards without the queen of the trump suit

5♠   Two key cards with the queen of the trump suit

Here is an example:

West		East
♠ A 10 8 6 3		♠ K Q 9 4
♥ A K		♥ Q 8 3
♦ 2		♦ A 8 6 3
♣ A K Q 6 3		♣ 8 2

WEST	NORTH	EAST	SOUTH
1♠	Pass	3♠	Pass
4NT	Pass	5♠	Pass
7♠	Pass	Pass	Pass

Using Roman Key Card Blackwood, East's response to West's bid of 4NT shows two key cards — the ♠K and the ♦ A — along with the ♠Q. That's all West needs to know to bid the grand slam.

Some partnerships reverse the meaning of the first two responses. Most partnerships also have agreements on how to ask for the queen of trump after a response of 5♣ or 5♦ and on the meaning of a subsequent bid of 5NT — usually asking for specific kings. It's important that the partnership is clear on the agreed trump suit before using Roman Key Card Blackwood. Since there are several variations of this convention, the partnership should be careful to discuss it in some detail before using it.

FINDING KEY CARDS
(Supplement to Chapter 6)

Other Responses to a Grand Slam Force

In the basic version of the grand slam force, a bid of 5NT asks partner to bid a grand slam with two of the top three trump honors, otherwise to bid a small slam in the agreed trump suit. Experienced partnerships prefer a more complicated set of responses, since it's sometimes important to know if partner has one of the top three honors. Unfortunately, the amount of bidding room left over 5NT to show the various combinations depends on the agreed trump suit. If the agreed trump suit is clubs, for example, then the only bid available over 5NT to deny two of the top three honors is 6♣, since any other bid would take the partnership beyond the small slam. If the agreed trump suit is spades, however, the responses of 6♣, 6♦, 6♥ and 6♠ are all available to show various holdings that don't include two of the top three honors.

One approach for responses to 5NT is the following:

If the agreed trump suit is clubs:
- 6♣ denies two of the top three honors.
- 7♣ shows two of the top three honors.

If the agreed trump suit is diamonds:
- 6♣ shows the ♦A or ♦K.
- 6♦ denies the ♦A or ♦K.
- 7♦ shows two of the top three honors.*

If the agreed trump suit is hearts:
- 6♣ shows the ♥A or ♥K
- 6♦ shows the ♥Q.
- 6♥ shows none of the top honors.
- 7♥ shows two of the top three honors.*

If the agreed trump suit is spades:
- 6♣ shows the ♠A or ♠K.
- 6♦ shows the ♠Q.
- 6♥ shows the ♠A or ♠K and extra length.
- 6♠ shows none of the top honors.
- 7♠ shows two of the top three honors.*

West		WEST	NORTH	EAST	SOUTH	East
♠ J 6		1♣	Pass	1♥	Pass	♠ A K Q 4
♥ A 8 6 2		2♥	Pass	5NT	Pass	♥ K J 8 7 5 3
♦ K Q 3		6♣	Pass	7♥	Pass	♦ —
♣ Q J 6 3		Pass	Pass			♣ A K 2

Using the above methods, West's response to the grand slam force shows either the ♥A or ♥K, but not two of the top three honors. South decides that's good enough to undertake the grand slam.

*Some partnerships always bid 7♣ when holding two of the top three honors, whatever the agreed trump suit.

Using the Grand Slam Force after Blackwood

When 4NT is used as Blackwood to ask for aces, 5NT can no longer be used as a grand slam force, since it would now ask for kings as part of the Blackwood convention. To get around this, Walter Malowan of New York suggested the following:

> After bidding 4NT as Blackwood and hearing partner's response, a bid of 6♣ is used as the grand slam force, unless the agreed trump suit is clubs.

For example:

West		East
♠ K Q 4		♠ A 10 8
♥ A J 8 7 5		♥ K Q 9 3
♦ 4		♦ A 7 5 2
♣ A K Q 3		♣ 10 3

WEST	NORTH	EAST	SOUTH
	Pass	1♦	Pass
1♥	Pass	2♥	Pass
4NT	Pass	5♥	Pass
6♣	Pass	7♥	Pass
Pass	Pass		

LEADS AND SIGNALS
(Supplement to Chapter 7)

Lavinthal Discards

On defense, most partnerships play that partner's first discard is an attitude signal — a high card is encouraging in that suit, a low card is discouraging. Some partnerships prefer to give a suit preference signal on their first discard. This is usually referred to as a Lavinthal discard, named after Hy Lavinthal, a bridge teacher from New Jersey.

For example, suppose declarer is playing in a heart contract and starts drawing trump after winning the first trick. Playing Lavinthal discards, if partner discards a low diamond, that's a suit preference signal for the lower-ranking of the remaining two suits, spades and clubs. If partner discards a high diamond, that's a suit preference signal for spades, the higher-ranking of the two remaining suits.

Lavinthal discards require considerable discussion by the partnership before being used, since there are many possible variations.

Upside-down Carding

The standard method of signalling attitude is to play a high card as an encouraging signal and a low card as a discouraging signal. Some players prefer to reverse the meaning of these signals. Now a low card is encouraging and a high card is discouraging. This is referred to as upside-down attitude signals. One advantage is that a defender doesn't have to waste a potentially valuable high card to make an encouraging signal.

A similar approach can be used when giving count signals. Playing upside-down count signals, a low card followed by a higher card would show an even number of cards in the suit. A high card followed by a low card would show an odd number of cards in the suit. The exact opposite to standard count signals.

A few players also use upside-down suit-preference signals, but this isn't nearly as common as upside-down count and attitude signals.

TWO-OVER-ONE
(Supplement to Chapter 8)

Exceptions to Two-Over-One Game Force

Some partnerships play two-over-one as forcing to game, except when responder bids and rebids a minor suit at the minimum level.

For example:

West	WEST	NORTH	EAST	SOUTH	East
♠ A Q J 8 6	1♠	Pass	2♣	Pass	♠ 4
♥ J 7 5	2♦	Pass	3♣	Pass	♥ 10 8 2
♦ K J 8 2	Pass	Pass			♦ Q 7 3
♣ 3					♣ A K J 10 7 4

Using this style, East's 3♣ rebid is invitational, not forcing. If East's second bid had been anything other than 3♣, the partnership would be in a game-forcing sequence. This approach is sometimes advantageous in distinguishing between weak and invitational hands for responder. With a weaker hand and a long club suit, East would start with a forcing 1NT response and then bid 3♣ over West's rebid. If the partnership did not have this exception, East would have to start with a response of 1NT with either a weak or invitational-strength hand, and the 3♣ bid would now be ambiguous.

There are other possible exceptions. Some partnerships allow the bidding to stop at 4♣ or 4♦ after a two-over-one response. Others use two-over-one as game forcing only when the opening bid is a major suit and the response is in a minor suit — for example, a response of 2♣ to an opening bid of 1♦ would not be game forcing.

The partnership must weigh any advantage of the various exceptions against the additional memory work required and the potential ambiguity in some auctions.

Constructive Raises

When the partnership plays 1NT forcing, there are two ways responder can show support for opener's major suit with less than the values for a limit raise: responder can raise directly to the two level or responder can bid 1NT and then show support after opener's forced rebid. This allows the partnership to play constructive raises. An immediate raise of opener's major shows about 8 to 10 points. A response of 1NT followed by preference back to opener's major shows 7 or fewer points.

GLOSSARY

1NT forcing —The conventional agreement that a response of 1NT to an opening bid of 1♥ or 1♠ is forcing for one round; often used in conjunction with two-over-one.

1NT response to 1♣ —A conventional agreement to use a higher range (8 to 10 or 9 to 11, rather than 6 to 10 points) for a 1NT response to an opening 1♣ bid.

2NT as a limit raise—See Truscott 2NT.

2NT as a non-forcing response to a minor —An agreement that a response of 2NT to 1♣ or 1♦ is invitational, showing 10 to 12 points.

2NT as an invitational response to a minor— An agreement that a response of 2NT shows a balanced hand of 11 or 12 points and is only invitational, not forcing. This is used when a response of 1NT shows 6 to 10 points and 3NT shows a balanced hand of 13 to 15 points.

3NT as a balanced forcing raise—The conventional use of a 3NT response to an opening bid of 1♥ or 1♠ to show a forcing raise with no short suit.

3NT as a weak preempt in either minor suit —The conventional use of an opening bid of 3NT to show a weak hand with a long minor suit; often used in conjunction with namyats.

ACBL Standard American Yellow Card (SAYC)—The list of conventions which must be used by a partnership in "Yellow Card" events and are a starting point for partnerships in other events. Frequently used by new partnerships playing on the Internet.

Acol—A bidding system popular in the United Kingdom featuring a weak notrump, four-card majors and limit raises.

Acol 3NT opening—An opening bid of 3NT based on a long, solid suit with stoppers in at least two of the other suits; this falls somewhere between the gambling 3NT opening and the more traditional strong balanced hand of 25 to 27 points.

Alert—A warning to the opponents that the last call by partner has been assigned a conventional message, rather than the natural or literal meaning they might expect.

Announcement—A word or phrase that directly describes the meaning of partner's call. This is part of the Alert process and is used in three cases: when the partnership's range for an opening bid of 1NT falls outside the range of 15 to 18 high-card points; when the partnership uses a Jacoby transfer bid; when the partnership uses a forcing 1NT response.

Astro—A conventional overcall of a minor suit after a strong or weak notrump, in the direct or reopening position, to show a two-suited hand. 2♣ shows hearts and a minor suit; 2♦ shows spades and another suit.

Attitude signal—An attitude signal tells partner whether or not to continue playing a particular suit. It can be used when one has a choice of cards to play in a suit that partner has led or when discarding in a suit. The conventional agreement is: a high card is encouraging; a low card is discouraging.

Becker—A conventional agreement to use an overcall of 2♣ over 1NT to show both minor suits and an overcall of 2♦ to show both major suits.

Bergen major-suit raises—See Bergen raises.

Bergen raises—A structure of major suit raises that puts the emphasis on quickly getting to the three level with four-card support.

Better minor—A bidding style in which the better (stronger) minor suit is opened when the hand doesn't contain a five-card major suit and the minor suits are of equal length.

Bidding box—A mechanical device which allows bids to be made silently, rather than verbally; often used in bridge clubs and at tournaments.

Blackwood—A conventional bid of 4NT after a trump suit has been agreed to ask partner to show the number of aces held: 5♣—0 or 4; 5♦—1; 5♥—2; 5♠—3. A subsequent bid of 5NT asks for the number of kings held.

Brozell—A conventional agreement that assigns the following meanings to overcalls of an opponent's 1NT opening bid: Double shows a one-suited hand (partner bids 2♣ to find out which suit); 2♣ shows hearts and clubs; 2♦ shows hearts and diamonds; 2♥ shows hearts and spades; 2♠ shows spades and a minor suit (partner bids 2NT to find out which minor); 2NT shows clubs and diamonds.

Bypassing diamonds—The conventional agreement following an opening 1♣ bid to bypass a four-card diamond suit when holding a four-card major suit.

Call—Any bid, double, redouble or pass.

Cappelletti (also called Hamilton, Pottage)—A conventional agreement that assigns the following meanings to overcalls of an opponent's 1NT opening bid: Double is for penalty; 2♣ shows a one-suited hand; 2♦ shows hearts and spades; 2♥ shows hearts and a minor suit; 2♠ shows spades and a minor suit.

Cheaper minor second negative—A rebid of 3♣ to deny strength following a strong artificial 2♣ opening, a 2♦ waiting response and opener's rebid of 2♥ or 2♠; if opener rebids 3♣, responder's 3♦ rebid denies strength.

Checkback Stayman—The use of 2♣ after opener's rebid of 1NT—or 3♣ after opener's rebid of 2NT—to ask about opener's major suit holdings.

Constructive raises—The use of an immediate raise of a major suit to the two level to show 8 to 10 points, rather than 6 to 10 points.

Control—A holding that prevents the opponents from taking a trick in a suit: aces and voids are first-round controls; kings and singletons are second-round controls.

Control Swiss—A variation of the swiss convention which focuses on the number of controls (aces and kings) held.

Convenient club—Another name for the bidding style in which the longer minor suit is opened with no five-card major suit; this term is used because opener bids 1♣ with three cards in both minors.

Convention—A call or play which may be artificial and which has a defined meaning for the partnership; it may not suggest playing in the denomination named.

Count signals (length signals)—A count signal tells partner how many cards you have in a suit. The standard conventional agreement to show length in a suit is: high-low shows an even number of cards; low-high shows an odd number of cards.

Cuebid—An artificial forcing bid in a suit in which the bidder cannot wish to play: a bid in the opponents' suit or a bid to show a control in a slam-going auction.

Cuebid as a limit raise—Responder's use of a cuebid of the opponent's suit following an overcall to show the values for a limit raise or better in opener's suit.

Deal—1. The distribution of the pack to form the hands of the four players. 2. The cards so distributed considered as a unit, including the auction and play.

Delayed Stayman—See checkback Stayman.

DEPO — This is a convention used to handle overcalls following a Blackwood bid. DEPO stands for Double Even, Pass Odd. A double shows zero, two or four aces; a pass shows one or three.

Distribution points—Hand valuation points that take into account the shape of the hand (see length points and short suit points).

DONT—A conventional agreement that assigns the following meanings to overcalls of an opponent's 1NT opening bid: Double shows a one-suited hand (usually not spades); 2♣ shows clubs and another suit; 2♦ shows diamonds and a major suit; 2♥ shows hearts and spades; 2♠ shows spades.

DOPI—When an opponent overcalls after a 4♣ Gerber bid or a 4NT Blackwood bid, the partnership can use D-O-P-I: Double is no aces; Pass is one; cheapest bid is two; next cheapest bid is three, etc.

Dormer 2NT—See Truscott 2NT.

Double-barreled Stayman—See two-way Stayman.

Double negative—A response that immediately denies strength in response to a strong forcing bid when responder also had the option of making a waiting bid.

Double raise—See jump raise.

Drury—A conventional response of 2♣ to an opening bid of 1♥ or 1♠ in third or fourth position, asking if opener has a full opening bid.

Dummy points—Valuation points for short suits when planning to raise partner's suit: void— 5; singleton—3; doubleton—1.

Extended Jacoby transfers—Use of 2♠ in response to 1NT as a transfer to 3♣ when holding a weak hand with either clubs or diamonds; with diamonds, responder then bids 3♦.

Extended splinter bids—Use of splinter bids in situations other than a direct response to an opening bid.

First-round control—An ace or a void in a suit contract.

Fit-showing jump—An agreement to use a jump shift in competitive situations to show a strong hand of at least nine cards in the two suits (partner's suit and the suit in which the jump is bid) and invitational strength. Usually shows five cards in the suit bid and four cards in support of partner's suit.

Five-card majors—A bidding style where opening bids of 1♥ or 1♠ usually promise a five-card or longer suit.

Flannery 2♦—A conventional use of a 2♦ opening bid to show four spades, five hearts and 11 to 15 points.

Flip-flop—The conventional use of 2NT by responder to show a preemptive raise after opener's minor suit opening has been doubled for takeout; responder's jump raise of opener's minor is then a limit raise. This is a reversal of the usual agreement when playing Truscott 2NT.

Forcing bid—A bid which requires partner to bid again if there is no intervening bid.

Forcing club system—A bidding system in which an opening bid of 1♣ is artificial and shows a strong hand.

Forcing for one round—A bid that requires partner to make a call other than pass, if there is no intervening call.

Forcing raise—A style of responding to an opening bid of one-of-a-suit where a jump raise to the three level is forcing to at least the game level.

Forcing Stayman—A variation of the Stayman convention in which a rebid of 2♥ or 2♠ by responder is forcing to at least 2NT.

Four-card majors—A bidding style where opening bids of 1♥ or 1♠ can be made on a four-card suit.

Four-suit transfer bids—Transfer bids into all four suits over an opening bid of 1NT: 2♦ for hearts, 2♥ for spades, 2♠ for clubs, 2NT for diamonds.

Fourth suit forcing and artificial —An agreement that the bid of the fourth suit by responder is artificial and forcing; usually played as forcing to game.

Gambling 3NT—An opening bid of 3NT based on a long, solid minor suit, rather than the more traditional 25 to 27 HCPs.

Game-forcing—A bid that, by agreement, commits the partnership to at least the game level.

Gerber—A conventional agreement that following a bid of 1NT or 2NT, a jump to 4♣ asks partner how many aces are held. Partner responds: 4♦ — 0 or 4; 4♥ — 1; 4♠ — 2; 4NT — 3. If the partnership holds all of the aces, a bid of 5♣ asks partner how many kings are held.

Grand slam force—An agreement that a bid of 5NT asks partner to bid a grand slam with two of the top three trump honors, otherwise, to bid a small slam in the agreed trump suit.

Grand slam force after Blackwood—An agreement that when 4NT is used as Blackwood to ask for aces, 6♣ (rather than 5NT) is used as the grand slam force, unless the agreed trump suit is clubs.

Hamilton—See Cappelletti.

Hand—The cards originally dealt to a player.

HCPs —The abbreviation for high-card points.

Herbert negative—The use of the cheapest available suit response to deny strength when opener has made a strong forcing bid. Often applied after responder has initially made a waiting bid.

High-card points—The value of the high cards in a hand: ace—4; king—3; queen—2; jack—1.

Informatory double—See takeout double.

Ingberman—See lebensohl over reverses.

Inverted minor-suit raises—A bidding style in which a single raise of opener's minor suit is forcing for one round while a jump raise shows a weak hand. Essentially, the meaning of raises to the two level and the three level are reversed from standard practice.

Invitational bid—A bid which encourages partner to bid again, but gives partner the option of passing with minimal values for what has been promised to date.

Jacoby transfer bid—A conventional response to an opening bid of 1NT where 2♦ shows hearts and 2♥ shows spades. Similar responses can be used over other notrump opening bids.

Jacoby 2NT—A conventional response to an opening bid of 1♥ or 1♠ which shows a forcing raise of the major suit.

Jordan 2NT—See Truscott 2NT.

Jump cuebid—An agreement to use a jump cuebid in the opponent's suit to show a hand with four-card or longer support for partner's suit and at least invitational strength.

Jump preference—Returning to partner's original suit at a level one higher than necessary.

Jump raise—A raise of partner's suit skipping a level of bidding (*e.g.,* 1♥ — 3♥).

Jump shift—A jump one level higher than necessary in a new suit.

Jump shift by responder—A jump in a new suit in response to an opening bid of one-of-a-suit.

Jump shift in other minor as a forcing raise—The conventional use of a jump raise in the other minor to show a forcing raise in opener's minor when a jump raise of opener's minor suit is used as a limit raise.

Kantar 3NT—A conventional opening bid to show a solid major suit with no side aces and at most one side king.

Key Card Blackwood—This version of Blackwood assumes that there are five key cards: the four aces and the king of the trump suit. The responses are: 5♣ — zero or four; 5♦ — one or five; 5♥ — two; 5♠ — three. See also Roman Key Card Blackwood.

Kock-Werner redouble—See SOS redouble.

Landy—A conventional overcall of 2♣ after an opposing 1NT opening as a request for a takeout to a major suit. Overcaller promises at least four cards in each major and usually has five.

Lavinthal discards—A complicated partnership agreement with many possible variations that calls for the first discard on defense to give a suit preference signal rather than an attitude signal.

Law of total tricks—An observation that the total number of tricks available to both sides in their best trump suit on any hand is usually equal to the total number of the trumps in each side's best trump suit. It is usually applied in competitive bidding situations.

Lead-directing double—Without specific agreements to the contrary, a double of an opponent's conventional bid shows strength in that suit.

Lead-directing double of 3NT—When the opponents have voluntarily bid to 3NT and the player not on lead doubles, this double conventionally asks partner to lead one of the following suits, in order of priority: a suit bid by the opening leader; a suit bid by the doubler; dummy's first bid suit if it wasn't rebid. When no suit has been bid, the double shows a solid suit which can take five tricks if the opening leader can find it. Without a clue, the opening leader will tend to lead a short major suit.

Lebensohl—A convention to handle interference after partner opens with 1NT (variations of this convention can be used in other situations).

Lebensohl over reverses—A conventional agreement for handling the auction after opener makes a reverse bid.

Leaping Michaels—An extension of the Michaels cuebid convention used following a weak 2♥ or 2♠ bid by the opponents. A jump to 4♣ shows at least five clubs and five cards in the unbid major. A jump to 4♦ shows at least five diamonds and five cards in the unbid major.

Length points—The value assigned to long suits in a hand: five-card suit — 1; six-card suit — 2; seven-card suit — 3; eight-card suit — 4.

Light opening bid—An opening bid on a hand that doesn't meet the standard requirements; for example, an opening bid at the one level on fewer than 13 points.

Lightner double—A conventional agreement that a double of a slam by the player not on lead requests partner to make an unusual lead, which hopefully would result in the defeat of the contract.

Limit raise—A style of responding to an opening bid of one-in-a-suit where a jump raise to the three level is invitational rather than forcing.

Longer minor—A bidding style in which the longer minor suit is opened when the hand doesn't contain a five-card major suit; 1♦ is usually opened with four cards in both minors; 1♣ is usually opened with three cards in both minors.

Mathe—A competitive conventional agreement following a strong, artificial 1♣ opening that a double shows both major suits and 1NT shows both minor suits.

Maximal double—A competitive double used by a player as a game try when the opponents' bids have left no bidding room to make any other form of game try.

Minor-suit slam try—A forcing bid in a minor suit asking if partner has interest in a slam contract in the minor suit.

Minor-suit Stayman—A conventional use of the 2♠ response to 1NT as an inquiry about opener's minor suits. Opener rebids 2NT with no four-card or longer minor, rebids 3♣ or 3♦ with one four-card minor suit and rebids the longer major — 3♥ or 3♠ — with four cards in both minor suits.

MUD—An agreement on how to lead from a suit containing three low cards — lead the middle (M) card; follow with the highest (Up) card, and finally play the lowest (Down) card — MUD.

Namyats—The conventional use of 4♣ to show a strong 4♥ opening bid and 4♦ to show a strong 4♠ opening bid; as a consequence, opening bids of 4♥ and 4♠ are weak preemptive bids.

Natural bid—A bid which suggests playing in the denomination named.

Negative double—A variation of the takeout double, used when an opponent overcalls at a low level.

Negative doubles after 1NT—The use of a double for takeout, rather than penalty, after a direct overcall by an opponent of an opening 1NT bid. It shows enough strength to compete and tends to show four cards in any unbid major suit.

Negative response—A response that denies strength when partner opens with a strong forcing bid such as 2♣.

New minor forcing—A conventional agreement that the bid of a new minor by responder is forcing after a 1NT (or 2NT) rebid by opener.

Non-forcing Stayman—The standard form of the Stayman convention where a rebid of 2♥ or 2♠ by responder is non forcing.

Ogust responses—A method of responding to weak two-bids that asks opener about both the strength of the weak two-bid and the quality of the suit.

Passed hand—A hand that was passed when it had an opportunity to open the bidding.

Penalty double—Double of an opponent's bid that suggests defending that contract for penalty.

Positive response—A response that shows some values when partner opens with a strong forcing bid such as 2♣.

Po[...] [...] bidding system centered around a conven-[...] strong hands of 16 or more points.

[...] made to interfere with the opponents' auction. [...]g suit and a weak hand.

[...]ive opening [...]d—Opening bid at the two level or higher [...] a weak hand; designed to interfere with the [...]

[...]ive re-raise—The conventional agreement where, after re-[...]er's suit to the two level, a further raise to the [...]mum-strength hand rather than an invitational,

Preempts—Bids that skip one or more levels of the bidding and are based on a long suit and a weak hand; designed to interfere with the opponents' auction.

Principle of fast arrival—A bidding concept that the faster a contract is reached, the weaker the hand that places the contract; conversely, the slower the approach, the stronger the suggestion that a higher contract might be appropriate.

Psychic call—A deliberate and gross misstatement of honor strength and/or suit length.

Puppet Stayman—A variation of the Stayman convention which can be used to discover whether opener holds a four-card or a five-card major suit.

Quantitative—A natural, limited, non-forcing bid. For example, a raise of an opening 1NT bid to 4NT—inviting opener to bid slam but not forcing.

Redouble—A redouble shows 10 or more points with interest in doubling the opponents for penalty. Responder usually won't have a good fit with opener's suit.

Responsive double—When partner makes a takeout double and the next opponent raises opener's suit, some partnerships agree to treat a double as responsive rather than as a penalty double. The responsive double acts like a takeout double, asking partner to pick a suit.

Reverse—A rebid of a new suit that prevents responder from returning to opener's original suit at the two level.

Reverse by responder—A bid of a second suit by responder that prevents opener from returning to responder's first suit at the two level.

Reverse Drury—A variation of the Drury convention in which opener rebids the major suit to show a sub-standard hand.

Ripstra—A conventional agreement to overcall 1NT with the better minor as a takeout for the major suits. Partner has the advantage of passing the overcall to leave the contract in the better minor suit when holding no fit for either major suit.

Roman Key Card Blackwood—A version of Blackwood that assumes five key cards: four aces and the king of the proposed trump suit. It also takes into consideration the queen of the proposed trump suit. The responses are: 5♣ — zero or three; 5♦ — one or four; 5♥ — two (or five) key cards without the queen of trumps; 5♠ — two (or five) key cards with the queen of trumps.

RONF—An acronym for 'Raise is the Only Non Force' when responding to a weak two-bid.

Rule of two and three—See rule of 500.

Rule of 5 and 10—A guideline for responding 2♥ over partner's 1♠ opening bid: responder needs at least five hearts and at least 10 points.

Rule of 15—A guideline for opening the bidding in fourth position on marginal hands: if the high-card points plus the number of spades adds to 15 or more, open the bidding; otherwise, pass.

Rule of 20—A guideline for opening marginal hands: if the high-card points plus the number of cards in the two longest suits adds to 20 or more, open the bidding.

Rule of 500—A guideline for opening preemptive bids based on the penalties for being doubled and defeated: a non vulnerable preempt should not risk being defeated more than three tricks; a vulnerable preempt should not risk being defeated more than two tricks.

Second negative—A rebid by the responder to a strong forcing bid that denies strength when responder initially made a waiting bid.

Second-round control—A king or a singleton in a suit contract.

Short club—A bidding style in which an opening bid of 1♥ or 1♠ shows a five-card or longer suit and an opening bid of 1♦ shows a four-card or longer suit. This style sometimes results in an opening bid of 1♣ being made on a two-card suit (4–4–3–2 distribution).

Short suit points—The value assigned to short suits in a hand (usually applied when showing support for partner's suit — see dummy points): void—5; singleton—3; doubleton—1.

Sign-off bid—A bid which partner is expected to pass.

Simple preference—Returning to partner's first suit at the cheapest available level when partner has shown two suits.

Smolen transfers—A convention for ensuring that the 1NT opener declares the contract when responder is 5–4 in the major suits.

Soloway jump shift—A conventional agreement that responder's jump shift falls into one of three types of hand: a strong single-suiter; a strong hand with a fit for opener's suit; a strong balanced hand.

SOS redouble—A redouble following a double for penalties in a low-level contract. It requests partner to pick another contract. (Partnerships must be clear when the redouble is for rescue and when it is strength-showing.)

Splinter bid—A conventional double jump in a new suit to show a fit with partner and a singleton or void in the suit bid.

Splinter raise—See splinter bid.

Stayman—A conventional response of 2♣ to an opening 1NT bid that asks whether opener has a four-card major suit and a 3♣ response to an opening 2NT to ask the same.

Step responses—A conventional set of responses to a strong forcing bid that shows the number of controls (aces and kings) held.

Stopper—A holding in a suit that is likely to prevent the opponents from taking all of the tricks in a suit (Q–J–3, for example).

Strong artificial (conventional) 2♣—The use of an opening bid of 2♣ to show a strong hand of about 22 or more points; commonly used in conjunction with weak two-bids.

Strong club—An artificial (conventional) opening bid of 1♣ to show a strong hand.

Strong notrump—An opening bid of 1NT that falls in the range of 15 to 18 HCP.

Strong two-bid—An opening bid in a suit at the two level to show a strong hand (21 or more points); it is forcing to game unless opener rebids 2NT or rebids the original suit at the three level.

Suit preference signals—A suit preference signal indicates a preference for one of the two remaining suits (it doesn't apply to the suit led or to the trump suit). A high card shows preference for the higher-ranking suit; a low card shows preference for the lower-ranking suit.

Super acceptance— A jump of a level when accepting partner's transfer bid to show a maximum-strength hand and good fit.

Support double—Used by opener to show exactly three-card support for responder's suit following an overcall on opener's right after partner has responded in a suit. By agreement, opener can redouble to show three-card support when the intervening call is a double.

Swiss—A conventional response of 4♣ or 4♦ to an opening bid of 1♥ or 1♠ to show a forcing raise of the major suit. (Not to be confused with Swiss teams, which is a method of pairing up teams with similar records in a bridge event.)

Takeout double—A double that asks partner to bid rather than defend for penalty.

Temporizing bid—See waiting bid.

Texas transfer bids—A conventional set of responses to an opening bid of 1NT or 2NT where 4♦ shows six or more hearts and 4♥ shows six or more spades.

Treatment—A natural bid that indicates a desire to play in the denomination named (or promises or requests values in that denomination), but that also, by agreement, gives or requests additional information on which further action could be based.

Trump echo—A high-low in the trump suit is commonly used to show three or more trumps.

Trump Swiss—A variation of the Swiss convention which focuses on trump quality.

Truscott 2NT—A conventional jump to 2NT after an opponent's takeout double to show a limit raise or better in partner's suit.

Two-over-one—A bidding style in which a new suit response at the two level is forcing to at least game after partner opens one-of-a-suit.

Two-way Stayman—A variation of the Stayman convention in which a response of 2♣ is non-forcing Stayman and a response of 2♦ is game-forcing Stayman.

Unusual notrump—A conventional agreement that a jump overcall of 2NT over a major suit shows a two-suited hand with two five-card or longer suits that promise to be weak. The majority of players use this bid to show both minor suits. Modern partnerships use the bid to show the two lowest-ranking unbid suits.

Unusual over unusual—An agreement that responder will take the following action when an opponent makes a two-suited overcall, such as Michaels or the unusual notrump, that takes away some of the available bidding room: double is penalty-oriented; raising partner at the cheapest available level is invitational; a bid of the suit not shown by partner or the opponent's bid is invitational; a cuebid of the lower-ranking of the suits shown by the opponent's bid shows the lower-ranking of the other two suits and is forcing for one round; a cuebid of the higher-ranking of the suits shown by the opponent's bid shows the higher-ranking of the other two suits and is forcing for one round.

Upside-down attitude signals—An agreement that a low card is encouraging and a high card is discouraging. The exact opposite to standard attitude signals.

Upside-down count signals—An agreement that a low card followed by a higher card would show an even number of cards in the suit; a high card followed by a low card would show an odd number of cards in the suit. The exact opposite to standard count signals.

Up-the-line—The practice of making the cheapest bid when responding or rebidding with two or three four-card suits (responding 1♥ to an opening bid of 1♣ or 1♦, for example, when holding four hearts and four spades).

Value Swiss—A variation of the Swiss convention which accommodates forcing major-suit raises with balanced hands.

Waiting bid—A bid asking for a further description of partner's hand while saying nothing specific about the bidder's hand.

Weak jump raises—Conventional use of a jump raise of partner's suit to show a weak hand with good support.

Weak jump shifts—The conventional use of a jump shift response to show a weak hand with a long suit.

Weak notrump—An opening bid of 1NT with a minimum-strength opening hand, usually 12 to 14 or 13 to 15 points.

Weak two-bid—The use of an opening bid of 2♦, 2♥ or 2♠ as a preemptive bid, usually showing a six-card suit with 5 to 10 points.

Wolff sign-off—A conventional method for allowing responder to sign off in a suit at the three level after opener's 2NT rebid.

ARE YOU A MEMBER?

The American Contract Bridge League (ACBL) is dedicated to the playing, teaching and promotion of contract bridge.

The membership of approximately 170,000 includes a wide range of players — from the thousands who are just learning the joy of bridge to the most proficient players in North America. The ACBL has long been the center of North American bridge activity. The organization celebrated its 75th Anniversary in 2012. The ACBL invites you to join in the excitement of organized bridge play.

The ACBL offers sanctioned games at local clubs, tournaments, on cruise ships and on the Internet! The ACBL is a service-oriented membership organization offering considerable benefits to its members, including reduced playing fees at tournaments!

If you are not a member of the ACBL, join today to take advantage of the reduced rates for first-time members and to receive our outstanding bridge magazine — "The Bridge Bulletin." You will receive an ACBL player number, and any masterpoints (the measure of achievement for all bridge players) you win at ACBL clubs and tournaments will be automatically recorded to your account!

You can enjoy the fun, friendship and competition of bridge with an ACBL membership. Join today by visiting our website **www.acbl.org** or by calling ACBL Headquarters. ACBL is a Great Deal!

American Contract Bridge League
6575 Windchase Boulevard
Horn Lake, MS 38637
662–253–3100 • www.acbl.org